Praise for
Mastering the Leadership Role in Project Management

"Alexander Laufer is one of the world's wisest authorities on projects and how they work. His cognitive authority is based on many years of studying and working at project-based organizations and universities. Based on Alexander's thoughtful judgment, this book—unlike so many anodyne and dull business texts—has the ring of 'ground truth' and authenticity that can't be bought or faked. It has to be earned. Projects are an old and a new form for designing work, and this book is a wonderfully readable and reliable guide to the new world of work, knowledge, and respect. Learn from it!"

—**From the Foreword by Larry Prusak,** Founder and Former Executive Director
of the Institute for Knowledge Management (IKM);
Currently teaching in the Information and Knowledge Program at
Columbia University

"I thoroughly enjoyed this book! The stories bring home the essence of what good projects need—good leadership. They present real women and men in very difficult situations, who succeed by doing what is right for the project and end up bringing the project team together to believe in the project. As valuable as project management's best practices are, they can't instill leadership. This book is the insight we need to pass on to the next generation. Thank you for writing this book!"

—**Charlene ("Chuck") Walrad,** Managing Director, Davenport Consulting, Inc.;
Vice President, Standards Activities, Board of Governors,
IEEE Computer Society

"Alexander Laufer's well-articulated and insightful stories helped me to identify subtle, but significant, opportunities for self-improvement that I have overlooked for so many years. I realized that small changes in my style can not only improve project outcome, but can also have considerable positive impacts on the rest of my team."

—**Robert J. Simmons,** Founder, CEO, CTO, ConXtech Inc.

"*Mastering the Leadership Role in Project Management* is truly a guilty pleasure to take the time to read. In today's fast-paced environment, Alexander and his colleagues have captured the essence of what project managers must do to deliver remarkable results—no matter where they work—by leading, not following, a scripted checklist. The book is written in bite-sized portions, so you can see what it takes to lead in today's world."

—**W. Scott Cameron,** Global Project Management Technology Process Owner,
Procter & Gamble Company

"Alexander Laufer's book on project leadership fills a long-standing void in management and leadership understanding. This book will teach and entertain anyone who has been in awe of great leaders and aspires to be a better leader. Readers will appreciate the recurring concept of 'unlearning' outdated concepts and practices. The book brings to life valuable lessons that are relevant to managers at every level in their career. *Mastering the Leadership Role in Project Management* is required reading for project managers who would like insights on how to improve their skills and get better project results."

—**Nadine Chin-Santos,** Senior Project Manager, Assistant Vice President, Parsons Brinckerhoff

"I was enthralled by the stories in this book on leadership in project management, as it corresponds to my recent focus on adaptive leadership. Stories help us to learn, and Alexander Laufer's book contains wonderful stories about leadership *by* great leaders. These are stories about real projects, from a cross-section of project types, which have two common themes: the dynamics of projects and the importance of giving priority to 'developing collaborative relations, fostering alliances, and giving people a sense of confidence in themselves.' If you want to lead projects, as opposed to administer them, then read these fascinating stories."

—**Jim Highsmith,** Executive Consultant at ThoughtWorks; Author, *Agile Project Management*

"We learn leadership best by observing great leaders, but most project managers rarely have an opportunity to do that…until now. In *Mastering the Leadership Role in Project Management*, Alexander Laufer introduces us to exceptional project leaders, the best of the best, and allows us to observe, in riveting narratives, how they plan, problem solve, and inspire their teams to deliver remarkable results."

—**Hugh Woodward,** Former Chair, Project Management Institute

"These stories tell how real people brought themselves fully to the management of uniquely complex and risky projects and found a way through. There is no easy success or bragging reported here. Rather, people tell in their own voice what they saw, how they understood the situation, and which factors shaped their actions. The terrain is challenging. Mistakes are made and lessons are learned. People grow as they find their way through. This would be a great book for project leaders to read and discuss, story by story, and learn from the practices reflected in each one."

—**Gregory A. Howell,** President, Lean Construction Institute

Mastering the Leadership Role in Project Management

Mastering the Leadership Role in Project Management

Practices that Deliver Remarkable Results

Alexander Laufer

Vice President, Publisher: Tim Moore
Associate Publisher and Director of Marketing: Amy Neidlinger
Executive Editor: Jeanne Glasser
Editorial Assistant: Pamela Boland
Operations Specialist: Jodi Kemper
Assistant Marketing Manager: Megan Graue
Cover Designer: Chuti Prasertsith
Managing Editor: Kristy Hart
Project Editor: Jovana San Nicolas-Shirley
Copy Editor: Ginny Munroe
Proofreader: Gill Editorial Services
Senior Indexer: Cheryl Lenser
Senior Compositor: Gloria Schurick
Manufacturing Buyer: Dan Uhrig

Publishing as FT Press

Upper Saddle River, New Jersey 07458

FT Press offers excellent discounts on this book when ordered in quantity for bulk purchases or special sales. For more information, please contact U.S. Corporate and Government Sales, 1-800-382-3419, corpsales@pearsontechgroup.com. For sales outside the U.S., please contact International Sales at international@pearsoned.com.

First Printing: April 2012

ISBN-10: 0-13-262034-0
ISBN-13: 978-0-13-262034-5

Pearson Education LTD.
Pearson Education Australia PTY, Limited.
Pearson Education Singapore, Pte. Ltd.
Pearson Education Asia, Ltd.
Pearson Education Canada, Ltd.
Pearson Educación de Mexico, S.A. de C.V.
Pearson Education—Japan
Pearson Education Malaysia, Pte. Ltd.

The Library of Congress cataloging-in-publication data is on file.

From Alex:
To Yochy, my dear wife and best friend,
and the loving family we have raised together

From Alex, Alistair, Dan, Don, Dora, Ed, Jeff,
and Zvi:
Our sincere thanks to all the project leaders
who allowed us to study their challenging projects
and to share their remarkable stories

Contents

Foreword: Larry Prusak xi

About the Author xiv

About the Contributors xv

Introduction: Learning from the Best Practitioners
Alexander Laufer 1
  Learning from Stories 1
  Stuck in the '60s 4
  Learning from the Best 7
  On Leadership, Management, and the
  Specific Context 8
  Description of the Cases 10
  Endnotes 14

**Chapter 1   Developing a Missile: The Power of Autonomy
             and Learning**
             Alexander Laufer, Dan Ward, Alistair Cockburn 19
  Doing Business More Like Business 19
  Six Is Not Seven 22
  We Would Shoot Granny for a Dollar 38
  We're Married Now 47

**Chapter 2   Building of Memory: Managing Creativity
             Through Action**
             Alexander Laufer, Zvi Ziklik, Jeffrey Russell 51
  Initial Stages: Making Progress by Splitting 51
  Middle Stages: Making Progress by Uniting 55
  Final Stages: Making Progress Through Versatility 65

Chapter 3 Flying Solar-Powered Airplanes: Soaring High on Spirit and Systems
Alexander Laufer, Edward Hoffman, Don Cohen 71

I Was the Enemy 71
Systems Are Our Best Friends 76
Change of Venue 87
People Matter the Most 94
Flight Party 100

Chapter 4 Transferring Harbor Cranes: Delivering a Bold Idea Through Meticulous Preparations and Quick Responsiveness
Alexander Laufer, Zvi Ziklik, Jeffrey Russell 103

The Entrepreneurial Phase 103
The Risk Reduction Phase 114
The Constant Vigilance Phase 118

Chapter 5 A Successful Downsizing: Developing a Culture of Trust and Responsibility
Alexander Laufer, Dan Ward, Alistair Cockburn 125

My Engineering Staff Shrunk from 80 to 12 125
Partnership 130
Constancy of Purpose 141

Chapter 6 A Peaceful Evacuation: Building a Multi-Project Battalion by Leading Upward
Alexander Laufer, Zvi Ziklik, Dora Cohenca-Zall 149

The Turbulent Birth of the Unilateral
Disengagement 149
The Systematic Preparations of the Israeli Defense
Forces 151
The Fight for the Makeup of the Battalion 156
The Speedy Implementation of the Evacuation 164

Chapter 7 Exploring Space: Shaping Culture by Exploiting Location
Alexander Laufer, Edward Hoffman, Don Cohen 171

"Good Enough" Is Good Enough 171
Nurturing the Culture of Location 175

A Gentle Touch. 183

When "Good Enough" Is Not Good Enough 189

Chapter 8   **Building a Dairy Plant: Accelerating Speed
Through Splitting and Harmonizing**
Alexander Laufer, Jeffrey Russell,
Dora Cohenca-Zall 193

Shifting from Park to Drive 193

Gaining Independence. 198

Splitting and Harmonizing. 203

Epilogue   **Practices for Project Leadership**
Alexander Laufer. 213

First Practice: Embrace the "Living Order"
Concept. 214

Practice Two: Adjust Project Practices to the
Specific Context 216

Practice Three: Challenge the Status Quo. 218

Practice Four: Do Your Utmost to Recruit
the Right People 222

Practice Five: Shape the Right Culture. 224

Practice Six: Plan, Monitor, and Anticipate. 227

Practice Seven: Use Face-to-Face Communication
as the Primary Communication Mode. 230

Practice Eight: Be Action-Oriented and Focus
on Results 232

Practice Nine: Lead, So You Can Manage. 236

Index 239

Foreword

We no longer work as we used to. By the mid-nineteenth century, new technologies produced in the U.S. and Europe (and later Japan) allowed complex tasks to be performed by a much larger number of employees than ever before. The older, artisan-based division of labor, as seen in Adam Smith's famous pin factory, with its paternalistic management structure, would never suffice for the railroads, cotton factories, chemical plants, steel mills, and munition works that were cropping up all over Western Europe and the Northeastern U.S. Something new had to be developed to manage this new form of work, to manage the new factories and mill workers, and to manage their final mass-produced products.

As Horace said, nothing ever comes from nothing. The management structures that were adapted to these new organisms were based on the only system that anyone had ever seen and that allowed for managing many men over time and space and enabled them to perform at least somewhat complex tasks. This, of course, was the military.

Now, the hallmarks of any military structure—at least up until the past 20 years or so—were command and control bureaucratic hierarchies with rigid rules and regulations and stiff penalties for non-compliance. This model was readily and quickly adapted to all sorts of manufacturing, mining, and shipping concerns and proved to be a great global success as far as wealth production. The gross output of the world increased approximately 12 times from 1880 to 1990—a record that is unlikely to ever be repeated. However, there is one great problem with this model in the twenty-first century. The fact is plain and clear: Most work today needs to be done very, very differently than it was done in these great industrial companies of the past century. Let's explore why and how this is happening.

For one thing, much of the wealth being created in the more advanced economies is based far more on knowledge and other intangibles than on the manipulation of any materials. This "knowledge economy" is every bit as "real" as the industrial one. Just think of the size and scale and output of some of the largest firms in our lives— Google, Microsoft, the medical, media, and finance giants, and even Apple, now the wealthiest firm on earth—whose competitive edge is based on design, a form of knowledge! Even in former manufacturing giants, such as Germany, the UK, and the U.S., less than 15 percent of the work performed in these countries is in manufacturing. And because form follows function, it stands to reason that the way plants were managed wouldn't be at all useful to any organization that is strongly or even moderately based on knowledge and its applications.

Knowledge workers surely do not want to be treated like modern versions of nineteenth-century mill workers. They not only want autonomy and respect, but they also want to work with peers in supportive knowledge-sharing environments where everyone can learn and contribute. No one wants to return to the world where Henry Ford famously asked: "Why do I want to pay for a worker's head when I only want the muscle in his arm?"

If we are all going to be working in organizations that develop and produce and extensively work with knowledge, then we also have to change the very way in which we structure the work. In many places, this is already going on. The most common new form of knowledge-based work where this is already going on is in projects—projects of every shape and form. And that is the focus of this wonderful book.

Alexander Laufer is one of the world's wisest authorities on projects and how they work. His cognitive authority is based on many years of studying and working at organizations and universities, which are project-based. Based on Alex's thoughtful judgment, this book— unlike so many anodyne and dull business texts—has the ring of "ground truth" and authenticity that can't be bought or faked. It has to be earned.

The book also highlights elements of successful project management that are scarcely found in standard texts. Social capital issues, such as trust, culture, and autonomy, are seen throughout the text, as they should be. Projects are an old and a new form for designing work, and this book is a wonderfully readable and reliable guide to the new world of work, knowledge, and respect. Learn from it!

—**Larry Prusak,** Founder and former executive director of the Institute for Knowledge Management (IKM) and currently teaching in the Information and Knowledge Program at Columbia University

About the Author

Dr. Alexander Laufer is a chaired professor of civil engineering at the Technion-Israel Institute of Technology, where he also served as the dean of the faculty. Currently he is also a visiting professor at the University of Wisconsin-Madison. He has served as the editor-in-chief of the *NASA Academy of Program and Project Leadership Magazine, Academy Sharing Knowledge,* and as a member of the advisory board of the NASA Academy of Program and Project Leadership. He has also served as the director of the Center for Project Leadership at Columbia University. He is a member of the editorial review board of the *Project Management Journal.* Dr. Laufer is the author or coauthor of five books; the two most recent ones are *Breaking the Code of Project Management* (Macmillan, 2009) and *Shared Voyage: Learning and Unlearning from Remarkable Projects* (NASA History Office, 2005).

About the Contributors

Dr. Alistair Cockburn is president of Humans and Technology, Inc. and was voted one of the "All-Time Top 150 i-Technology Heroes" in 2007 for his pioneering work on use cases and co-creation of the agile software development movement. He is an internationally renowned IT strategist and an expert on agile development, use cases, process design, project management, and object-oriented design. He is the author of *The Crystal Agile Methodologies*, three Jolt-awarded books on software development, and coauthor of *The Agile Manifesto* and *The Project Management Declaration of Interdependence*. He is known for his lively presentations and interactive workshops. His articles, talks, poems, and blog can be found online at http://alistair.cockburn.us.

Don Cohen is managing editor of NASA's *ASK Magazine*, devoted to stories of project management and engineering excellence. His articles on organizational knowledge and social capital have appeared in *Harvard Business Review, California Management Review, Knowledge Management, Knowledge and Process Management,* and other journals. His chapter on "Designing Organizations to Enhance Social Capital" appears in the *Handbook of Knowledge Creation and Management*, Oxford University Press. He created and edited *Knowledge Directions*, the journal of the IBM Institute for Knowledge Management. He is also coauthor of *In Good Company: How Social Capital Makes Organizations Work* and *Better Together: Restoring the American Community*. He received both his BA and M.Phil in English from Yale University.

Dr. Dora Cohenca-Zall is an independent project management consultant, particularly for large infrastructure projects in their early phases of project definition, strategic planning, and procurement strategies. In recent years, she was involved in two of the largest projects in Israel: the Carmel Tunnels project in Haifa and the Light Rail Train project in Tel Aviv. Prior to these projects, she worked as a consultant to the UN in large organizational change projects in Paraguay, South America. She teaches project management courses to graduate students at both the Technion-Israel Institute of Technology and the University of Haifa. She obtained her BS in civil engineering in Paraguay and her M.Sc and Ph.D. at the Technion in Israel.

Dr. Edward J. Hoffman is the director of the NASA Academy of Program/Project and Engineering Leadership (APPEL) and NASA's Chief Knowledge Officer. He works within NASA as well as with leaders of industry, academia, professional associations, and other government agencies to develop the agency's capabilities in program and project management and engineering. Dr. Hoffman has written numerous journal articles, coauthored *Shared Voyage: Learning and Unlearning from Remarkable Projects* (NASA, 2005) and *Project Management Success Stories: Lessons of Project Leaders* (Wiley, 2000), and speaks frequently at conferences and associations. He serves as adjunct faculty at The George Washington University. He holds a Doctorate, as well as Master of Arts and Master of Science degrees from Columbia University in the area of social and organizational psychology. He received a Bachelor of Science in Psychology from Brooklyn College in 1981.

Dr. Jeffrey S. Russell, P.E., is Vice Provost for Lifelong Learning and Dean of Continuing Studies at the University of Wisconsin-Madison (UW). In this role, he is responsible for leading the university's programs and services for lifelong learners and nontraditional students. Prior to assuming his current position, Dr. Russell served as Professor and Chair in the Department of Civil and Environmental Engineering (CEE) at the UW. He served as editor-in-chief of the American Society of Civil Engineers (ASCE) *Journal of Management in Engineering* (1995–2000) and as founding editor-in-chief of the ASCE publication *Leadership and Management in Engineering* (2000–2003). He has published more than 200 technical papers in addition to two books. He has been honored with a number of national and regional awards, as well as nine best paper awards. He has advised over 100 graduate students, including 26 Ph.D. students, and served as principal or coprincipal investigator for more than $14 million of publicly and privately funded research. Dr. Russell served on the ASCE Board of Directors (1997–2000), was recently elected to the National Academy of Construction, and is presently Chair of the ASCE Committee on Academic Prerequisites for Professional Practice.

Lt. Col. Dan Ward is chief of acquisition innovation in the Air Force's Acquisition Process Office at the Pentagon. His background includes laser research, satellite projects, communication infrastructures, imagery exploitation systems, and social networking for the military. His writings have appeared in *Defense AT&L Magazine, SIGNAL, Harpers, Gilbert,* and the *Information Systems Security Association Journal.* He is also the author of seven books, including a design book titled *The Simplicity Cycle.* He holds a BS in electrical engineering from Clarkson University, an MS in engineering management from Western New England College, and an MS in systems engineering from the Air Force Institute of Technology.

Dr. Zvi Ziklik is the general manager of the Haifa branch of A. Epstein and Sons, a Chicago-based international company. His company specializes in managing the design and execution of very large and highly complex construction projects in Israel. Previously, he served as the vice president for Engineering for Druker Construction company, at the time, one of the fastest growing companies in Israel. When Drucker was acquired by the largest construction company in Israel, Solel Boneh, he became vice president for Marketing. He holds a BS and a Ph.D. in industrial engineering from the Technion-Israel Institute of Technology, where he is currently a senior adjunct lecturer.

Introduction

Learning from the Best Practitioners

by Alexander Laufer

Learning from Stories

"In late December 1995, I got a call to come in and talk to one of my bosses at the Eglin Air Force Base. At the time, I was program manager for the Joint Direct Attack Munition (JDAM) missile. As soon as I got there, I was informed that I was being switched off JDAM to run the Joint Air-to-Surface Standoff Missile (JASSM) program, and I wasn't happy about it at all..."I knew that at JASSM, I would have to start over and would probably have to cope with a more difficult environment. The original program manager of JASSM... was given two major mandates. The first was not to repeat any of the mistakes of the past, meaning the TSSAM program. The Tri-Service Standoff Attack Missile (TSSAM) had been cancelled after six years and several billion dollars in cost overruns... The second mandate was to get started quickly..."...Most of my peers in program management think that the most important aspects of our job are making decisions, conducting reviews, and controlling performance. In contrast, my priorities are to develop collaborative relations, foster alliances, and give the people who work for me a sense of confidence in themselves."I stumbled into an understanding of this when I got involved in program management many years ago. At first, I gravitated toward an analytical approach because of my background in operations research. I was brought up in the Robert McNamara school of management, where everything is

quantifiable—if we can't build a model of something, then it doesn't exist. "It didn't take me long to figure out that this idea was bankrupt. Programs move ahead because of the activities of people, but none of the models I was using measured that critical ingredient for success. I could do the fanciest calculations in the world, but did they have anything to do with determining whether the project was going to be successful? Not at all..."Experience was my greatest teacher. I had managed to deliver several major projects successfully by implementing practices that were designed to fit the world as I saw it and that often differed from the accepted practices..."...I called a meeting the first day back after New Year's with the 20 people who were working on JASSM. They were in a state of disbelief after learning that their boss had been fired over the Christmas holiday. He had worked with them on this program from the beginning and was well liked. Out of the blue, I showed up and told them, 'We are going to get this program on contract within six months. If we don't do it in six months, there is no program.'"...The truth is that I pulled the number six out of my hat. I would have been happy to be on contract at the end of seven months, or even eight months, but I would never have told the team that."What I wanted to do was set a goal that would challenge these folks to look at things in an entirely new way. I didn't want a schedule that they felt they could achieve just by working on weekends or figuring out a handful of inventive ways to do things. I wanted something so outrageous that it would cause them, first, to essentially give up, but then—once they figured out that giving up wasn't an option—to step back and examine all their assumptions, all their beliefs, all the things that were in their heads as a result of their experiences and what they had been told in the past, and to ask themselves with a clean slate, 'What do I really need to do to achieve this goal?'"

This is an excerpt from the story of Air Force program manager Terry Little, who was drafted to turn around a program that appeared to be on its way to swift cancellation. Yet, at project completion, Terry's team received the highest acquisition honor of the Department of

Defense. The full story is one of the eight remarkable cases presented in this book.

We all know that most people love to read stories and that a good story can serve as a very powerful learning tool. Stories can stimulate curiosity, convey easily digestible complex messages, convert tacit knowledge to explicit knowledge, induce reflection, and be remembered easily.[1]

By reading the eight stories and reflecting on them, you can acquire rich knowledge about two related subjects:

- **Project leadership:** Its different facets, how it relates to project management, and how it is fulfilled in different circumstances

- **Project practices:** The specific practices that successful project managers apply in exercising their leadership and management roles, and how these practices are implemented in different circumstances

However, prior to learning, it is sometimes necessary to first go through a process of *unlearning*. As Terry Little tells us, "At first, I gravitated toward an analytical approach, where everything is quantifiable—if we can't build a model of something, then it doesn't exist. It didn't take me long to figure out that this idea was bankrupt."

You will see when you read his full story, as well as all the other stories in the book, that the beliefs and practices of project managers and their team members are often influenced by outdated concepts that must first be abandoned. The use of stories becomes more important for unlearning purposes because they are usually far more effective than analytical explanations or dry principles. People's minds are changed more through observation than through argument, and real-life stories told by credible and successful managers may serve as an effective substitute for observation.

Yet, the learning process, and even the unlearning process, will evolve primarily from the experiences accumulated by applying the practices. *The Fifth Discipline Fieldbook* explains it vividly: "Buckminster Fuller used to say that if you want to teach people a new way of thinking, don't bother trying to teach them. Instead, give them a tool, the use of which will lead them to new ways of thinking."[2] Using the new tool naturally triggers reflection, and the unlearning process usually requires more than a few cycles of using the tool and reflecting on the new experience. The practices described in the cases throughout this book will quickly become your new tools, and by applying them and reflecting on them, you will gradually master a leadership role in your projects. As Ray Morgan, the project manager in the Pathfinder case (see Chapter 3, "Flying Solar-Powered Airplanes: Soaring High on Spirit and Systems"), tells us: "This new approach didn't immediately solve my problems, but it started me down the right road... [I] felt like I was not only a different man, but a better manager. What's more, I had finally begun to be a leader..."

Stuck in the '60s

The great British leader Winston Churchill once said, "We are shaping the world faster than we can change ourselves, and we are applying to the present the habits of the past." A half a century later, and one can say that nothing has changed regarding the validity of Churchill's painful insight. This is how, in 2001, the British management business leader and philosopher Charles Handy vividly described the pace of change, "All of the world's trade in 1949 happens in a single day today, all of the foreign exchange dealings in 1979 happen now in a single day, as do all the telephone calls made around the world in 1984. A year in a day is exactly how it feels sometimes."[3]

Yet, in spite of these vast world changes, the theory of project management has remained largely unchanged. Just as Churchill astutely observed how we are stuck in our ways, so did the British executive and a professor of project management, P.W.G. Morris, note more recently that, "Modern project management... emerged... in a period that was more inflexible and less complex and where events changed less rapidly than today... it [the theory of project management] is in many respects still stuck in a 1960s time warp."[4]

Practitioners must recognize that the prevailing theories and the basic assumptions of their discipline have a great impact on their own thoughts and practices. Albert Einstein explained it very succinctly: "It is the theory that describes what we can observe." Peter Drucker added that the basic assumptions about reality largely determine what the discipline—scholars, writers, teachers, practitioners—assumes to be reality.[5]

Thus, a theory stuck in the '60s might not be just old and irrelevant, but it might also adversely affect our performance. Indeed, in his 2005 seminal article, "Bad Management Theories Are Destroying Good Management Practices," Sumantra Ghoshal cites Kurt Lewin's argument that "nothing is as practical as a good theory." Ghoshal stresses, however, that the "obverse is also true: Nothing is as dangerous as a bad theory."[6] This is exactly what Koskela and Howell claim in their paper "The Underlying Theory of Project Management Is Obsolete," "In the present big, complex, and speedy projects, traditional project management is simply counterproductive; it creates self-inflicting problems that seriously undermine performance."[7]

If conventional methods of project management can exacerbate rather than alleviate project problems, then we should not be surprised to learn about the widespread poor statistics of project results. For example, a recent study that examined ten large rail transit projects in the United States found that the projects suffered from an average cost overrun of 61 percent, whereas the average cost overrun of eight large road projects in Sweden was 86 percent.[8] Results of software projects have received great attention in this regard. For example, in their study of software project failure, Keil and his colleagues reported that, "Based on a survey of 376 CEOs... roughly 50 percent of all information technology projects fail to meet chief executive expectations."[9]

Research by the Standish Group, which has been doing surveys on information technology projects since 1994, shows that overrunning the budget is common and that delivering projects late is normal. Delivering less functionality than was originally planned is also nothing out of the ordinary. In short, project failure in the information technology world is almost standard operating procedure. The Standish Group's 2006 survey showed that nearly two-thirds of all the information technology projects launched in that year either failed or ran into trouble.[10]

These unsettling statistics beg the question of why management theories are still stuck in the '60s. One possible reason is that the research is detached from practice. This problem has not been confined only to researchers in project management. In research concerning general management (that is, with a focus on permanent organizations rather than on temporary ones), researchers are chronically wrestling with the problem of how to find ways to develop what is termed "relevant research." Yet, this is the simple and painful conclusion reached by Sandberg and Tsoukas in 2011: "There is an increasing concern that management theories are not relevant to practice."[11] Attempting to respond to this concern in project management research, Cicmil et al. suggest that: "...what is needed to improve project management practice is not more research on what should be done... we know very little about the 'actuality' of project-based working and management."[12]

Learning from the Best

Studying the "actuality" of projects is exactly what I have attempted to do for more than two decades. Instead of asking: "Why don't practitioners use what researchers know?" I have reversed the question and asked: "Why don't researchers use what practitioners know?" In this long learning pursuit of striving to develop a "theory of practice," I have collected firsthand data by alternately employing three different, yet complementary, approaches:

- Field studies in advanced organizations using structured research tools, particularly interviews and observations of practitioners
- Case studies and stories collected from more than 150 project managers in over 20 organizations
- Consulting work to test interim results

All of my studies were focused on the most competent practitioners affiliated with a great variety of "advanced" organizations, among them: AT&T, Du Pont, General Motors, IBM, Motorola, NASA, Procter & Gamble, Skanska, and the U.S. Air Force.

My focus on a selective sample of the best practitioners rather than using a sample representing the entire population of project managers is highly recommended by prominent authorities in management research. The common arguments for this research approach are:

- Management practitioners live in a world of extremes; therefore, population averages are meaningless to them. What they need to know is how to differentiate between good and bad managers.
- Excellence is a better teacher than mediocrity. Management is best learned by emulating exemplary role models.[13]

On Leadership, Management, and the Specific Context

Based on my studies, I was able to uncover the common practices employed by successful project managers in order to cope with our dynamic environment. These practices of planning, control, collaboration, and communication have been described in four previous books that I authored or co-authored.[14] However, only in recent years and with the help of the contributors to this book, I was able to better understand the crucial role of project *leadership* in project success, as well as the meaning of project *management* in this dynamic environment.

In my studies, I found that even the most effective planning, control, and risk management systems cannot eliminate the need for coping with frequent unexpected events and numerous problems throughout the life of a project. Most of the problems encountered throughout project life are *technical*; that is, they can be solved with knowledge and procedures already at hand. Although solving problems such as how to accelerate project speed or replace a contractor might require great flexibility and high responsiveness, these issues can be accomplished without challenging conventional habits and practices. They just require good *managerial* skills.

Other problems, however, are *adaptive*, that is, they are not so well defined, do not have clear solutions, and often require new learning and changes in patterns of behavior. For example, adaptive problems might require the project manager to bypass company procedures in order to ensure that the best contractor in town will be selected to cope with an infeasible design or in order to instruct the designer to think outside the box and develop creative solutions to cope with unreasonable cost constraints. In order to address these adaptive problems, the project manager must be willing and able to make significant changes and to challenge the status quo. These problems require *leadership*.[15]

The studies also reveal that while all projects require both leadership and management, the way in which leadership and management are exercised depends on the specific context of the project.

Peter Drucker argues that several assumptions regarding the realities of management have been held by most scholars, writers, and practitioners since the study of management first began in the 1930s. He maintains, however, that today these assumptions must be unlearned, particularly the assumption that "there is (or there must be) *one* right way to manage people." Drucker further argues that this assumption is totally at odds with reality and totally counterproductive. Johns presents evidence that management researchers are inclined to downplay the context or the specifics of a given situation. According to Johns, it seems that context-free research is somehow perceived as being more scientific and prestigious than context-specific research.[16]

For the most part, the project management literature has not given explicit treatment to context issues and has thus implicitly endorsed the "one best way" approach, which was the favorite phrase of Fredrick Taylor, the father of "scientific management." Thus, the emphasis in the literature has typically been on the "standard" or the "common," rather than on the "unique." Melgrati and Damiani make this point very eloquently: "Project management ideology is paradoxical because it focuses on repetitive aspects and 'marginalizes' the uniqueness and originality that should instead characterize the project."[17]

However, there have been some notable exceptions, such as proponents of Agile Project Management, giving voice to a new approach that challenges the "one best way" and recommends tailoring the project management process to the situation.[18]

Description of the Cases

This is precisely the rationale behind the design of this book: to help the reader understand how successful project managers tailor practices, such as planning, control, collaboration, and communication to the unique context of their projects. Thus, eight very successful projects, four from the U.S. and four from Israel, were selected for this book. The uniqueness of the projects was assured by their geographic location and by the wide range of their industry and product settings (space, weapons development, construction, and transportation).[19]

The eight projects selected are divided into four groups, with two projects in each group, one from the U.S. and one from Israel. The key aspect defining each group is its uniquely different nature:

- New Product Development
- Repeated and Risky Tasks
- Organizational Change
- Complex Projects (large projects composed of many diverse components, widely dispersed geographically)[20]

Upon reading each of the eight projects in this book, it will become clear that there is no "one best way" for leading and managing a project. Rather, the project manager must tailor the project practices to the project's unique context. Yet, when considering the different types of projects, it will also become evident that in projects sharing common characteristics and coping with similar challenges, the project managers use many practices in a like manner.[21]

Following is a brief description of the eight projects and their key challenges:

New Product Development

Developing a Missile: The Joint Air-to-Surface Standoff Missile program was established to replace the cancelled Tri-Service Standoff Attack Missile program, which had exceeded its budget estimates by record levels. The contractor, Lockheed Martin, was told by the U.S. Air Force: "We don't have the time, we don't have the funds, and we don't have the answers. We want a missile in half the time for half the price. You will have the freedom to put together your approach that meets our three key performance parameters. The objective is a dramatic reduction in acquisition time and funds. You either understand that or you are out of the game." Thus, it became clear very quickly that the only way to produce an affordable missile was to stop doing "business as usual."

Building a Museum: Yad Vashem, the official Israeli memorial complex for the victims of the Holocaust, was embarking on the addition of a new history museum. Following an international competition, with the participation of ten of the best architects in the world, Moshe Safdie from Canada was selected. During the early phases of the project, the project manager found that the design required the development of a revolutionary and very challenging product that had never before been implemented. Indeed, the building appeared to call for sculpturing more than construction, and at times it seemed that its execution was just not feasible.

Repeated and Risky Tasks

Flying Solar-Powered Airplanes: The Environmental Research Aircraft and Sensor Technology program, established by NASA, was charged with the task of converting Unmanned Aerial Vehicles (UAV) into research platforms. The know-how required to overcome the extraordinary difficulty in controlling the risks involved was enough to put most companies off. Aero-Vironment, one company that was brave enough to embark on the adventure with NASA, did indeed find that it faced a daunting technological challenge: to operate an aircraft that was both light enough to fly and large enough to be powered by the sun and carry meaningful payloads. If this was to be done, it would be through careful attention to the design of the aircraft and its systems—and by doing business in an entirely new way.

Transferring Harbor Cranes: The Israeli Ports Authority issued a bid for transferring four huge harbor cranes from the port of Haifa to another port in Israel. The traditional method is to dismantle the cranes, each weighing up to 400 tons and reaching as high as 40 meters, into about 70 pieces each. They are then transported over land on huge trucks, recomposed through a very meticulous process, and tested and licensed by the manufacturer. One company decided to employ a pioneering method never before attempted anywhere in the world: transferring the cranes by sea, thereby skipping altogether the lengthy and costly process of dismantling and recomposing the cranes.

Organizational Change

Downsizing: The Advanced Medium Range Air-to-Air Missile program of the U.S. Air Force was rife with problems, not the least of which was the mandated drawdown plan that had not been met. When the new project manager arrived, she discovered that not everyone at the base was keen on change. Still, despite strong pressure to maintain the status quo, she was motivated by a desire to do the right thing. She soon found herself in the center of a maelstrom, as the reforms she had in mind entailed a partnership with her industry counterpart (Raytheon), which was on a dramatically different management path.

Evacuation: The former Israeli Prime Minister, Ariel Sharon, was for years the greatest activist behind the Jewish settlements in the Gaza Strip. So the announcement of his decision to abandon the Strip, uproot the settlements, and evacuate all the inhabitants was met with shock by many and threatened to tear apart the Israeli population. The implementation of his decision led to the largest series of demonstrations in Israel's history. Due to the enormity of the mission, Sharon called on the Israeli Defense Forces (IDF), rather than the police, and 12 battalions were specially organized to carry out this unique mission. The charge was accepted quite reluctantly, as described in the story of a Lieutenant Colonel and his team who headed one of the battalions.

Complex Projects

Building a Spacecraft and Scientific Instruments: Under a novel co-leadership arrangement between NASA and Caltech, three large organizations with marked geographical and cultural differences were faced with the development of a complex product within a fixed timetable. The project had barely started when it already appeared to be quickly outspending its resources, and it was soon in jeopardy of being cancelled.

Building a Dairy Plant: When Tnuva, Israel's largest food manufacturer, launched the biggest dairy plant in the Middle East, the vision called for a "dream dairy" that would be equipped with the most advanced technology in the world. However, two years following the launch, the company learned that its greatest rival was about to embark on a new dairy line that would threaten Tnuva's domination in the field. Tnuva's management decided to make a radical change, downgrading many features of their original design and adopting an emergency schedule. However, not everyone involved in the project, in particular the German firm designing the equipment, was so willing to abruptly abandon their state-of-the-art design.

You are now ready to embark on an enjoyable voyage of learning from eight remarkable stories. Through these vivid stories, you are going to live through the experiences of the best project managers. Inevitably, you are going to reflect on their challenging problems, creative solutions, and effective practices, and at times, you might find yourself "dialoging" with yourself and with these successful project managers. Their decisions and actions, their successes and failures, and their learning and unlearning will undoubtedly affect you. They will empower you, inspire you, and gradually facilitate a change of mind and a change of practice. Most of all, they will help you become both a better project manger and a better project leader. Bon Voyage!

Endnotes

1. R.C. Schank (1990). *Tell Me a Story: A New Look at Real and Artificial Memory*. New York, NY: Charles Scribner's Sons, p. 12. A.L. Wilkins (1983). "Organizational Stories as Symbols to Control the Organization." *Organizational Symbolism*, eds. L.R. Pondy, P.J Frost, G. Morgan, and T.C. Dandridge. Greenwich, CT: JAI Press, pp. 81–92. R. Nisbett and L. Ross (1980). *Human Inference: Strategies and Shortcomings of Social Judgment*. Englewood Cliffs, NJ: Prentice-Hall. M.R. Jalongo and J.P. Isenberg (1995). *Teacher's Stories: From Personal Narrative to Professional Insight*. San Francisco, CA: Jossey-Bass Publishers, pp. 50–1, 78, 143. Numagami suggests that the objective of management studies should be changed from a search for invariant laws of practical use to the encouragement of a reflective dialogue between researchers and practitioners and among practitioners, and that the case study is an excellent vehicle for such a dialogue. T. Numagami (1998). "The Infeasibility of Invariant Laws in Management Studies: A Reflective Dialogue in Defense of Case Studies." *Organization Science*. 9, 1: 2–15. H. Mintzberg (2004). *Managers Not MBAs—A Hard Look at the Soft Practice of Managing and Management Development*. San Francisco: Berrett-Koehler Publishers Inc., p. 254.

2. P.M. Senge, A. Kleiner, C. Roberts, and B. Smith (1994). *The Fifth Discipline Fieldbook: Strategies and Tools for Building a Learning Organization*. New York, NY: Doubleday Currency, p. 28.

3. C. Handy (2002). *The Elephant and the Flea: Reflections of a Reluctant Capitalist*. Boston, MA: Harvard Business School Press, p. 101.

4. P.W.G. Morris (1994). *The Management of Projects*. London, UK: Thomas Telford Services, p. 217. Indeed, a group of software developers, who were dissatisfied with the traditional project management approach, took the initiative and developed, formalized, and implemented a new project management approach called the Agile method. See: B. Boehm and R, Turner (2004). *Balancing Agility and Discipline*. Boston, MA: Addison-Wesley Professional.

5. P.F. Drucker (1999). *Management Challenges for the 21st Century*. New York, NY: Harper Collins, pp. 5 & 17.

6. S. Ghoshal (2005). "Bad Management Theories Are Destroying Good Management Practices." *Academy of Management Learning and Education* 4, 1 (March): 75–91.

7. L. Koskela and G. Howell (2002). "The Underlying Theory of Project Management Is Obsolete." *Proceedings of PMI Research Conference*. Seattle, WA: pp. 293–301. Williams, focusing on complex projects, also finds a need for a new paradigm. T.M. Williams (1999). "The Need for New Paradigms for Complex Projects." *International Journal of Project Management* 17, 5: 269–73.

8. B. Flyvbjerg, N. Bruzelius, and W. Rothengatter (2003). *Megaprojects and Risks: An Anatomy of Ambition*. Cambridge, UK: Cambridge University Press, p. 44.

9. M. Keil, A. Rai, J.E. Cheney Mann, and G.P. Zhang (2003). "Why Software Projects Escalate: The Importance of Project Management Constructs." *IEEE Transactions on Engineering Management* 50, 3: 251–61.

10. The Standish Group (http://www.standishgroup.com/) has been doing surveys on all types of IT projects since 1994. Its research is published under the title CHAOS.

11. R. Gulati (2007). "Tent Poles, Tribalism, and Boundary Spanning: The Rigor-Relevance Debate in Management Research." *Academy of Management Journal* 50, 4: 775–782; J. Sandberg and H. Tsoukas (2011). "Grasping the Logic of Practice: Theorizing Through Practical Rationality." *The Academy of Management Review* 36, 2: 338–360.

12. S. Cicmil, T. Williams, J. Thomas, and D. Hodgson (2006). "Rethinking Project Management: Researching the Actuality of Projects." *International Journal of Project Management* 24, 8: 675–86. Richard Daft, relating to management researchers and not particularly to project management researchers, said back in 1983: "As a reviewer of papers, it becomes painfully clear that many authors have never seen or witnessed the phenomena about which they write. Authors cannot give an example to illustrate a point." R.L. Daft (1983). "Learning the Craft of Organizational Research." *Academy of Management Review* 8, 4: 539–46.

13. W. Bennis and P.W. Biederman (1996). *Organizing Genius—The Secrets of Creative Collaboration.* Reading, MA: Addison-Wesley. J.C. Collins and J.I. Porras (1994). *Built to Last—Successful Habits of Visionary Companies.* New York, NY: Harper Collins. B. McKelvey (2006). "Van de Ven and Johnson's Engaged Scholarship: Nice Try, But..." *Academy of Management Review* 31, 4: 822–29. T. Peters and R.H. Waterman (1982). *In Search of Excellence: Lessons from America's Best-Run Companies.* New York, NY: Harper & Row.

14. A. Laufer (2009). *Breaking the Code of Project Management.* New York, NY: Palgrave Macmillan; A. Laufer, T. Post, and E.J. Hoffman (2005). *Shared Voyage: Learning and Unlearning from Remarkable Projects.* Washington, DC: NASA; A. Laufer and E.J. Hoffman (2000). *Project Management Success Stories: Lessons of Project Leaders.* New York, NY: John Wiley & Sons; A. Laufer (1996). *Simultaneous Management: Managing Projects in a Dynamic Environment.* New York, NY: AMACOM, American Management Association.

15. R.A. Heifetz (1994). Leadership without Easy Answers, Cambridge, MA: Harvard University Press.

16. P.F. Drucker (1999). *Management Challenges for the 21st Century.* New York, NY: Harper Collins, pp. 9 & 16. The "one best way" approach came under sharp attack by Henry Mintzberg as well. In *The Rise and Fall of Strategic Planning,* Mintzberg discusses forms of organizations: "Throughout this book, we have repeatedly criticized the 'one best way' thinking in the management literature." H. Mintzberg (1994). *The Rise and Fall of Strategic Planning: Reconceiving Roles for Planning, Plans, Planners.* New York, NY: Free Press, p. 397. G. Johns (2001). "In Praise of Context." *Journal of Organizational Behavior* 22: 31–42.

17. A. Melgrati and M. Damiani (2002). "Rethinking the Project Management Framework: New Epistemology New Insights." *Proceedings of PMI Research Conference.* Newtown Square, PA: Project Management Institute, p. 371–80.

18. J.A. Highsmith (2000). *Adaptive Software Development—A Collaborative Approach to Managing Complex Systems.* New York, NY: Dorset House Publishing, p. 85. W. Royce (1998). *Software Project Management: A Unified Framework.* Boston, MA: Addison-Wesley, p. 209. See also: K. Beck (2000). *Extreme Programming Explained: Embrace Change.* Boston, MA: Addison-Wesley, p. 172. A. Shenhar and D. Dvir (2007). *Reinventing Project Management: The Diamond Approach to Successful Growth & Innovation.* Boston, MA: Harvard Business School Press.

19. Athough there are clear differences between the U.S. and Israel in terms of size, history, and security, culturally they seem as if they are not so far apart. A comprehensive comparison study of culture in 62 societies found that the "cultural distance" between the U.S. and Israel is quite small. For example, regarding Uncertainty Avoidance, although the distance between the highest and the lowest scores was 2.49, the distance between the U.S. and Israel was only 0.14. Similarly, regarding Power Distance, although the distance between the highest and the lowest scores was 1.91, the distance between the U.S. and Israel was only 0.15. Regarding Human Orientation, the distance between the highest and the lowest scores was 2.05, but the distance between the U.S. and Israel was only 0.07. See: R.J. House, P.J. Hanges, M. Javidan, P.W. Dorfman, and V. Gupta (Eds.) (2004). *Culture, Leadership, and Organizations: The GLOBE Study of 62 Societies*. Thousand Oaks, CA: Sage Thousand Oaks.

20. The data for these cases was originally collected by Dora Cohenca-Zall, Edward Hoffman, Alexander Laufer, Todd Post, and Zvi Ziklik. The original focus of the previous study was on project context, disregarding the issue of leadership. Together, with the coauthors of the current book, the original data was revisited, additional data was collected, and the cases were completely rewritten, this time with a focus on leadership and management.

21. Because stories are highly context-sensitive, their use should facilitate the required shift from a context-free mindset to a context-specific one. Indeed, in comparing the "one best way" approach with a story-based approach, various researchers have reached the same conclusion that context is ever present in narrative thinking (the narrative account of an experience). See: H. Zukier (1986). "The Paradigmatic and Narrative Modes in Goal-Guided Inference." *Handbook of Motivation and Cognition*, R. M. Sorrentino and E.T. Higgins (Eds.). New York, NY: Guilford, pp. 465–502. D.J. Clandinin and F.M. Connelly (2000). *Narrative Inquiry: Experience and Story in Qualitative Research*. San Francisco, CA: Jossey-Bass, p. 32.

1

Developing a Missile: The Power of Autonomy and Learning

by Alexander Laufer, Dan Ward, and Alistair Cockburn

Doing Business More Like Business

Air Force Program Manager Terry Little's reputation as an innovative program manager preceded him when he was drafted to turn around a program that appeared to be on its way to swift cancellation. The Joint Air-to-Surface Standoff Missile (JASSM) program had been launched in April 1995 and only nine months later was already in big trouble.

"In late December 1995, I got a call to come in and talk to one of my bosses at the Eglin Air Force Base. At the time, I was program manager for the Joint Direct Attack Munition (JDAM) missile. As soon as I got there, I was informed that I was being switched off JDAM to run the JASSM program, and I wasn't happy about it at all. I had started the JDAM program, and I was quite content there. I asked about the person who I would be replacing, and the answer was simply, 'He wasn't up to the task.'

"I knew that at JASSM, I would have to start over and would probably have to cope with a more difficult environment. The original program manager of JASSM was put in place at the start and given two major mandates. The first was not to repeat any of the mistakes of the past, meaning the TSSAM program. The Tri-Service Standoff Attack Missile (TSSAM) had been cancelled after six years and several billion dollars in cost over-runs. It was considered an unmitigated disaster, and all subsequent missile programs had to establish early on that they were not going to repeat the same mistakes made by TSSAM.

"The second mandate was to get started quickly. Unless the program established quickly that it was serious about getting on contract, it was unlikely that money would be made available through the next fiscal year. Still reeling from the TSSAM debacle, the attitude down at the Office of the Secretary of Defense (OSD) was: Show that your program is serious, and show it fast—or don't expect to be around long.

"The immediate objective was to award contracts to two competitors that would spend the next two years developing a system under the watchful eye of the government. At the end of the two-year evaluation process, one contractor would be awarded production of the missile. My predecessor and his team had worked on the contract since April, but they couldn't find a way to make the source selection quickly. Too many things still needed to be done, and it looked as though it was going to take the government team another year. That was unacceptable to senior management, especially at OSD.

"When I was brought on, we still needed to get the formal requirements approved by OSD, focus the contractors on making a serious proposal, field their proposals, and do the evaluation. Five companies were interested in competing for the two contracts: Hughes, Texas Instruments, Raytheon, Lockheed Martin, and McDonell Douglas.

"'You just go down there and do your thing,' I was told as I left my boss's office. Nothing more than that in the way of concrete detail. The rest was up to me, I guess. During the few days left until I actually joined JASSM, I started collecting some information about the status of the program. It became apparent that the JASSM team did not grasp the extent of the dissatisfaction with their achievements. As in other times throughout my career, I realized that my first challenge would be to change the way in which the team perceived reality.

"Most of my peers in program management think that the most important aspects of our jobs are making decisions, conducting reviews, and controlling performance. In contrast, my priorities are to develop collaborative relations, foster alliances, and give the people who work for me a sense of confidence in themselves.

"I stumbled into an understanding of this when I got involved in program management many years ago. At first, I gravitated toward an analytical approach because of my background in operations research. I was brought up in the Robert McNamara school of management, where everything is quantifiable—if we can't build a model of something, then it doesn't exist.

"It didn't take me long to figure out that this idea was bankrupt. Programs move ahead because of the activities of people, but none of the models I was using measured that critical ingredient for success. I could do the fanciest calculations in the world, but did they have anything to do with determining whether the project was going to be successful? Not at all. I had some difficulty convincing the people with whom I worked that it was not the right approach because they, like me, had been brought up to believe that a sharp analytic mind can arrive at a solution for any problem.

"Experience was my greatest teacher. I had managed to deliver several major projects successfully by implementing practices that were designed to fit the world as I saw it and that often differed from the accepted practices. It had been a bit easier to implement these practices in my previous projects because of the classified nature of the projects.

"However, my most recent project, JDAM, had been completely different. It was a high-profile Defense Acquisition Pilot Project, which was part of a wide reform movement in the defense establishment. This pilot program was given a clear mandate: *Do business more like business.* In order to do business differently, I assembled a group of people who were change agents. The main qualities required were the ability to think differently and the energy and zest to do something different. I sent the whole team for a two-week training session and for industry visits to Boeing Commercial Aviation, Motorola, Apple Computers, and Florida Power and Light, primarily to reinforce the fact that acquisition reform was not just a buzzword. It meant throwing out their old paradigms and embracing a new one."

Six Is Not Seven

At JASSM, Terry intended to apply the same principle that business would no longer be done as usual: "I called a meeting the first day back after New Year's with the 20 people who were working on JASSM. They were in a state of disbelief after learning that their boss had been fired over the Christmas holidays. He had worked with them on this program from the beginning and was well liked. Out of the blue, I showed up and told them, 'We are going to get this program on contract within six months. If we don't do it in six months, there is no program.'"

Brian Rutledge, the JASSM financial manager, was already familiar with Terry's no-nonsense approach when he took over JASSM, as they had worked together on a previous project. He recalls that same day from the perspective of the project members:

"I knew some of his antics, so I was half expecting something dramatic on his first day. He didn't let me down. It was January 3, and a lot of people were still on Christmas and New Year's leave, but Terry scheduled a mandatory meeting and required that everyone show up. He came into the room where we had assembled and, before even introducing himself, said, 'We're going to be on contract by July, and anybody who's not on board with that might as well look for another job.' He scared a lot of people. Some people weren't sure they would still be in the JASSM program office by the end of the month. He had a reputation, perhaps unfairly, of not hesitating to fire people when he thought it necessary."

Terry's objective was to empower the team, as a group, to rise to the challenge, impossible as it may have seemed at the time:

"After some initial cries of resistance—'there's no way, you really don't get it'—they realized that I was counting on them. I told them, 'We have to figure out how to work together to make this happen. First you need to put aside all of your paradigms and start with one basic assumption: that it's going to be done in six months. My job, as the leader here, is to facilitate things, to do whatever's necessary to make the bureaucracy move out of our way, so that it parts like the Red Sea parted for Moses—that's my job. But here you are giving up, and you haven't even started.' That silenced them, literally stopped them in their tracks."

Lynda Rutledge, the project's systems engineer (and Brian's wife after the first two years of the project), describes those early days when she had only known Terry for about a month:

"We had done a draft of the Single Acquisition Management Plan (SAMP) in the fall of 1995. The SAMP is the document that lays out how a program will be managed. It's a project plan, basically, and it seems as though everybody in the OSD needs to sign off on it. Terry read what we had written before he arrived and deemed it 'a piece of junk.' I remember him closing his office door and disappearing for about five days to rewrite it. This impressed me more than anything else about him. I'd never seen, or even heard of, a program manager writing his own SAMP. Normally, they farm it out to their leads who have no idea how their piece will be integrated into the whole.

"Terry wanted to present a concise, unified plan. I think that he rewrote 90 percent of our original draft and cut it down by more than half. But when the document came back from the OSD, it had grown bigger than he'd wanted. Terry didn't want a lot of detail. He didn't believe that you need to, or for that matter even can, spell out every detail about a program at its start. He pushed back on OSD, but ultimately decided to give in. In a case like this, you can't do anything more than push and push against the system, and in the end it's going to be a Pyrrhic victory at best if it distracts you from the main task at hand—getting on contract. He was not going to fall on his sword over a handful of paper. One thing about Terry Little is that he knows when to pick his battles.

"As I later learned, in his previous project, JDAM, where Terry had the luxury of selecting his own team and sufficient time to ensure that everyone on board understood and embraced the principles of the reform, he had served only as the project integrator, while the plan was actually prepared by the team. This time around, Terry had to adapt his approach to the new conditions under which JASSM was forced to operate: a shortage of time and a team unfamiliar with the reform. Still, Terry didn't shut anyone out and in fact sought input from people, occasionally popping out of his office and showing up at peoples' desks, like mine, to ask questions.

"When I joined JASSM, which was before Terry's arrival, the project had already formed working groups for each critical project area. Meetings in my area were conducted with the purpose of reaching some consensus on the models, measuring weapon effectiveness to be used by the five companies competing for the contract award. In the first meeting for my area, I was surprised to find close to a hundred people in the room. My notion about successful working groups was that they should be small, so I told the contractors that from now on, I intended to limit the number of people who could attend the meetings.

"Now you have to understand that up until that time, the companies had managed to get what they wanted from the original project manager by whining. Every time they complained, he tried to appease them, even at the expense of the other team members. So when the contractors went back to the program director and complained about me, he said that he was shocked by my behavior. I can't tell you what a big relief it was after starting to work with Terry that I could finally make decisions without having to worry anymore about being overruled every time one of the companies complained. A lot of bosses talk the talk about letting you take risks, but when something goes wrong, they punish you. Not Terry; he's not afraid to fail, and that's why he takes chances."

Indeed, Terry's management philosophy is based on autonomy and trust:

"When it comes to making decisions on the technical aspects of a program, I seldom intervene or get involved in the details. Sometimes people let me know what was decided, and other times, they don't. There are program decisions being made every day without my prior approval. When someone is new and I haven't taken the full measure of them yet, I will ask him or her to let me know what's going on, what they've decided— but after I am comfortable with their judgment, I believe in giving them the freedom they need to do their job. People who want to work for me are the kind of people who are not afraid to be accountable for results. I think that the key to getting the most out of people, whether they are on the government side or the contractor side, is to have a high expectation for results."

Regarding commitment and trust, Brian Rutledge explains:

"Terry expects you to defend your position. If you can't defend it, he'll tear you apart. In the first project we worked on together, I replaced a major who was just fired by Terry. The reason he got fired was because he couldn't figure out Terry's personality. Terry had challenged him on his cost estimate—Why did you do this? Why did you do that? After several rounds of this, my predecessor finally said, 'I give up, what number do you want?' But that's not what Terry wanted to hear. You don't ever say to Terry, 'What do you want?' So after three months, I had to go in and defend my estimates to him. We went head to head and he challenged me on every little thing, but I stood my ground. From then on, when I brought something to him, he trusted me, and that trust grew. About a year later, I got promoted."

Mutual accountability and a sense of project ownership are essential to Terry:

"Earlier in my career, I had a conversation with a colleague who had a tremendous impact on how I manage and why I place so much importance on establishing goals for the project and ensuring that each member fully embraces them. Late one night, we were driving together and got involved in a car accident. Neither of us was hurt, but the car was wrecked and we had to call for help. As we were waiting on the side of the road for the police to come, I was joking with him about all the things that he was insisting I do in his area. He was in charge of security on the program, but he could have been any functional type person. 'You are going to bankrupt the program,' I said. 'We are going to have all the security we could possibly need, but there won't be a program anymore.' 'That would suit me just fine,' he told me, and he was serious. 'The rest of the program is not my job; it's not what I get measured against. Security is my job.'

"Looking back on this, I remember it being such a shock to me that he would say, in effect, 'I really don't care about the program. That's your job. I only care about my own sandbox.' His comment led me to start questioning some of the people with whom I worked. I had assumed that everyone I was working with looked at things from the perspective of what was good for the program overall, that they wanted the whole program to be successful, and that their own special area was secondary.

"What I found out was that he was not unique—virtually none of the people who worked with me had the same goal that I did. Their expectation was that I, as the project leader, would integrate all of these different narrow vertical goals. It was my job alone to care about what was good for the program as a whole. That was an enlightening experience for me, and it's why I believe that it is so critical to make absolutely sure everyone has a clear understanding of what we are trying to do and feels ownership for the goals of the entire project."

Jackie Leitzel, the contracting officer for the U.S. Air Force, recalls:

"Before Terry arrived, we were just spinning our wheels, so I understood what he was saying about the problem of people having different goals. Before he came, Logistics might be saying one thing while Testing was saying another, and I would have to go to the program director to ask which version we were going with—and even then I still didn't get a clear-cut answer. At one of the first meetings after Terry came on board, he showed us several charts about teaming and shared goals. Terry got us focused fast with the same goal to get on contract in six months. Suddenly we knew what we were aiming for."

Not only did Terry get everyone to agree on the same goal, he encouraged their input on how best to reach it:

"I held weekly meetings with representatives from each of the five companies competing for the contract in order to give them an update on where we stood, what had changed since the last time we spoke, where we were having problems in the program office, where the requirements stood, and what approvals we still needed to get from my upper management. After these group meetings, I would meet with each of the five contractors separately—not to tell them something, but to listen to what they had to say. When they were with the four other competitors, they were all guarded and careful about what they disclosed. Nobody wanted to give away their competitive edge or reveal any weaknesses. They started out reserved in the one-on-one meetings, but as they saw that I wasn't just doing this for my health or because it was polite, they began to approach these meetings much more seriously.

"From my point of view, I was trying to learn—as opposed to just trying to squeeze information out of them. I would ask, 'Give me some feedback. Tell me specifically about this requirement. Does the path we're headed down seem right to you? Is there a requirement—or two or three or four—which you think is not going to be consistent with us getting a low-cost system? What I want to know is: Are we spinning our wheels in some area that we don't really understand, and what are the implications?'

"For example, we suggested a requirement to put this weapon on a number of different kinds of airplanes. A couple of the companies said, 'We've looked at that, and we can do that, but it's going to take a really long time to go through all of the engineering details. If we could just start off putting it on one or two planes and get this thing built and fielded, and then modify it if we need to, we would be much better off in terms of overall cost, overall schedule, and overall performance.'

"By and large, the government frowned upon doing things that way at this stage of a program. Its view was that once you decide on your requirements, then you call in the contractor and say, 'Here is exactly what we are going to do, we've got it all figured out, and now it is up to you to go and respond.' But I didn't believe that was the way to get the most bang for the buck. I wanted the five companies who were going to bid to be involved in the process of refining the requirements. Because they were the ones who had to respond to whatever innovations we pitched, it didn't seem to me to be in their best interest—or ours—to say, 'Okay, this is what we're going to do, and you companies are going to learn how to adjust.' I thought that the best way to improve our chances of getting a quality product was to allow for some give-and-take at this stage, when our vision for the missile was still in flux.

"The fact of the matter is that most requirements are just made up by someone. Typically, a requirement starts off as somebody's opinion or view of what would be good, but what often happens is that everybody then begins to march as if it's a law of nature that you've got to meet this requirement. The prevailing assumption is that however much time and however much money it takes, it doesn't matter because the requirement is the requirement. Once a requirement is established and everyone has signed on to it, the requirement becomes an expectation, which is extremely difficult to change. As such, it is much easier and much better to carefully think about requirements before they are formulated, rather than after they appear to be cast in stone.

"One of the major reasons for schedule slippages and cost over-runs is uncontrolled growth in requirements. So I allow, and even encourage, flexibility regarding requirements, but only up to a certain point. Once I am convinced that we have taken the necessary steps to formulate requirements that meet the needs of the customers and which are fully understood by them, I have found it useful—and this doesn't come easy to me—to create a very bureaucratic process for changing requirements. Basically, I say there will be no changes in requirements until the customers understand the cost and schedule implications of the change and explicitly agree to those implications. It is quite amazing to see how a process that simply establishes accountability for requirements growth promotes better discipline and yields a more realistic schedule and budget."

Throughout the entire process, Terry stressed to his team that part of a technical requirement has to be cost:

"Cost is a technical issue, and to treat it as something different is crazy. Imagine a car manufacturer telling its engineers, 'Go and design the next generation whatever-kind-of-car,' then after it is designed ask, 'Okay, now can we sell it? Is there a market for something that costs this much?' It's a question of establishing the affordable price for a system and then trading off either performance or schedule to meet that price as long as the Key Performance Parameters are met. The trick is to define performance in a way that permits the team to meet the requirements of the system within the constraints of affordability.

"Our aim was to demonstrate that we could produce this missile for low cost. What I did was make cost an intrinsic part of the technical requirements for designing the missile. You have to do that to make sure the engineers understand that the success or failure of their activity depends on what the ultimate cost is. The thing about engineers is that they generally do not accept ownership of cost and schedule. They accept ownership of performance, but cost and schedule are somebody else's problem.

"We ran into this problem with 'radar cross section,' which is a critical performance parameter that has to do with how visible the cruise missile is on radar. Ideally, you would want it to be totally invisible. You can spend infinite amounts of money on this, so you have to decide what you are willing to accept and can still afford. The way I saw it, the question was: How much better should we go? We had engineers who were very eager to go four or five orders of magnitude better on this parameter. Then there were the cost people saying, 'We don't need to be any better than the predecessor program. We don't want to reach for something and spend a lot of money and then not make it. Let's stay on ground that we know will not collapse beneath us.' Ultimately, what I decided was somewhere in between the engineers and the cost people. The engineers whined that I wasn't being ambitious or aggressive enough, while the bean counters whined about the risk. Nobody was really happy. In the end, it turned out to be a good match of cost and performance."

As the financial manager, Brian knew that the program could not move forward without the approval of the Cost Analysis Improvement Group (CAIG):

"They're the cops of the cost world, and they are there to challenge your assumptions. The head cop at the CAIG was the one who had to sign off on the program, and he was known for grilling people hard about how they put together their cost estimates. What I did was invite one of his deputies to work directly with my cost team. I had him interfacing with all of our engineers and anybody we were working with to help build the cost estimates. My hope was that by making him a member of our team, rather than an adversary with whom we had to struggle to get the program going, he would feel accountable for the product.

"To invite him in was a risk because I couldn't control what he was going to see, but I had worked on other programs before JASSM, and I knew that the worst thing you could have happen was for someone on the CAIG to say, 'I don't understand all your data or where your numbers are coming from.' Even though he was doing an independent estimate in parallel, he knew that our data was good because we shared all of it with him. He, in turn, went to his boss and said, 'They have credible numbers.'"

Brian knew that getting the job done required the ability to adapt to the situation, even if it sometimes meant a willingness to deviate from the norm:

> "Our plan called for completing the source selection in three weeks. Three weeks to review the proposals and choose the two companies who would compete for the next two years. Three weeks, and then breathe.
>
> "I had one person helping me to crunch numbers. When I recruited him, he wasn't in high demand. In fact, a lot of people around Eglin Air Force Base thought he was off the wall—and he was. He was definitely high maintenance, but he was intelligent and had a passion for what he did. If you ask me, those two things can overcome just about anything.
>
> "All he needed was a little direction, so I kept him focused on which way to go. He loved the intensity, and we worked insane hours during those three weeks. The only thing that slowed us down was his chain smoking. We'd be the only ones in the building at 11:00 at night and he'd be smoking like a fiend. Each time he lit up, he had to leave the office and go outside the building. Finally, I said, 'You're not leaving! Open the window and smoke. I'll take the heat for it.' The person who managed the building complained, 'We're going to throw you out of here if you keep this up.' Fortunately, the source selection was done before he could mobilize the bureaucracy against us.
>
> "Other people would never have considered recruiting this guy for their team, but I knew he would get the job done. The room reeked of cigarettes, but we got the job done. I suspect that

he never enjoyed himself as much as he did those three weeks during source selection. You have to get the right people for the right job at the right time."

As Lynda Rutledge discovered, sometimes keeping the right people in the right job at the right time is a hard call to make:

"Terry gives women more latitude than he does men, and I took him to task for it once, much to his chagrin, I think. A woman in a leadership position on our team was vanishing for long periods without any explanation. One day Terry asked me, because he knew I had the most contact with her, if I thought her absence was having a negative effect on the program. I told him that I thought it was.

"Then he asked me what I would do. So I told him, 'I'd get rid of her.' I said it wasn't worth sacrificing the morale of the rest of the team to keep her on. The program was a roller coaster ride as it was, and it was bad for morale when someone whom you relied on to make decisions was disappearing for long stretches and holding people back. 'But technically she's good,' he said. 'When she's here,' I pointed out.

"'Well, I just like to give women more latitude,' he explained. That's when I told him, 'You're a male chauvinist.' I could tell he was mortified. 'What do you mean?' he asked. 'You treat women differently than men,' I said. He still wasn't getting it.

"'We don't want to be treated differently,' I said. 'What kind of example does that set for junior people when they see somebody senior behaving that way? Is that the example you want to set for future leaders? It's unacceptable. It's just not worth the technical benefit she brings to the program.' He listened to me, but he didn't get rid of her, and the problem didn't go away either, as he continued to compensate for her absences."

When it came to devising the process for selecting the two contractors, though, Lynda and Terry were in complete harmony about the need to change the usual way of doing source selection and the need to cut down the enormous amount of information requested by the government team. Considering that the selection was to be equally based on their past performances and their current proposals, Lynda describes the need for less paper and more personal interaction:

> "Many people in the government don't want to talk to contractors prior to source selection. They think we should write an all-encompassing Request for Proposal, hand it over to contractors, get an all-encompassing document back, and then go read the thing in our hole and say, 'We pick you.'
>
> "Personally, I think it's absurd to choose a contractor without talking to them and finding out who they are, what their strengths are, and how you're going to team with them. Let's face it, a contract is like a marriage, and to do that sight unseen, I mean, I just think that a decision worth billions of dollars should not rely on a piece of paper. Terry fought to have the companies do oral presentations instead of simply turning in a written proposal. When all was said and done, we had managed to cut a 1,000-page proposal down to what could be adequately addressed in a four-hour oral presentation."

Although they did get their oral presentations, Lynda tells how the process was not without its problems:

> "Upper management worried about our ability to evaluate live performances, and the companies argued that scheduling the presentations on different days meant that some of them would have more time to prepare than others. In the end, the compromise was to have them all turn in videotaped presentations at the same time. Unfortunately, that defeated the whole purpose of doing an oral presentation because we missed out on the dialogue.

"Nobody was more anxious about the oral presentations than the companies who were doing them. They worried that their engineers weren't going to be effective presenters or go off on a tangent and never get back to the point. They got nervous after the dry runs, which were face-to-face with government evaluators. There was plenty of dialogue then. We raised hands, asked questions, and cut in. We had the ability to say to our counterparts on the contractor side, 'Hey, I don't get what you're saying. I've never heard this before. I don't understand what you're talking about.' And then they would respond back, 'Well, the reason we are doing it this way is...' That was invaluable, and that's what you really need to do in order to evaluate and understand somebody's proposal.

"When we got the final presentation tapes, some of the contractors had hired professional actors to narrate. In other cases, the companies' engineers, bless their hearts, gave acting a shot. I wasn't the only person who considered the videotaped presentations a waste of time. The companies all submitted written slides to accompany their presentations, and most of us who were doing the evaluations turned off the tapes and did our evaluations based on the slides."

Terry had his way of making sure everyone stayed on message. Brian Rutledge recalls a small gesture that took on far greater meaning than he ever thought it would:

"After Terry said that we were going to be on contract in six months, he directed someone to make a viewgraph stating this goal: *Be on contract by July 1, 1996.* That was it. He wanted it pinned up in everybody's cubicle. At first, I thought, 'Oh man, this is goofy. I know what we're doing. I don't need to have a reminder on the wall.' When I talked to other people working in the program office, I just rolled my eyes. 'What's this guy thinking?' I said. 'It's like we're in kindergarten.'

"But after a few months, I had to admit that there was something to it. I saw it there every day when I walked up to my desk. I eventually found myself stopping to think, 'What am I doing to get to that point, and what can I cut out of my work that's preventing me from getting there? How am I getting distracted from the goal?'"

An unexpected admission by Terry revealed the essence of his philosophy:

"The truth is that I pulled the number six out of my hat. I would have been happy to be on contract at the end of seven months or even eight months, but I would never have told the team that.

"What I wanted to do was set a goal that would challenge these folks to look at things in an entirely new way. I didn't want a schedule that they felt they could achieve just by working on weekends or figuring out a handful of inventive ways to do things. I wanted something so outrageous that it would cause them, first, to essentially give up, but then—once they figured out that giving up wasn't an option—to step back and examine all their assumptions, all their beliefs, all the things that were in their heads as a result of their experiences and what they had been told in the past, and to ask themselves with a clean slate: 'What do I really need to do to achieve this goal?'

"As they ran into hard times, they wanted to negotiate. There were a lot of people saying, 'Hey, we've figured out ways to work faster, but does it really have to be six months, or can it be seven?' 'No,' I said, 'because the difference between six months and seven months is that seven months isn't the goal.'

"The result was that problems didn't remain unsolved for long. People no longer scratched their heads and asked one another, 'How should we make the right decision?' Now, there was a level of commitment that meant any problem had to be attacked with a sledgehammer. The team addressed all problems, no matter whose area it was in. They wouldn't let any given problem cause the rest of the team to fail. When a problem was detected, everybody marshaled their energies together to try to figure out quickly, 'How do we move forward? How do we either solve the problem or get around it?'

"Even after they got to the point where it became fairly certain that they were going to meet the six-month deadline, they were so imbued with energy and passion for achieving the goal that instead of saying, 'Okay, now let's coast,' they kept working on it every day to figure out, 'What is it that we've got in front of us to do, and is there a quicker way to accomplish it? How can we cut another day, another two days, another three days?'

"We kept a chart to measure our progress. But, it wasn't a chart to mark off this event, that event, and so on. Forget about chronology; it was a chart that graphed how much we had accomplished and how much we had left to do. Some days we put our progress at 70 percent, and the next week, having run into some kind of unanticipated problem, our mark would go back down to 60 percent. People would look at that and say, 'Oh no, we've got to step it up!'

"What we achieved was something even better than six months. At the end of the day, we completed the source selection in less than five months. People were proud of themselves, and with good cause. When we talked about it afterwards, what the team discovered was that they hadn't known how capable they could be if they just quit thinking about things in the way they had always thought about them. They achieved what they did as a result of passion, commitment, and focus, as opposed to being smart, making good decisions, following the rules, and making sure that they didn't make any mistakes."

We Would Shoot Granny for a Dollar

Jackie Leitzel describes the Program Definition and Risk Reduction phase of the JASSM, which started in June 1996 at the end of the six-month source selection process:

> "The two defense contractors finally chosen to compete in the Program Definition and Risk Reduction phase were Lockheed Martin Integrated Systems and McDonnell Douglas Aerospace. Each of the companies was awarded contracts totaling $237.4 million and will go head-to-head over the next two years to win the final contract. At the end of this phase, the Department of Defense will award one of the contractors approximately $3 billion for the development, testing, and production of at least 2,400 JASSMs."

Brian Rutledge explains the process further:

> "What was unique about JASSM was that we let the companies decide what they were going to do during the two years. Every six months, the government conducted a two-day review of the design of each company, brought the best experts, and provided candid feedback. However, we didn't present to them a Statement of Work and say you have to do A, B, C, D, and E. Because they were at different stages of maturity, we gave them the opportunity to tailor what it was they were going to do over the next two years. At the end of the two years, we would judge them on that and pick the one we believed was best able to carry us on through the rest of the program. We let the competition give us the assurance that we were going to get good value for the money.
>
> "When we down-selected from five companies to two, I switched from being the financial lead in the government program office to being program manager on a helper team for McDonnell Douglas. The role of a helper team was to assist your company in winning the contract at the end of the two

years. When we began, six government people were assigned to each of the helper teams. We all came from the JASSM program office at Eglin Air Force Base. Winning was the goal. Forget about the old goal of getting on contract in six months. We had a new goal.

"I stayed in that position for the duration of the competition, and about halfway into it, McDonnell Douglas merged with Boeing. Our program office was then absorbed into the Boeing organization, and I started splitting my time between Eglin in Florida and the company's main facility in St. Louis. Soon after we moved into our offices in St. Louis, Terry asked the vice president at McDonnell Douglas/Boeing in charge of JASSM whether he wanted to reconsider having government helpers. 'Oh no, I want to continue this,' he said, 'these people are integral in helping us make decisions.' And we were. He often asked for my advice on how we should present this or that problem to the government team back home. When I was with the government team, my job was to show why my company earned an "A" grade on the evaluation criteria. At this point, you could say I might as well have been wearing a company uniform. Winning was everything. Naturally, I couldn't do anything illegal, but all else was fair game. I'll say this, it was the best job I ever had working for the government in terms of having a clear direction."

Terry describes his role in the competition:

"I picked the helpers. Their job was to support their respective company—not to look after the government's interest, not to make sure the company didn't do something stupid, not to bring home secrets to me—just to help that company win, period. And the reason that was in the government's interest was because at the end of the two years, we wanted to face a difficult decision when we selected the winning company.

"The government's role should be to ensure the success of the project, and the way to do that is not to oversee or second-guess the contractor—the way to do that is by helping the contractor. Help the contractor to do things that the contractor can't do or that the government can do better. The helper teams set the stage for what I wanted the government's role to be two years later when we got down to one contractor. When we finally got down to the one company that was going to do the job, I wanted to have already established a working relationship in which we were open, straight, candid, and—most of all—trusting of one another. I clearly understood that you can't do that by just saying it is so. It just doesn't work that way.

"Now, there were a lot of people above me who were against this. Their view was, 'The guy who loses will protest or create a legal problem for us because he will argue that you gave him weak people or that his competitive position got inadvertently disclosed by these government people.' But the companies had the capabilities to get rid of any government person they chose at any time for any reason. In other words, the companies were the ones deciding what 'help' was and whether or not they were getting it. If they had thought that they needed someone else with a different talent or expertise, I would have done whatever I could to get it for them."

Larry Lawson, the project manager for Lockheed Martin Corporation, reflects on the need to stop doing "business as usual:"

"Before acquisition reform, the government said to its contractors, 'Follow these military standards and everything will be okay.' From a contractor's point of view, that was a comfortable place to be. Contractors understood the 'old way' of business, where we knew what the government wanted. There was more time, less risk, and more money.

"Then came along Terry Little, who was quick to say, 'We don't have the time, we don't have the funds, and we don't have the answers. We want a missile in half the time for half the price. This is what's important to us. We have three key performance parameters: system effectiveness, range, and carrier operability. These things are not tradable; everything else is. You will have the freedom to put together your approach that meets our three key performance parameters, and along with that, we will ask for a long-term, bumper-to-bumper warranty to back up the quality of your approach. The objective is a dramatic reduction in acquisition time and funds. You either understand that or you are out of the game.'

"Terry took a very aggressive approach on standards and detailed specifications. He told me, 'Larry, throw all the military standards out. You don't have to follow them. I don't want you to reference a single military standard.' This was an extreme approach intended to force change—the type of change that was required if we were going to make unprecedented inroads in cutting the time required to field weapons. Suddenly we found ourselves in an environment where our customer was saying, 'If you want to win, you can't do things the old way. Here's the way it is now. We did the last down-select 50 percent on past performance. Now the rules are different. Affordability is going to be foremost. The contractor who can provide the best price—and is somebody that we can work with—is going to win.'

"That was a wake-up call to me. I remember realizing that we were going down the wrong road. We were moving ahead with a performance-oriented agenda. We had to change what we were doing and drive everything toward affordability, and we did. One of our engineers was quoted a few months later as saying, 'We would shoot granny for a dollar.'

"Of course, change is seldom comfortable. We were in a purely experimental space, which is a disconcerting place to be at times. We moved forward with the vision to create a significantly different model for the missile design, system test, subcontracting, and production, but change was slower to happen in some areas. As a contractor, it is sometimes frustrating when you are going down an acquisition reform path only to find out that it isn't possible. Looking to place blame for the cost and schedule impacts could have split our team, but we took our lumps and moved on.

"We were not known as a cruise missile producer, so most of our team wasn't burdened with preconceptions of how to proceed. Using the customer's overarching vision, we opened our eyes to all possible methods, which allowed us to synthesize the design that stands today. The folks that couldn't get the vision moved on. Those who remained understood the Air Force vision, and we shaped our own.

"We recognized that we had to dramatically reduce cost while still keeping the performance bar high. A fully integrated systems design approach to meet performance at the defined cost targets was our only hope of obtaining a reliable and affordable solution. For instance, it was understood that cruise missiles were built in sections and then integrated in final assembly. That approach wasn't affordable and didn't contribute in any way to performance. We decided on a uni-body approach, which would reduce material cost and assembly labor, and we were not going to build the missile fuselage out of metal. We said, 'We're going to build it out of composites, and we're going to use boating industry processes.'

"Acquisition reform forced us to take a whole new look at the way we did things. We outsourced work any time we realized that we could do something more affordably with suppliers. I won't deny that there were conflicts within the organization, but we were able to convince people that this was what it took to win—taking a risk and not surrendering to political pressure.

"For example, we normally would have built the composites at our legendary Skunk Works facility in Palmdale, California. Now, because affordability meant everything, we went with a supplier instead. It would have been lower risk and superior quality to do it at Palmdale, but it was going to cost us more money.

"We found a company outside of Boston that had been in the business of making baseball bats and golf club shafts. They had never built a military product, but they knew how to weave carbon fiber and were open-minded, and we were committed to making them successful. So we took this small company from being a baseball bat provider to being a cruise missile supplier, and it was a remarkable transformation.

"The first prototype they built took a long time, and the end product didn't measure up. When they built the second one, they had learned what things they didn't have to do or be concerned about, and so the second prototype was a better product that took about half as long to build. By the time they started work on the sixth one, they knew exactly where they had to be concerned with the strength of this thing as they were putting it together and they knew exactly where they could reduce their cost.

"I have to give the credit to the folks at Palmdale. In spite of the fact that they were going to lose the work, they found the Boston company for us. They also helped find a supplier for our missile wings. One of the fellows at Palmdale knew about a company that built surfboards. He said, 'Hey, look, I think this wing is the same kind of thing that they do with surf boards.' We went down to their factory in a disadvantaged section of Los Angeles and bought the equipment for them. Now they make cruise missile wings using surfboard technology.

"From my perspective, even though we at Lockheed Martin faced the challenge of not having a platform to start with, we were in a better position of being responsive to the government's objectives. Success was realized by creative, highly motivated people who were not locked into accepted solutions or preconceptions defined by military standards."

In that same competitive spirit, Terry visited one of the contractors' suppliers and asked him, "What is the prime making you do or causing you to do that you think is worthless or not value-added enough to offset the cost?" As he tells it:

"A representative from the prime was present, and so there was a little bit of nervousness on the part of the supplier. I told the representative from the prime to go get a cup of coffee. I ended up with about three pages full of stuff that the supplier said was causing him headaches.

"As I was writing all this down, he asked, 'What are you going to do with that?' And I said, 'Not to worry.' I made it clear to him that I was going to protect him, and I think he accepted this. Legally, I couldn't do a thing, and he knew that, but I knew that he wouldn't have told me any of this stuff about the prime if he hadn't believed me. How did I gain his trust?

"Well, for one thing, I was there. A government program manager does not normally go to visit the suppliers of a prime contractor. The fact that I was there and willing to spend a whole day looking at his facility, meeting his people, and talking to them about the program and how important their contributions were—that was a big deal to him. A lot of these people never see any government people, except for inspectors, so when I showed up at their facility, they understood that it was because I wanted to know about what they were doing.

"Typically, the government says, 'Our contract is with the prime, and we don't have a contract with these suppliers.'

Maybe that's true, theoretically, but think about this in terms of common sense. A large part of the success of the program depends on what the suppliers to my contractor are doing. Am I just going to close my eyes to that? We have two big companies putting together a cruise missile, and there are all kinds of smaller companies that provide the engine, the warhead, the fuses, and so on. I believe it's important to communicate with everybody involved in the outcome of a program.

"I understand that I can't go to these suppliers and start making demands, do this, do that, because I don't have an official means, an actual legal relationship with them. But for me to just say, 'Well, that's not my problem,' or 'I'm not very interested in any of them'—to me that seems insane. Yes, it is true that we can't be in there undermining the relationship between the prime and the suppliers, but it doesn't mean that I can't, as the government program manager, go to them and say, 'Tell me what I can do to help you do your job better.'

"I gave the three pages to the prime without any explanation other than, 'This is what he told me.' A week later, this guy from the prime came back to me and explained how they'd addressed everything on the list except for one thing, and he gave me a detailed and satisfactory explanation as to why the one thing was still important to do. That was fine. I had no problem with that."

On the need to be aggressive in cutting costs, Brian tells us:

"At this stage of the game, the affordability of the missile was rated higher than its technical capability. This was no secret. At the end of the two years, the government would select a contractor who promised technical competency at a good price. In everything the companies were doing in this phase, they had to work to convince the government that they had gotten the price of this missile down.

"As one of the Boeing helpers, I told them where I thought they should be in terms of a production price at the end to win the contract. They had the resources to be very aggressive in pricing the missile. Historically, they'd been the cruise missile contractors, and I think they did not take the stance of being aggressive enough on their pricing, and I tried to get them to change. I kept arguing, 'That's not good enough to keep out the other guy, who is very hungry and wants to get into the cruise missile business. We need to find some other ways to get this price down lower than he is willing to go.' I could not convince them that they had to be more aggressive in their production pricing, and this was something that frustrated me throughout the process. In the end, the DOD chose Lockheed Martin Corporation."

Terry recalls:

"When it came to choosing which company would be awarded the contract, we would have liked for it to have been a difficult decision. However, it was not a difficult choice. One company was clearly the stronger of the two. The one that lost didn't do a bad job. They had good engineers, they used disciplined processes, but when they got feedback from the government, instead of listening to us and looking at what they were doing, they argued—'But you just don't understand.' It was as though they had their plan and nothing was going to cause them to deviate from that.

"The other company listened to our feedback, and after their reviews would go back and decide, 'What is it that we need to change? Where is it that we need to put more emphasis? Where is it that we need to get rid of people? Where is it that we need to spend more money?' Every time they got feedback, they saw it as an opportunity to adapt. There was no doubt that by the time we got to the last review, everybody knew who was going to win.

"The company that lost also had another big problem. Eventually they overcame it, but by then it was too late. Their suppliers complained that the prime was unwilling to give them the money to build prototypes. Somebody should have asked, 'How do we convince ourselves that we know how to build this in an affordable way?' You do prototyping up front and then see if something works like you think it will. Sometimes it will, most of the time it won't, but then you learn from that. The company that won was not afraid to learn from its mistakes, and prototyping was an essential part of their strategy.

"Prototyping is a wonderful way of learning, yet we don't do enough of it because we would like to believe that if we simply get enough smart people together, we can run through the numbers, put them in the model, do the simulation, and it will all come out just like it is supposed to. But guess what? In the real world, it rarely happens the way we predict with our models. The reason people want it to be that way is because prototyping is not cheap—it is not cheap in terms of the money or the time required to do it. It is messy and sometimes you are embarrassed with the results, but eventually you reach your goal. In the long run, it saves you money."

We're Married Now

Lockheed's Larry Lawson discusses the change in the way his team had to interact with the government team after winning the contract:

"Soon after we won the contract to be the sole source provider on JASSM, Terry and I realized that the majority of his people needed to become helpers—not just the handful who worked with us during the rolling down-select. Their job up to this point had been to measure us and to critique us so that they could do a source selection. For the program to continue moving ahead, his people could not be in the critique mode any longer. We had to all play as a team now, all responsible for the success of the program.

"The first thing I did was bring several of the government folks into our facility. I invited them to all of our meetings, and I also made Terry's deputy my number two person. He moved his office into our facility and sat across the hall from me.

"Whenever Terry or I felt like his people were reverting to their traditional role of overseeing the contractor, we met with the key individuals involved to talk about it. Invariably, this led to an offsite with the whole team. At our first offsite after the contract award, Terry got up to speak and said, 'Let me be clear, we're married now. We must work together—so don't come to me with a bunch of domestic squabbles. Divorce would be devastating.'

"Our offsites were crucial in maintaining the focus and reinforcing the message that we were all working together as a team. And they were invaluable in other ways. People got to know one another and realized that they weren't slimy contractors or inconsiderate government employees. These were real people with real commitments to what they were working on. Were they all motivated to make this program successful? Almost universally, the answer was yes.

"After months of working seven-day weeks, our first missile launch after the contract award failed. Our first launch! This worried me because up until that point, some of our innovative designs were unproven other than through extensive subsystem testing and detailed modeling. Everything before flight testing is substantiating data and simulation. The competitive phase didn't allow either team to fly.

"A tremendous effort had gone into that first shot, and the team was shaken. At that moment, we all questioned ourselves, 'Are we up to it or not?' We were all determined to get it fixed, and we turned the failure into a challenge to correct the problem by the next scheduled shot date. We would not break the schedule.

"It was the defining moment for the program. The status quo response would have been, 'We need six months to figure this out.' Terry could have said, 'I don't trust you, and I want to have an independent technical review. Oh, by the way, I want a report every day.' But that's not what he said. Terry did the right thing. He did not roll in on us. He did not send his people in to stand over our shoulders and say, 'You really messed up here. We don't trust you.' Instead, he asked me if I wanted some help. I asked him to send down three or four people from his test organization who had expertise in specific areas. He sent them down, and they went to work.

"It turned out that there was nothing inherently wrong with the system. The problem was associated with some test-related analog circuitry requested by the safety team. But the failure focused the team on challenging all requirements and on testing every detail prior to flight. We redesigned the circuit, and six weeks later shot a missile and it flew beautifully. That was no doubt one of the most pleasing moments in my career.

"Teams are defined by how they react in adversity—and how their leaders react. Terry's reaction, I think, was absolutely right. He decided, 'I'm going to let you solve this problem.' His decision demonstrated trust, and it set the tenor for how we moved forward as a program. The lessons learned by this team about how to respond to adversity enabled us to solve bigger challenges and keep the remainder of the test program on track."

And stay on track it did. Jackie Leitzel sums up the success of the U.S. government-Lockheed Martin JASSM team:

> "Although the estimated unit cost of JASSM when the program was launched in 1995 was $800,000, the contract was awarded to Lockheed Martin in 1998 for a cost of $400,000 per unit. In June 2002, the team received the DoD's highest acquisition honor, the David Packard Excellence in Acquisition Award, which was presented by C. Pete Aldridge, the Undersecretary of Defense for Acquisition, Technology, and Logistics, in recognition of their exemplary innovations in the defense acquisition process."

2

Building of Memory:
Managing Creativity Through Action

by Alexander Laufer, Zvi Ziklik, and Jeffrey Russell

Initial Stages: Making Progress by Splitting

Yad Vashem is a memorial site to the six million Jews killed by the Nazis. The 45-acre site located near Jerusalem contains several museums and various research and educational centers. The largest museum on site is the new Holocaust History Museum, which opened in March 2005. The architect of this museum, Moshe Safdie, who is a leading international designer, concludes his book *Yad Vashem—The Architecture of Memory* as follows:

> "No design I have ever undertaken was so charged with sym- bolic associations. It seemed that every move, form, shape, and sequence elicited multiple interpretations and endless debate. Now that the public has possessed the complex, I am amazed at the diversity of interpretations and reactions. When I am there, I often become a voyeur and watch visitors' reactions and listen to their conversations. I have always wondered if architecture is capable of evoking the same emotions that we experience lis- tening to music. At Yad Vashem, I am constantly aware of how intensely personal the feelings provoked are and how individual

and particular. It is at these moments that I feel architecture can, however rarely, move us as deeply as music can."

Shimon Kornfeld, the project manager of the Holocaust History Museum, recalls another kind of music that prevailed when he was appointed to lead the project from the early stages of the design. Loud voices and even shouting were known to accompany the passionate and intense debates about the fundamental concepts of the design that constantly took place between the chief curator of the museum, Avner Shalev, and the architect Moshe Safdie.

Shimon was already an experienced project manager at the time and was used to internal conflicts in his project teams. Over the years, he had learned to appreciate such conflicts because of their eventual positive impact on the quality of the team's decisions. But this time was different. These conflicts often sounded more like a competition between two fierce opponents rather than a healthy debate between two members of the same team. Shimon was worried that such rivalry would hurt collaboration between the other members of the project team and that it would eventually hamper project progress. It was also difficult to reconcile diverging opinions in an analytical way because at this creative stage of the project, most decisions were based more on ideas and less on facts. Shimon realized that navigating between these two strong personalities and their respective teams would require a great deal of creativity on his own part as well.

It should be noted that both the chief curator and the architect enjoyed a unique and powerful status in the project. Avner, the chief curator, also served as chairman of the Yad Vashem Directorate of the Holocaust Martyrs' and Heroes' Remembrance Authority. That is, he was a member of the project team and head of the client organization at the same time. Safdie, who is regarded as a world renowned architect, had been awarded this project through an international competition, and his proposal had been selected by an independent committee composed of highly esteemed experts and public figures.

Thus, Shimon, the project manager, could not have dealt with these two designers like he would have any other member of the project team. They were simply too powerful. Because of the nature of this project—remembering the Holocaust—both designers were totally committed to the success of the mission, but each one felt that the other side was somehow attempting to "own" the entire project. The concern on the curators' side was that the spectacular design of the building would be so dominant that it would stand by itself as a memorial and would overshadow the central role of the exhibitions. Ironically, therefore, the unique shape of Safdie's structure worrying the curators was the very reason that his design had been chosen.

The truth is that Shimon himself was also very concerned about the design of the structure:

> "The museum's central bloc was designed as a prism that penetrates into the ground and 'erupts' from it, at varying angles, as an unsupported protrusion. The walls of the prism envelope had a unique architectural design based on 'exposed concrete' elements with no external cladding or coating. We were worried that certain components of this unique and extraordinary monument might be impossible to execute."

The architect explained his radical demands:

> "I was determined to cast the entire museum monolithically, jointless, unadorned—without any exterior waterproofing or cladding or any interior insulation or finishes. I wanted just the basic structure—concrete walls and floors and glass to let the light in from above."

Thus, it is no surprise that Shimon came to the following conclusion: "The contractor will be required to 'sculpt' the concrete elements in order to realize the architect's wild dream." Shimon approached an expert in executing complex elements made of "architectural concrete" and asked him to examine the feasibility of executing the proposed design. The expert provided a list of recommendations to render the execution more feasible, but only a few of his recommendations were accepted by Safdie.

Safdie reiterated his opinion that the project must be imparted with a unique character and that he himself, as well as other leading architects around the world, had designed buildings of similar character that had been successfully executed and that served as a source of inspiration and a place of pilgrimage. In an attempt to convince Shimon, Safdie suggested that they visit a few of these sites abroad. Undertaking this tour, however, did not alleviate Shimon's concerns: "On the tour, we saw structures that were amazing in their complexity, but the structure designed for Yad Vashem seemed to me to be more problematic than they were. I really did not know how one can build the external envelope of this unique building."

Even the director general of Yad Vashem, Ishai Amrami, was not fully satisfied with the design of the building: "During the project, I had some harsh arguments with Shimon and with Shimon's predecessor about the management of the design and particularly about our proceedings vis-á-vis Safdie. I felt that they avoided confrontations with the famous architect and in several cases, chose to 'sacrifice' the functionality of a certain area for the 'benefit' of an 'architectural whim.'" Still, despite some discomfort on the part of the client, the curators, and the project manager with some aspects of the design, the architect seemed to have the power and the determination to stick to his design.

Although the new Holocaust History museum was the heart of the new development at Yad Vashem, it was only one component of it. The project that Shimon was managing was much larger and covered additional buildings and infrastructure work throughout the Yad Vashem site. The cost of the entire project was estimated at 100 million dollars, but at that time only 45 million dollars had already been procured. Given that the estimated cost of the museum building was about 40 million dollars, Ishai requested that Shimon split the construction of the museum building from the rest of the project and issue the tender for it as early as possible:

> "I was aware that the design of the electrical, mechanical, and other systems in the building had not been completed. However, Yad Vashem finances all its projects from donations, and accelerating the beginning of construction was crucial for obtaining financing for the project. Potential donors tend to respond more favorably to our appeals when they can see real action on site and when the actual structure starts rising on the site."

Surprisingly, Shimon responded favorably to Ishai's request. Even with the difficulties of starting construction on the building before design of all the systems was complete, Shimon felt that creating a *fait accompli* would put a quicker end to the bitter conflict between the curators and the architect. Moreover, Shimon explained that decoupling the building of the museum from the rest of the project would allow him and his team to focus all their attention on execution of the most difficult component of the entire project, the one with the radical design and stringent requirements. Thus, the gap in needed resources and the splitting process unexpectedly turned out to be a huge help for Shimon, enabling him to cope better with the many unique challenges posed by execution of the design.

Middle Stages: Making Progress by Uniting

Shimon surprised Ishai again when he insisted on an unconventional process for selecting the contractor who would build the new museum. Yad Vashem, like most public organizations, generally chooses its contractors via the traditional process, in which any and all contractors are invited to submit their proposals, and the one with the least expensive proposal is the one selected for the job. That was exactly what bothered Shimon. He was worried that for such an extremely complicated project, selecting the least expensive contractor rather than the most suitable one would not only severely compromise the quality of the product, but would lead to disastrous financial results:

> "It was very clear to me that not every contractor would be able to cope with the ambitious and intricate design of the building and its stringent and 'quality-based' requirements. As a matter of fact, I was sure that only a few contractors could meet these extremely radical demands. Moreover, I envisioned that the contractor would have to cope with endless changes during construction—changes because more than a few components in the architectural design were simply not feasible, and the architect refused to change them and changes because the design of the building systems was far from ready and would inevitably call for changes in the current design of the building. Also, the curators were still debating fundamental conceptual ideas regarding the design of the exhibitions, and it was clear that the late submission of their detail requirements would lead to additional changes in the design of the building. The chances that a contractor selected on the basis of cost alone would be able and willing to stay responsive to such a stream of changes and still maintain high-quality requirements would certainly be extremely low."

Shimon recommended that the client embrace an unconventional approach for selecting the contractor. According to this approach, various criteria for prequalifying the bidders would have to be met, and the winning contractor would be selected on the basis of multiple factors, not only the total cost of construction. He presented his ideas to the client, explained his rationale, and shared his successful past experience with unconventional approaches to selecting a contractor. Yet, the client preferred to stick to the traditional approach, primarily to avoid taking any risks. Shimon was fully aware that this unconventional approach was not free of risk and that he would be blamed in the case of failure.

Nevertheless, he was determined to reverse the decision:

"After several fruitless meetings, I realized that more arguments would probably not help me change their minds. I decided to try a new approach by providing them with concrete evidence through observation. This required my finding a site where selecting the contractor based on cost alone was clearly detrimental. The search turned out to be very quick."

Shimon organized a visit to a nearby large construction site, the Ben-Gurion International Airport, and invited the client to join him. They met with site management and learned that all the contractors had been selected strictly on the basis of cost, which enabled many unqualified contractors to join the project. Many contractors had declared bankruptcy, with extremely negative outcomes for both project quality and schedule. Shimon had the satisfaction of getting approval for his unconventional approach from Yad Vashem's management, who were convinced of its virtues after observing firsthand the poor results of a project that had considered cost alone in selecting a contractor: "Where endless solid arguments in the office failed, one brief site visit did the trick. Apparently, seeing *is* believing."

The first tender to get underway was also the largest and most important one in the entire project—the tender for execution of the skeleton and structure envelope. The selected contractor was supposed to function as the "general contractor" for the project and coordinate the activities of the various electrical, mechanical, and other specialty contractors, who would be appointed later to work in parallel with the general contractor.

Shimon understood the pivotal role of selecting the general contractor: "I was of the opinion that selecting the right general contractor was by far the most important factor for the success of the project.

I was therefore determined not to err in this selection process, and I was prepared to invest every effort necessary to make it work."

Thus, Shimon carefully designated a three-stage selection process:

- **Preliminary screening:** Criteria included the bidders' financial robustness, experience with similar projects, recommendations from former clients, and a presentation by their proposed management team. Only those bidders who met the criteria continued on to the next stage.

- **Implementation test:** The bidders were required to present their proposed methodology for construction and to execute a sample mockup of the special concrete elements of the structure (a small model that included an exposed concrete wall, door, and window details).

- **Monetary bid:** Only those contractors who successfully passed the first two stages were granted the right to continue to the final stage and to submit their monetary bids.

Both the client and many of the competing contractors did not fully understand the purpose of the second stage, which is exactly why Shimon included it:

"It was important to me to see whether the contractor was treating the project and the mockup as an important engineering challenge or just as a folly of the client's which could be changed later on. I knew that for this challenging project to be successful, the contractor would have to demonstrate an extremely high degree of competence, commitment, and flexibility. I also knew that the best way to learn about these attitudes and capabilities would be by observing the contractor in action."

Based on these criteria and after reviewing all of the proposals received, Shimon selected the company most likely to be awarded the job as contractor. However, beyond the selection of the contractor, it was important to him to participate in the determination of the contractor's management team as well. He selected Israel Chaskelevitch, the project manager proposed by one of the earlier bidders (whose offer had been rejected for financial reasons) as the person most suited to be project manager:

> "Israel was the same concrete specialist who we had approached in the initial stages of the project for a professional opinion as to the feasibility of the architectural design. At this early stage, he gave us feedback on the design as well as ideas for changes in the design to render it more implementable. I recalled that I was very impressed with his competency as well as with his creativity. I felt that I could rely on his professionalism, resourcefulness, and integrity. Based on my early and current impressions of Israel, I indicated to him that he should try to join the company that seemed to be the winner. At the same time, I applied pressure on the director of the company and informed him that his chances would increase if Israel were to be included in their team as project manager. To my delight, I got a positive response from the company. Apparently, at this stage, he was willing to agree to any request of ours as long as he was awarded the project."

Ishai, the Director General, was also concerned about the issue of staffing the contractor's management team and supported Shimon's intervention:

> "I had already failed in the past with large and promising contracting companies that chose to assign unsuitable project managers at the head of the pyramid. The project manager on behalf of the contractor must be a person with a 'head that doesn't stop working.' I fully trusted Shimon. I did not rush him, and I gave him a free hand in his efforts to shape the staffing of the contractor's management team."

The contractor's on-site preparations for the onset of the work brought into sharp focus another key problem: how to enable visitors to continue touring the Yad VaShem site without affecting or being affected during the intensive construction activity. The original solution called for a step-wise execution of the museum complex, with relocation of the visitor access roads accordingly. Yet, realizing how taxing this solution would be on site management time and focus, a second solution was adopted. Two temporary overhead pedestrian entrance bridges were built, enabling visitors to come in 'above the construction.' Ishai explained that "this solution not only prevented safety hazards; it eventually saved the project a great deal of money and endless headaches."

Yet, Shimon's headaches were only just beginning:

"Now that I was able to select a contractor and a project manager that fit the unique challenges of the project, I was supposed to be relaxed. However, I was not. With the ambitious architectural design, many building details remained unclear or were especially expensive to execute, and some were even impossible to execute. I did not have any doubt that we would have to cope with a stream of design changes during construction. I realized that we would be unable to provide the contractor with execution drawings for all the project areas, and I knew that entering into the execution stage in such a state would open the door to monetary claims by the contractor. But I was counting on Israel to refrain from abusing the situation."

For his part, Israel observed:

"Shimon was in great distress due to the extensive design changes that the architects could not seem to stop introducing. I knew that I could easily confront Shimon and demand supplements to the contract for all those changes. Yet I decided not to do it, at least not for the moment. I tried to persuade the architect to change some especially complex and problematic execution details, but did not succeed. The architect suspected that I was trying, from the very beginning, to 'pull' the project in directions that were undesirable for the client and refused to cooperate. I estimated that the client, although he approved the drawings, did not in fact understand what he was signing."

Two camps were actually forming, with the designer on one side demanding absolute adherence to the original design regardless of whether it was at all feasible, while the contractor on the other side was adamant about his inability to execute many of the design details. In between the two was Shimon, the project manager, who was trying to reconcile both sides without compromising the project.

Israel himself was also looking for a creative way to put an end to the conflict:

> "I was debating as to how to help the architect off his high horse without offending him or damaging the project. I understood that in order to 'remain viable,' I had to make a move as soon as possible to gain the trust of both the architect and the client. I was constantly seeking creative ideas for alternative solutions that would protect the interests of all those involved—solutions that would not be inferior to the original design, but that would, at the same time, allow us to shorten the execution time and reduce the financial cost. I chose to first tackle the issue of the architectural concrete elements in the prism structure."

Thus, the prism design for the museum's central hall, which was to be cast entirely of special architectural concrete, was the first problem to put the architect's versatility to the test. Due to the massive quantity of concrete required, the contractor needed a very large number of special and expensive forms in order to execute the castings within the set time schedule. But, as Israel explains, even the most expensive forms did not yield a final product of the quality anticipated by the architect:

> "All of my attempts and efforts to find an applicable and economic solution for the prism's concrete elements were in vain. At that critical point in time, it was important for me to check the architect's willingness to compromise, and this time I was

ready to fight if my demands were rejected. After much exploration, I decided to request that the architect move from a conventional execution of the prism walls by on-site casting to a pre-cast execution. I proposed that the pre-cast elements be made separately at a makeshift factory and be assembled using joining bolts.

"In order to enable the architect to experience the proposed solution, I built a mockup of the proposed pre-cast solution. The joining bolts that protruded from the pre-cast panels initially bothered the architect. After a week of deliberation, however, the bolts started to grow on him and he even became 'enamored' with the solution. Finally, my proposed solution was unanimously approved by the architect, the client, and the project manager.

"We all benefited from the change. The client benefited from a shorter execution time; the project manager benefited from easier on-site supervision made possible by the simple pre-cast execution; the architect benefited professionally from adopting the solution (several months later, he presented this solution at an international architecture conference); and we all benefited from saving a great deal on expenses."

The contractor's success in persuading the architect, at this early stage of the project, to agree to such a fundamental change in the execution details of the prism walls was a kind of "decisive event" in the project in terms of developing a trust-based relationship between the contractor, the architect, and the client. Israel took this success and ran with it:

"The successful solution for the execution of the prism's architectural concrete elements made me try and dare again, this time with respect to the synagogue building. The circumferential concrete wall of the main prayer hall was originally designed to be executed in a unique conic manner. Despite our many efforts, we could not succeed in casting this concrete element at the required level of quality. I proposed to the client to change the design and substitute the concrete wall with a drywall-clad steel structure, the final result of which would be identical in shape to the original concrete wall design. To my delight, the architect again agreed to my proposal after being convinced that his original design simply could not be executed. Again, all of the parties benefited from my proposed solution, since I agreed to significantly decrease the unit price on this item following the change in execution method."

The concrete work took about a year and involved 240 different castings. Throughout construction, several mockups, some full-scale, were tested to make sure that the casting process and concrete quality met specifications. Israel recalls the difficult environmental constraints of the work:

> "We had to embrace a mindset of 'versatile' formwork. For example, we had to build a scaffold system up to 80 feet high to support the cantilever over the forest and access road during construction. We had to work above the Jerusalem forest without damaging it, and we were allowed to cut down only three trees."

Another example of the contractor's creative thinking that eventually led to a brilliant solution was seen in the Hall of Names, situated at the heart of the museum. In this hallowed hall, the names of all the communities annihilated in the Holocaust are commemorated on the peripheral walls. The architect treated this room with the appropriate reverence, and the complex itself was designed as an architectural focal point of extreme importance. In the middle of the floor, there would be a deep conic well whose walls were to be made of special architectural concrete castings. The well walls were to be illuminated with special lighting, and so the execution had to be meticulous and the joints between casting interruptions had to be highly accurate.

However, Israel again anticipated problems with executing the design:

> "In my opinion, it was impossible to execute the concrete walls at the depth of the conic well according to the architect's design. Even had we gone to extreme lengths, we would not have achieved the required accuracy. I proposed an original solution: to carefully excavate the conic well in the rock and leave it in its natural form, without the concrete cladding. The proposed solution initially led to serious arguments with the architect, but the final result, after the peripheral lighting was completed, was so impressive that the client and architect not only approved the solution, but also thanked us for our initiative."

If at the beginning of the journey, the architect and client had been reserved and suspected that the contractor's primary purpose was to find shortcuts and cut costs, Israel managed to win their favor after proving himself to be part of the solution rather than part of the problem. Cooperation and mutual trust continued to increase as work on the project progressed.

Shimon was thrilled with Israel's contribution to the project:

> "Early on, I worked tirelessly to ensure that the prequalification process would help us to select a contractor high in competence, commitment, and flexibility. We were very lucky and got them all. Israel excelled in that he managed to identify the architectural design problems and, in parallel, present us with proposals for their solution. He invested time and money in finding practical solutions, which were often crucial for transforming challenging design concepts into reality. I felt that the brilliant solutions Israel proposed were considerate of the architect's extreme sensitivity about the unique design and at the same time met the client's expectations regarding the quality of the final product."

Safdie himself praised the contractor's commitment and creativity:

"It would take many experiments, mockups, novel engineering techniques, and a dedicated contractor to realize the building. The stainless-steel buttons that conceal the post-tensioning anchors at both ends of the prism are visual testimony of the ingenuity involved."

Final Stages: Making Progress Through Versatility

Avner Shalev, the chief curator of the Holocaust History Museum, describes the underlying concept for the design of the exhibition:

"My starting point and basic assumption was that as the years advanced, individual mourning would dissipate, the feeling of severed limbs would become dulled, and the memory of the Holocaust would become like that of any other historical event. In order to prevent this drift and enable future generations to connect to a memory with inherent significance for their identity and values, a memory with the capacity to shape the future, I realized that we would have to place educational work at the center of our endeavors."

The group of curators embraced this vision and developed a very ambitious and innovative objective: educating the young generation by personalizing the abstract concept of the Holocaust. Thus, unlike the exhibition in the old museum at Yad Vashem, which was primarily composed of photographs, the new exhibition would be composed of a multimedia presentation incorporating personal artifacts. It was designed to span 10 exhibition halls, each devoted to a different chapter in the history of the Holocaust. The exhibits would be set up chronologically, with the testimonies and artifacts accentuating the individual stories. All together, the museum would present the personal stories of 90 Holocaust victims and survivors and would include approximately 2,500 personal items, such as artwork and letters.

The curators focused on preparations of the various exhibits, and only on them. They behaved as if there were two different and quite independent projects: the building and the exhibitions. As a result, they treated the exhibitions as a 'once in a lifetime project' without any regard for time constraints in their decision-making process. It did not take Shimon long to realize that the curators did not care much about the project schedule, even though he needed their timely input in order to maintain construction progress:

> "Infrastructure preparations for the exhibitions and displays required joint teamwork between the exhibition curators and the construction designers, since various kinds of piping (electricity, lighting, communications, computers, security, etc.) had to be passed through the structure's floors and walls. The piping had to be positioned in its final locations in the forms before the walls and floors were cast; otherwise, excavation or sawing of the concrete would be required. But the curators wished to maintain as much flexibility as possible in light of the fact that the exhibition program was still being worked on."

However, as the project advanced, the flexibility and degree of freedom remaining for the curators gradually declined. Before each of the critical stages (casting of walls and floor, closing of roof openings, tiling of floor, and so on), the struggle between the curators and the project manager flared up anew. As Shimon recalls:

> "I tried to leave the curators enough time to make decisions right up until close to casting time of the various concrete elements, when I had to get the data and force a decision."

Just leaving the curators enough time, however, was not always enough. When Israel, the contractor, realized that some of the curators had difficulty in reading architectural drawings, he took the initiative to assist them. Shimon describes how Israel's versatility contributed to expediting their decision making:

> "Some of the curators did not understand the complicated design of the spaces designated for the exhibitions. In order to help the curators familiarize themselves with the relevant spaces, Israel prepared computerized simulations as well as 1:1 mockups made of wooden boards and geotechnical fabric. These models clarified, in a tangible manner, the joining of the portable partitions, the hanging of the pictures, the hanging alternatives of the lighting fixtures, and so on."

Ishai, the director general, highlights another example in which Israel went out of his way to help the curators:

> "One of the spaces in the exhibition area was designated for a re-creation of the death train that transported victims to the gas chambers. I was not really clear on what the curators wanted to create in this space, and it seemed to me that it was not clear enough to them either. The contractor decided to take the initiative and, early on, proposed to bring the original train car and tracks and display them so that their true dimensions could be experienced. The effect of the physical model was especially great, and it enabled the curators to reach timely decisions regarding the design of this sensitive space."

Israel's commitment to the success of the entire project, of serving the needs of the client, was again demonstrated in the conflict between the curators and the architect over lighting. The architect, striving toward controlled and constant lighting, had designed the structure's envelope so as to allow only a minimal amount of natural light to penetrate into the interior spaces. The curators, on the other hand, were interested in installing large skylights in order to get as close as possible to the natural state in which light, with all of its variability, penetrates into the structure throughout the entire day.

However, this time, Israel decided that the best way to expedite progress would be to wait:

> "The issue of the skylights troubled me greatly. I had in my possession supposedly approved execution plans, and I could have gone ahead and ordered all of the special glass components. I was witness to the vigorous and incessant confrontations between the architect and the curators regarding the desired amount of light, and it was clear to me that if I progressed with my approved plans, I might 'trip up' the client. I preferred to wait with the execution, and this ended up saving the client a lot of money since the design of the skylights changed drastically later on."

Ishai noted that: "One can't overemphasize the extreme importance of the teamwork between Shimon, Israel, and me for overcoming or eliminating problems, and eventually for the success of the entire project." However, when it was time to begin the finishing work in the exhibition areas (including multimedia, construction of displays, acoustic ceilings, and other special infrastructure elements), the curators persuaded Ishai to entrust this activity to their exclusive care, releasing the project manager from any involvement. Under pressure from the curators, the client informed Shimon that he would be taking this issue upon himself and did not require Shimon's services.

This time, due to the unique stage of the project, Shimon did not put up any resistance and respected the client's decision. The utmost commitment and intensive involvement of the curators was required for the finishing work, and Shimon felt that without the client's support, he was not in a position to impose his own participation on them:

> "It was clear that at this stage, Ishai could not overcome the curators. Thus, I did not object to Ishai's suggestion to leave the responsibility for the finishing work in the exhibition areas in their hands."

After about two months of status quo in this matter, Shimon realized that the client was having difficulties making decisions. The issue
of the construction of displays had become critical and was starting to
delay the envelope contractor of the building:

> "Only after I explained the grave situation into which we had
> got ourselves to Ishai, did he manage, after much effort, to per-
> suade the curators to transfer this area of responsibility over
> to Israel and so, in fact, opened up the bottleneck that had
> formed."

After the problem of the construction of displays in the exhibition
areas was solved, Ishai continued to manage the other components
of finishing work. When another four months had passed and the
work was still not progressing according to schedule, Shimon warned
Ishai that the execution of the elements was moving slowly and in an
uncontrolled manner. In the end, the client finally decided to entrust
Shimon with the responsibility for managing the unique elements and
the area of multimedia.

The outstanding versatility and commitment to the success of the
project on the part of the execution team paid off. On March 15, 2005,
the dedication of the new Yad Vashem Holocaust History Museum in
Jerusalem, Israel took place, with leaders from 40 countries attend-
ing the inauguration. Glowing reviews applauded "the supportive and
complementary relationship between the architectural dimension
and the exhibition design." Another remarked on the fact that "the
collaboration and counterpoint between curatorship and architectural
design remain admirably balanced and harmonious."

Shimon reflects on the long process to completion:

> "The visitor sees the end result, the harmony, the music that
> Safdie was talking about in his book, unaware that it all started
> with an extremely noisy and squeaky music of endless shouting
> and conflict. It appears that the two designers, the architect and
> the curators, must have worked together in great harmony all

along, when in fact this transformation was accomplished only through the constant dance between ideas and action. It was the ingenuity, and indeed the creativity, of the implementers, who enabled each creative entity to flourish and nurtured the fusion of the two separate disciplines into a united and eternal cradle of memory."

3

Flying Solar-Powered Airplanes: Soaring High on Spirit and Systems

by Alexander Laufer, Edward Hoffman, and Don Cohen

I Was the Enemy

"'Where's the rest of the plane?' That was my reaction when I saw the Pathfinder," says Jenny Baer-Riedhart, program manager at the Dryden Flight Research Center, NASA's Center for aeronautical research located in California. "I had just been named program manager and was seeing the plane up close for the first time. I had to ask, 'Will it fly?' It was an odd-looking bird."

Pathfinder was AeroVironment's solar-powered airplane and one of four aircrafts that were part of NASA's Environmental Research Aircraft and Sensor Technology (ERAST) program launched at the end of 1994. It was constructed of state-of-the-art composites, plastics, and foam. The upper surface of the aircraft's 100-foot wing was covered almost completely by thin solar-cell arrays that collected the sun's energy and converted it into electricity, which, in turn, powered six small motors with propellers.

Reflecting on the risky nature of the program, Jenny explains:

> "Unmanned Aerial Vehicle (UAV) technology is inherently risky and not considered an especially sound investment. This was particularly true in 1994, when we kicked off the ERAST

program. The idea behind ERAST was to minimize the risks as much as possible by joining forces with the best companies in the industry.

"ERAST represented a whole new way of doing business for NASA. The agency had been involved in similar partnerships before, but they were all university-led. This would be the first industry-led alliance of its type. NASA would provide some funding to the companies, but the companies would also have to pony up their own resources. If the alliance was successful, then NASA would be able to demonstrate the viability of UAVs for atmospheric science, and the companies would be able to apply their work toward commercialization. Now all we needed was approval for the budget from NASA's headquarters in Washington.

"But as it turned out, securing funding for this project would prove to be no easy task and would require a lot of persistence, commitment, and flexibility. I had just finished up another program to develop a next-generation UAV. Even though the plane had crashed, nobody was ready to give up on this technology. The knowledge was there to build UAVs; it was the cost and operational factors that made them unpopular.

"I made several appearances at NASA Headquarters to brief higher-ups about the status of the ERAST program. Early on in this endeavor, I learned a key lesson in working with multiple customers: Always know the folks you're meeting with, and always tailor what you're going to say based on who you know will be there.

"At my first ERAST meetings, I wasn't as attuned to the personalities in the room as I should have been. I didn't know what their requirements were or what their problems might be with what I was selling. I had anticipated some resistance, but I naively thought that all I had to do was explain how successful the program was and, voilá, I would win them over. I believed in my heart of hearts that ERAST was important for NASA and that I could convince them of that.

"Instead, I was perceived as a threat, even as the enemy. They weren't interested in hearing anything about a program aimed at developing UAVs. From their standpoint, I represented someone who would suck up the resources that they needed in other areas.

"What I failed to recognize was that people are not convinced just because the seller believes in the product. The seller needs to understand what the buyer wants from a product. I realized that the only way I was going to cultivate supporters was by putting myself in other people's shoes and learning what they wanted to get out of the program.

"I imagined that I was on the other side of the table, with a tight budget, and that I was looking at having to cut programs. What would I want to hear if I was in that position? I would want to make sure that the program was viable, successful, even unique, that I could get recognition and congressional backing for it, and that it didn't come with a big price tag. And that was how I packaged it.

"But before I went anywhere near NASA Headquarters again to make my pitch, I did some serious training. I got in shape. You might even say that I went to boot camp. I met with people from Dryden who frequently gave presentations at Headquarters about their programs, and I used them as a sounding board. I found people from my Center and the ERAST alliance with areas of expertise similar to those I would address at Headquarters and set up role-playing sessions, or what we endearingly referred to as 'murder boards.' I briefed them with the charts that I was going to take, and when they told me what I'd be killed on, I changed what I had to in order to stay alive.

"I gathered information from NASA's own reports and figured out what mattered most to them. Then I said to them, 'This is how I can deliver what you're looking for.' I brought charts that were worth more to them than an original Picasso. Talk about visual aids—I had one with forty pictures showing all the things that we were doing and how they related to existing programs. The audience was blown away.

"There are times when the role of the project leader is simply to sell the project. The most compelling sales pitch you can make is not that you have something wonderful to sell. It is, 'I understand what you need.' So projects can, and do, succeed or fail because of politics. But 'politics' doesn't have to be a dirty word if it means working closely and openly with your customers and stakeholders."

Bob Whitehead, the associate administrator for Aeronautics at NASA Headquarters, tells the same story from his perspective:

"In Aeronautics, our focus was on potential economic impact, and that was to be found in subsonic transports and technologies that supported Boeing, Honeywell, McDonald Douglas, and the other 800-pound gorillas. When you're trying to sell programs in this kind of political pressure cooker, other things can be viewed as distractions. I wasn't the person telling Jenny Baer-Riedhart to take her solar-powered airplane and go back home to Dryden. She came in at the level of people who work for me. Those people knew our strategy, and it was easy for them to say, 'Whitehead doesn't want this.'

"Everyone tries to get a piece of the agency's budget, but it's not a fair fight. Aeronautics made up about 10 percent of the total NASA budget in 1995 when I was associate administrator at Headquarters. To put that in perspective, 60 percent of the budget went to the Human Space Flight division, which wasn't doing anything about the economy once you got beyond Teflon and Tang. But then there was Aeronautics—and it was all about the economy.

"Jenny and her colleagues at Dryden showed up at NASA Head-quarters and stuck their noses in, pushing what they had to offer. They were clearly willing to take risks and challenge the status quo—in short, they were behaving like entrepreneurs ready to do whatever it took for the success of their project! They got turned away the first time, came back with a new message, got pushed aside again, but wouldn't go away—and they deserve a tremendous amount of credit for that—until finally we said, 'Okay, if we fit this ERAST thing into the budget, then you'd better take it and run with it.' And that's exactly what they did.

"When you live in the world that I lived in at NASA Headquar-ters, selling programs to the Administrator, Congress, and the White House, you are always looking to spice things up. One day the right answer is to sell them on economic impact. Then the wind shifts and they want to know what cool, exciting things you're doing. Turbine engines are no longer the answer.

"So when someone suggested that the projects we were propos-ing weren't anything to get excited about, I had to ask, 'Is there any more spice out there? What about some innovation?' Then one of my guys said, 'These whackos at Dryden came here talk-ing about 100,000-foot airplanes and solar power.' Well, why don't we look at that? Can we broaden the appeal? It wasn't that I was some genius sitting at Headquarters who suddenly looked out, saw the light, and understood what the ERAST folks were doing. It was more like, 'Hey, this fits the recipe.'"

Systems Are Our Best Friends

Even after NASA approved the budget, some of the other companies involved were not quite as enthusiastic as Bob Whitehead. Ray Morgan, vice president of AeroVironment Design Development Center, recalls the reservations of the companies in the alliance: "Initially, the other companies considered Pathfinder to be too impractical. We at AeroVironment believed that our solar plane was uniquely suited to the extreme duration and altitude goals of the ERAST program, and they almost voted us out of the alliance."

But AeroVironment had an advantage over the other companies in terms of technical know-how. As Ray explains:

> "What persuaded them to let us stay was our experience. Compared to the other three companies, we were old timers in the UAV industry. The Pathfinder was by no means AeroVironment's first foray into solar-powered aircraft. We had been developing UAVs for over 13 years and had seen all the ways to crash them. The other alliance members had less experience than we did in developing UAVs, and they probably didn't have as much appreciation for learning from the past.

> "One problem that many small UAV companies shared at that time was the 'silo' syndrome, which simply meant that they attacked each task as if they were the first ones who had tried to solve a particular problem. As a consequence, the industry as a whole was plagued by the duplication of stupid mistakes and problems that had been encountered and solved many years earlier. In the end, the other companies recognized that learning from others was perhaps the only way to avoid repeating their mistakes.

> "Although most of us knew the others from prior experience, working together in a collaborative way would be an entirely new way of thinking about our relationship to one another. For

one thing, we were all rivals in a fairly ruthless and highly competitive industry. The 'big four,' as we came to think of ourselves, had lost out to each other on prior programs. I tended to see us as four hungry dogs looking at the same piece of meat. That may sound a bit harsh, but it was that kind of industry.

"Like most new relationships, the alliance went through an initial courtship phase, followed by a few spats, before it settled into an ongoing relationship that worked, more or less, for the good of all. I think it was best said (I've forgotten by whom), 'If I have a dollar and you have a dollar, and I give you mine and you give me yours, we each still have a dollar. But if I have an idea and you have an idea, and I give you mine and you give me yours, then we both have two ideas.'

"NASA provided AeroVironment with valuable advice about how best to implement redundant systems in its critical components, particularly when the system had to automatically determine which sensors were working properly and which were not. In the first prototype of Pathfinder, built in the early 1980s, we had relied on single thread systems across every major component of the UAV. This meant that there was only one of any given component, and if that one component failed, then the whole UAV would likely fail. NASA's input was critical as AeroVironment began focusing on system optimization.

"NASA also brought to the table its vast experience in risk management. This was something AeroVironment had never formally approached, but it was old hat to the folks at NASA Dryden who were on the review team. Assigning a quantitative measure to a subjective judgment of risk is a difficult concept, but it is critical in conducting flight tests safely. It used to be joked that UAV manufacturers put 'more holes in the desert than Arnold Palmer.' However, for these large, expensive, one-of-a-kind UAVs with NASA logos and public scrutiny, crashing could not be taken lightly.

"Because ERAST was a different way of doing business, we had to tailor almost everything about the program, and that included how we did reviews. In a typical NASA contract, you wouldn't rely on the contractor saying, 'We're good to go,' while NASA nods its head and says okay—but that's what we did. The companies could take NASA's advice or they could ignore it altogether.

"For the ERAST reviews, NASA would bring in people with experience in a particular area of aircraft development and testing, even though they often had no prior background with UAVs specifically. Despite not being familiar with these particular types of light wing structures, they were still experts in physics and engineering, and the atmosphere we were operating in was the same. Many times they provided the most value by simply asking questions. The point was that NASA had within its ranks a wealth of experience and judgment in developing and testing unique air vehicles, particularly at high altitudes."

However, not all of the companies in the alliance were willing to accept NASA's advice. Jenny Baer-Riedhart illustrates the consequences:

"The companies who were not as open about accepting NASA's advice faired worse in this alliance. One of these companies we will call X. On paper X was a superb company. Man for man, employee for employee, every one of them was a genius in his own right. Still, despite their superior IQs, they crashed their UAV—twice, actually.

"Generally, their attitude towards NASA was negative. They chose not to discuss their problems, share information, or see reviews as something that they might learn from. The unfortunate thing is that had X listened to what NASA's experts pointed out during the reviews, their crashes might well have been avoided.

"When X crashed its UAV, the precipitating cause was the failure of a single thread component. NASA had spotted this and warned them of the catastrophic consequences of not switching to a redundant system. X ignored the advice. When the component failed during a flight test, the UAV flew out of control. With no backup means of recovery short of an act of God, the UAV was doomed to crash, and so it did.

"Another company in the alliance, call them Y, also crashed their UAV. They, too, rejected NASA's advice about developing a redundant system for a critical component. In this case, the UAV had two data links. To conduct one particular operation during flight, they had to switch from the primary data link to the secondary data link. But each time that the data were switched between the links, the data coming down disappeared for about six seconds. When a critical component failed during one test flight, the pilot on the ground noticed that the sensor was not updating properly, concluded that no data was coming down, and switched from the regular link to the backup. After six seconds the data were still screwy, but by then the aircraft had rolled upside down.

"Here again, NASA had pointed out that using a redundant system would safeguard against a catastrophic turn of events should the critical component in question fail. But by the time the pilot finally realized that the lost data was not merely the result of the switch between the regular data link and the backup, it was too late—the UAV was pointed straight down and could not be recovered."

John Del Frate, deputy project manager at NASA Dryden Flight Research Center, illustrates how using a simulator for training can even contribute to the risk of crashing when discrepancies in the system are not resolved:

"Flying these airplanes was risky, and the pilots needed 'stick time,' as we called it. The companies used simulators to practice their operations and procedures. It should be self-evident, but remarkably often it is not, that if you are going to use a simulator, it needs to mimic the actual flight hardware as accurately as possible.

"In one instance, a pilot practiced on a simulator with an instrument gauging the behavior of his plane on descent. The instrument, a rate meter, told him how many feet per minute he was descending. It turned out that his ground control station, in essence the cockpit, didn't work the same way as the simulator. In the cockpit, the rate meter didn't measure descent greater than 2000 feet per minute. We had a problem on a flight and had to shut off the engine and glide down into a dry lake bed. The pilot ended up coming down too fast. When he finally realized this, it was too late—he broke the landing gear. There were other ways in which he could have known that the plane was exceeding safe speed and was in danger of crashing, but he wasn't paying attention to them. This flawed training cost the company nearly a year of repair work."

Ray Morgan explains the way in which procedures should be developed and refined:

"For the longest time, we weren't procedures-oriented at Aero-Vironment. One guy at the top typically wrote our flight procedures, and often he would leave out a lot because—after all—he's just one guy, and there were things he didn't think about.

"Hence, we realized a couple of common sense things to help refine our methods of writing flight procedures: First, one person is not as smart as a group. Second, a person at the top may not understand things in the same way as someone looking at it from a different perspective, such as a technician who is actually performing the task. If you bring together all the people who understand parts of the system, you will develop better procedures by using each of their areas of expertise.

"Another problem that stemmed from having one guy write the procedure was that different nomenclatures were being used. If the person writing a procedure had gotten used to calling something by a nickname, that's how he would identify it in the procedure. But not everyone who had to use the procedure was familiar with that particular nickname, making it a recipe for frustration, not to mention potential disaster.

"The most significant problem we found with autocratically handing down procedures was that people were far less likely to follow procedures that they neither created nor could change. Procedures are tools, and like tools, they need to be sharpened and honed. All good craftsmen like to sharpen their own tools. What's more, people feel less stress when they can control how they perform their tasks. Our first rule was always to 'put the person closest to the problem closest to the solution.'

"Thus, whenever possible, the person(s) who actually performs the task creates the procedure for it. Providing this type of ownership is invaluable and is also the most efficient way to create the procedure. Certainly, we had people cross-checking their procedures with coworkers, but even so we recognized that we had to provide a way to handle inevitable mistakes.

"The process for the refinement of procedures at AeroVironment starts with reading through the procedure with a group of people who were involved in writing it. We also invite other people who were not directly involved to provide some objectivity. We get a number of changes from that—and that's generally where we catch inconsistencies in nomenclature. On the next iteration, the labeling is usually very close to being error-free.

"Next, we get everyone together for another read-through. This time we have the actual hardware in front of us, and we practice just as we would if we were going through a flight—a prototype of sorts. At this stage, correcting any discrepancies that we might catch is the responsibility of whoever 'owns' that procedure, usually the pilot or a stability and control engineer. Our next meeting is with the same people at the ground control stations, where we do the last run-through of the whole process before the actual flight, using the latest rewrite.

"After the flight, we get a group together to look at whether there were any abnormalities that could be attributed to a procedure, and we discuss any 'red-marked' changes to a procedure made during the flight. The person who 'owns' the procedure makes note of any issues that come up and corrects the procedure before the next practice.

"This process of continuous improvement by the 'owner' of the procedure accelerates the rate of development of the procedure by allowing both the 'owner' and the users to rapidly refine a procedure and to respond quickly to changes in the system during the flight test program."

John Del Frate reiterates how crucial following a well-developed set of procedures can be to the outcome:

"One cannot say enough about developing and documenting a good set of procedures and practicing them and analyzing them, then rewriting them if necessary, and practicing them again and again until they run as predictably as clockwork. It is grueling work, it takes lots of time, and it requires an incredible amount of coordination with team members. But you have to do it because this is the time when you discover discrepancies that can make the difference between saving a plane and crashing it.

"I saw a lot of cases where maintaining the project schedule started to become a problem, and some of the companies started to basically skimp on the amount of time that they spent practicing their procedures. Not AeroVironment...they were religious about how they developed procedures. When I showed their procedures to some of the guys at NASA Dryden who were in the flight-test business, they were blown away by how precise the details were."

AeroVironment also developed a unique system for collecting, documenting, and sharing all the data that were used and developed by the team. Jeffrey Bauer, chief engineer at NASA Dryden Flight Research Center, describes this system and how he benefited from it:

"Data memos were intended to communicate to everyone in the program what was going on with the Pathfinder project. Everyone in the alliance had access to the database, and the idea was to make it easy for anyone to generate a data memo. Aside from the title block, there was no format required. Even notes jotted on scraps of paper proved worthy of making it into the file.

"When I joined the ERAST program in 1995, first as chief engineer and later as deputy project manager, I had a lot to keep track of—four flight projects and numerous technology development initiatives. My background was in flight research, not solar power, and certainly not with such a unique vehicle as the Pathfinder. What allowed me to stay abreast of their progress was AeroVironment's system of using project data memos."

Another tool used for communication in the Pathfinder project was the PERT (Program Evaluation and Review Technique) chart. This is one of the most common tools employed by project managers and the planning and control staff. Here, Ray Morgan also adopted the PERT chart for communication purposes in order to keep everyone focused on "the big picture," thereby rendering it as a tool used by all the team members:

> "We put our chart on the side of a large container right in the hangar, next to the flight test crew and the airplane. When posted, it becomes a valuable, graphic depiction of the work plan, interdependencies, milestones, and people on the critical path, as well as which ones may need help. It also allows the team to mark it up interactively, adding tasks that come up when necessary and checking off tasks as they are completed. We usually incorporated these changes into a computer model and reprinted it once or twice a week during flight tests.
>
> "The chart was much more than window dressing, as we often referred back to it in team meetings to help redefine the importance of a current task and to see how it fit into 'the big picture.' This became a critical tool for the team. Enthusiasm for accomplishing the next goal was reborn each time we looked at the graphics on our wall. The fact that these charts were actually updated, and did not just become faded wallpaper, validated them to the team."

Overall, this kind of openness set an important precedent for what would become common practice among all the members of the alliance. As Ray Morgan recalls:

> "When we were approached by NASA about becoming part of this alliance, it seemed difficult to believe that even if we shared with the other companies, our rivals, they would share equally with us—whether it was shared data, hardware, money, or you name it. Initially, we felt that we were the only ones living up to the letter of the agreement, but over time we started seeing others get into the spirit.
>
> "The importance of working together as an alliance to the success of the Pathfinder cannot be overstated. In 1995, the first

full year of the program, we ran out of money. We had on the order of $3 million, but we simply hadn't gotten through the low-altitude tests before we had spent it all. Our goal was to fly into the stratosphere, and we had not yet flown above a thousand feet.

"NASA, being a sophisticated customer, understood the risks involved in developing and testing new technologies. They understood the vagaries of it all and how hard it is up front to predict what's going to happen. NASA also recognized that there are unknowns, which cannot be identified during a program and that a flexible budget is needed to compensate for them. When you're doing things you haven't done before, it's hard to predict what it will cost.

"With NASA's help, specifically Jenny's, we were able to borrow money from the other members of the alliance who hadn't spent all of their funds. Thanks to this, we were able to reach our performance goal for the year. In September 1995, Pathfinder soared to 50,000 feet into the stratosphere during the first solar-powered high-altitude flight. This 12-hour flight not only broke a world record but was a triumph for everyone in the alliance because as a program we were able to point to our impressive performance as a reason to continue funding the program. We billed it as an ERAST accomplishment instead of AeroVironment's: 'All for one, and one for all.' That's why, when I think about the 50,000 feet we reached in September 1995, I also view it in terms of the stratospheric leap we'd made as an alliance."

That success in working as an alliance is what helped Ray and his team to overcome another unforeseen crisis in the month following their memorable flight:

"When we set the world altitude record for solar aircraft in September 1995, we knew the risks involved and took every precaution possible. But when the airplane was in a hangar on the ground, we assumed that it was inherently safe and that we didn't need to worry about procedures for its safety. We were shocked out of this assumption fairly dramatically.

"In October, we were asked to display the Pathfinder at the Edwards air show, where it would be parked in a hangar near two classified aircraft, the B-2 and the F-117. The day that we brought the Pathfinder to the hanger, our crew chief told the attendant in charge that our plane was much more fragile than the others and that the attendant needed to be particularly careful when moving it or moving the other planes around it. He emphasized the Pathfinder's susceptibility to wind because it was so large and light. (It had a 100-foot span but weighed less than 600 pounds.) The hangar attendant seemed responsible, and we had no reason to doubt that he would do anything less than what we had asked. All went well until the show ended.

"During the night, an Air Force crew moved the B-2 and the F-117 to a different hangar. The guy we had talked to about our plane wasn't on duty and hadn't talked to the people who were moving the planes. They opened the hangar doors on three sides to give themselves more room to work. As they were working, a windstorm blew through the base, exceeding 30 knots, and with the three doors open, the hangar became a giant wind tunnel. The Pathfinder was blown across the hangar and got wrapped around the F-117 next to it. In the collision, the spars of two mid-panels on the Pathfinder were broken, and much of the solar array on these panels was destroyed.

"The next morning when I learned about the accident, it occurred to me that we might be finished. We didn't know whether NASA would give us the funding we needed to rebuild. The agency sent a management team to conduct an investigation into the incident. When the report came in, it was just as we had already determined. The guys who left the hangar doors open didn't know how fragile the Pathfinder was, and no one but us could be blamed for the accident.

"Lucky for us, we were able to secure funding from NASA to rebuild the airplane because we had already proven ourselves on our test flights and had demonstrated our ability to learn from our mistakes. By remaining focused on learning from our mistakes, an unexpected benefit of the accident was that we learned a tremendous amount about our plane. While rebuilding, we got to experiment with an improved structural design and turned out a better plane that was stronger and more durable. We were able to do so because we had a team that refused to be broken by adversity and a knowledgeable and rational customer that understood the risks for flight-testing unique aircraft. Even more importantly, we recognized that we needed improved procedures to protect the Pathfinder on the ground as much as in the air.

"Above all, the process made us stronger because it proved that we could count on each other in the worst of times as well as the best. Had we not been as successful a team as we were at that point, we would not have recovered from the tremendous setback. For many projects, an accident like that could have been catastrophic. But for us, it laid the foundation for pushing even higher into the stratosphere."

Change of Venue

In early 1997, Pathfinder and the entire ERAST program were deployed to the U.S. Navy's Pacific Missile Range Facility (PMRF) on the Hawaiian island of Kauai. Although the official explanation for doing so focused on the right weather conditions in conjunction with other operational requirements necessary for testing UAVs, there were additional reasons related to the 'organizational environment' that alienated Jenny Baer-Riedhart and her team. Jenny explains:

> "Ironically, just as we were starting to demonstrate success with the Pathfinder project and gaining more support at NASA Headquarters and in Congress for ERAST, the harder it became to operate out of our home base at the Dryden Flight Research Center. Because of the nature of the Joint Sponsored Research Alliance, the private companies handled most of the flight activities. NASA engineers weren't directly involved. Dryden 'hosted' the program, providing the facilities and some limited oversight and guidance, while the companies did the primary work. The attitude around Dryden was, 'Want to cut us out of the picture? Then do it all yourself.'

> "Moreover, the culture at Dryden didn't value UAVs in the same way as the other aircrafts there. At Dryden, traditionally, test pilots figured prominently in the programs, and here we were bringing in unpiloted planes. Understandably, there was some ambivalence, if not open resentment, toward a UAV program competing for precious airtime and flight resources. Still, it was disappointing.

> "Things never got openly hostile, but at the same time the message wasn't subtle. For example, we needed to schedule flights with the solar-powered Pathfinder at around 8 or 9 AM to take advantage of the sun and the wind conditions. Dryden wouldn't let us fly after 8. We could fly later on weekends, but we had to spend extra money to bring people in to support the activity.

> "The situation was exacerbated in other petty ways. We'd send a document for review, and it would never come back. I would schedule a meeting with Dryden personnel who needed to be there, and no one was available. While it was just a matter of time before we left Dryden in any case, the problems there accelerated our departure, and we turned our attention to Hawaii."

Ray Morgan describes the cultural barriers that they encountered in the process of moving their operations:

> "We'd chosen the island of Kauai because of the favorable conditions there for high-altitude flight tests. To take advantage of these conditions, we had to overcome obstacles that were far more down to earth.

> "The residents of Kauai share a natural apprehension about outsiders. Visitors need to be wary of making an inappropriate, if unintended, impression. It helps to have someone willing to serve as your entrée into the community. Dave Nekomoto, a fourth-generation Japanese-American born and raised in Hawaii, was our man in Kauai. He was a former executive officer at the Navy base where we were conducting the flight tests. Dave introduced us to the unique culture of Kauai and helped us 'fit in' and establish a good rapport with the local community.

> "Dave was well connected and helped smooth the way for us by cutting through red tape in dealing with the local authorities. Like many Kauaians we met, Dave had more than one job. Although he considered the support he gave us to be part of his job(s), he made it clear that the real reason he did favors for us was because he liked us. That was a main ingredient we found in all the business dealings we did on Kauai. It was a culture where your personality took you further than the size of your billfold. With Dave, we endeared ourselves to him right away. Among other things, we devoured all the tasty food that he and his friends Vince and Johnny cooked for us in their giant (and I mean giant) woks. Not only that, we sang with him. Yes, that's right—we sang.

> "Dave had—how shall I say it?—a thing for karaoke. This was Dave's way of relaxing at the end of the day, and he had quite an elaborate setup at his place for it, including microphones, speakers, and acoustics that any garage band would kill

for. Plus, he must have owned the tracks for every song ever recorded. All you had to do was punch a button on a computer and the music started up, with the lyrics flashed across a television screen. It was up to you to provide the vocals, and heaven help you if you were bashful.

"Anybody who was tight with Dave spent time with him at his house singing. No one on the Pathfinder team had a Sinatra voice, but we managed to get everyone to sing something. Even those who were painfully shy managed a few lines of 'Happy Birthday.' It was all in good fun and, more importantly, it showed that we weren't afraid to risk embarrassment and we all trusted each other with our most precious possession—our egos."

Jeffrey Bauer reiterates the importance of the karaoke ritual:

"Hula Pie is a dessert at one of the restaurants near the hotel where we were all staying in Kauai. It consists of an Oreo cookie crust, macadamia nut ice cream, and four inches of whipped cream. Everyone on the project who came to Kauai had to eat a piece of this pie. Call it an initiation, a hazing of sorts; it was the project's way of letting you know when you got off the plane that you weren't walking into this tropical paradise without paying an entry fee first.

"Singing karaoke was another must. Jenny had made it clear to all of the team members that we needed to be sensitive to cultural differences when we were on the islands. But singing? I don't sing. 'We have to go,' Jenny told me. 'And we're going to sing, too.'

"I traveled to Kauai for the first time to attend an alliance meeting and to scout out potential operating locations. I spent my first two days there locked away in all-day meetings. Dave Nekomoto was there. Following the second day of meetings, he suggested that we go over to his house to sing karaoke.

"Anybody who was nervous about singing picked a song that everyone else knew. That way they could help you out. People who absolutely refused to do a whole song were still expected to sing one verse. One guy from AeroVironment sang so badly that everyone was rolling on the floor laughing. But he was one of the project leaders, and to show that kind of vulnerability, to stand up in front of his subordinates and look silly, that was a great exercise in team building.

"What I found also was that it gave the project a history that people could cite whenever things were getting tense and we needed to remind ourselves of something fun. Someone might be stuck on a problem, but he could always turn to his colleague and say, 'I'm stuck, but at least I don't sing as bad as you.' They'd get a good laugh about it, and that was a nice break from dealing with the problem at hand.

"For many reasons, I cannot possibly overstate the importance of these karaoke nights at Dave's place. The whole NASA and AeroVironment team was there, along with spouses, children, and other friends that had come over for a visit. It brought the team together, and we made friends with our Hawaiian and military hosts. Dave invited folks from the base who we worked with each day and who we never would have gotten to know personally otherwise. Without Dave's karaoke parties, we probably would have been accepted by the community eventually, but developing a social relationship certainly broke the ice quicker and formed a basis of trust."

Jenny Baer-Riedhart describes more about the social environment on the island:

"In planning our marketing strategy on the islands—yes, we had a marketing strategy—we developed educational programs in the schools and put together displays at the local museum. We helped to write the lesson plans, and the NASA public affairs staff led training workshops for the teachers in order to show them what we were doing so that they could share this information with their students.

"We involved the Kauai Community College by hiring students to work for us at the Pacific Missile Range Facility (PMRF) and introducing them to advanced solar technology. This was done on Dave Nekomoto's advice, and he put us in direct touch with the right people at the college—it helped that his brother-in-law was the Dean of Instruction there.

"From Dave we learned invaluable things about the Kauaian culture—for instance, the high regard that Kauaians have for those who educate their children. Working with the base commander and the PMRF public affairs office, the NASA and Aero-Vironment team orchestrated an open house that brought in approximately 1,000 local schoolchildren to see the Pathfinder, its payloads, and key parts of the PMRF support equipment. It was tremendously successful, and students and teachers from all across the state participated. We jokingly called this event the '1,000-Kid March,' and the name stuck.

"Dave was also quick to let Hawaii's political machine know what was going on with our project at PMRF, which resulted in Hawaii's entire congressional delegation sending a letter to NASA commending us on the success of our program. Not only that, money that hadn't been available before suddenly appeared at our doorstep.

"The community, to put it immodestly, fell head over heels in love with us. 'This Pathfinder is a good thing,' people were saying. 'These people are doing something special.' That kind of talk has a way of making things happen. People on the island who worked at the hotels, restaurants, and airline and car rental agencies that we used all got to know many of the team members. When we had to make travel arrangements that were subject to change with events in our flight schedules, this relationship proved invaluable.

"Many times in our projects, we think that just being smarter than someone else or having the best idea is all we need. That helps, no doubt, but you've got to understand the human side of things. We came to Kauai not knowing how the human dimension would figure into our activities, but we understood that however it worked itself out was going to be critical to our success. That's why we set aside money in our budget specifically for those kinds of activities. Call it marketing or public relations, but whatever you call it, by the time we left Kauai, we had probably spent 20 percent of our project time on it."

Other activities of the project focused on testing microminiaturized sensors that can be carried out by the remotely operated aircrafts and that can serve the science community. Dougal Maclise reflects on how connections were made with scientists on the island toward this end:

"Ostensibly, the purpose of our project was to look at broad swaths of vegetation on Kauai from our high altitude perch on Pathfinder. By the brightness of the infrared bands in the images we captured, scientists could check the health of the plant life below. To help scientists understand the potential value of our data to them, I went on marketing trips around the islands. I met scientists who had no idea about aerial photography and what it could do for them. I tried to explain to them how chlorophyll reflects infrared more than it reflects green, what the camera was capturing, and how it showed the stress of the plants. My other objective was to look for new ideas, new ways to use our information. For example, we planned to take pictures of the forests to collect data on agriculture. We learned where to go to get a shot of a broken irrigation line, where an outbreak of something was occurring, where there appeared to be an immature crop or anything else that someone asked to see.

"Building on earlier visits to sugarcane producers, I went for a ride with one in his helicopter and took pictures of crops to demonstrate the value of the project and to whet his appetite for wider-scale images available from Pathfinder. He pointed out areas where he wanted me to take pictures as we were flying. Later, when I showed him the pictures, he pored over them. Within a day he was using the information we'd collected to fix broken irrigation lines. Word of that got around to other parts of the community, for example to the coffee growers, who began to see how useful aerial photography could be to them. It led to some of the work that's going on now."

People Matter the Most

In sharing their impressions of Ray with great affection and admiration, Jeffrey Bauer and Dougal Maclise attributed his success in leading the team to his unique ability to focus on people, treat them as equal, and enable them to contribute and learn. They stressed the strong trust and commitment that Ray was able to build within the entire team, including AeroVironment, NASA, and later on with the larger community on the island. But this knack for inspiring mutual support didn't always come naturally for Ray. In fact, prior to becoming the kind of leader who fosters individual and project growth, Ray Morgan had to be in control of everything and everyone. It is only over time that his unique managerial style has evolved in response to his own experiences and self-development on the job:

"In 1980, I was hired to lead a project for AeroVironment, a small company run by a man named Paul McCready, who was known as the 'Father of Human-Powered Flight.' McCready was a visionary, a genius inventor, but he was not a project manager. That was going to be my job.

"McCready had gotten Du Pont interested enough in his activities to sponsor a solar airplane that would fly from Paris to London. Solar power was still in its infancy, and nothing like this had ever been tried. In some ways it was a stunt, but if we could pull it off, it might be seen as a groundbreaking event in the development of solar aviation technology.

"AeroVironment was an environmental consulting company, and all of McCready's projects with airplanes had been worked on outside the company. He wanted somebody to put together a team, do this project, and then disappear. I was working at Lockheed in Burbank, California, but I took a leave of absence to join the project. To me it was the dream of a lifetime, something I never thought I'd get a chance to do. There are hundreds of reasons why project managers accept an assignment, and we all have ones that are important to us. Solar power was one of the last frontiers in aviation. It was pioneering in the truest sense of the word. I told McCready when we were negotiating my terms of employment, 'If I had another way to support my family, I would do this for free.'

"We would develop two planes. The first was a test bed called the Gossamer Penguin, which had a solar panel placed above the wing and aimed at the horizon so that we could fly and test it in the early morning sun. By learning as much as we could from those tests, we were going to design the airplane that we planned to call the Solar Challenger.

"When I was hired by McCready in January, I didn't have a building to work in—let alone people on the project. To be on schedule, I had to demonstrate solar-powered flight on the Penguin by May, and we had a lot of ground to cover. I tried to do what I thought a good manager would do to get a project started—I found a building, had lights installed, and shelves built. But McCready wasn't happy. 'Let's get going, and get something in the air,' he told me.

"The first time we went out to flight test the Penguin, I set up the same procedures we had used at Lockheed. I was in the hangar at daybreak going through a checklist before we began the flight. McCready pulled the Penguin out of the building, telling me: 'You can do that after the flight. Let's get it in the air before the sun comes up too high.' He was right to be concerned about timing because as the sun rose higher, the turbulence would make the plane less stable, and then we wouldn't be able to control the fragile airplane. However, his dismissal of even the most minimal safety procedures would prove to be more costly in the long run. We crashed the plane with varying severity over and over, often for the same reasons—broken parts not found and repaired, cables not properly connected, etc.

"The most alarming aspect of putting the plane in the air without more rigorous reviews and precautions was that—by McCready's edict—the test pilot was his 12-year-old son, Marshall. McCready reasoned that because his son only weighed 80 pounds, we could get away with fewer solar cells on the airplane. Without a great deal of introspection, I relied on what McCready told me and what I learned from the few people left over from his earlier programs. I let them guide me, listening to what they said and—often against my better judgment—going along with it.

"One April morning, Marshall took off and began to fly our standard racetrack pattern. With the crew following on bicycles, Marshall climbed to about 25 feet above the concrete runway and began a left turn. No sooner had the plane begun to bank when it suddenly began spinning around the left tip. The wing tip crumpled onto the ground with McCready's son inside the cockpit. As the wings folded up and collapsed, the boy fell out the side of the plane, and that was fortunate—because a carbon fiber spar from the left wing pierced the cockpit where his head had been only seconds earlier. It could have killed him. That was disaster number one.

"Disaster number two was my reaction. I said never again, never, ever again would that happen while I was managing a project. I couldn't believe what I had done. I had almost killed a 12-year-old boy. Never mind that his father wanted him to be the pilot—I should have known better. I don't think I could have been any more traumatized had it been my own child in that airplane. And thus began an eight-year period for me where I became exactly the kind of boss that I said I would never be.

"I stayed on at AeroVironment. We flew the Solar Challenger from Paris to Kent, England, and Du Pont loved it. McCready asked me to stay on and lead a new division of the company to develop solar applications. I couldn't pull myself away. The kinds of projects I was working on were intoxicating. We did about 25 projects over the next several years—incredible stuff, all types of flying things, including props for the movie industry. This was the sort of job that, 10 years earlier, I wouldn't have believed I could ever have.

"From the outside, it looked like the ultimate job. But on the inside, I was a mess. Some days I felt so much stress in the morning driving to work that I almost threw up. The tension was so palpable that I could feel it when I walked in. I thought I had to control everything. Nothing happened without my approval. I had people lined up outside my office waiting for decisions because I made them all. I wouldn't trust anybody to do anything. I was not only killing the morale of everyone I worked with, I was killing myself. I was working 80- to 100-hour weeks. I worked weekends. I never took vacations.

"People came to work for me almost crying because they were so grateful to be there, and in two or three years they were burned out. I was probably as bad a manager as you could be, and it was out of sheer desperation that I finally started to figure out that I needed to quit—or find a better way. That better way was about to present itself when I heard about night school classes being offered at UCLA on W. Edwards Deming's revolutionary 14-point management system. 'The 14 points all have one aim," wrote Deming, 'to make it possible for people to work with joy.'

"I had a longtime employee, one of the few that I could call a friend, whom I talked to about this. I said, 'How can I go to night school? I don't have time to go to night school. I'm barely sleeping.' And he said, 'You don't have time not to go to night school.'

"I took one class at UCLA. At first, I thought this was the biggest waste of money. The guy that taught the class never told us anything; he just asked us questions. But as time went on, it dawned on me: This was how the instructor worked. He was demonstrating the power of using the brains of the people around you through the way he was teaching. I asked myself, 'Why can't I get this out of my people?'

"Taking the first class at UCLA was just the beginning. I continued for two more semesters. Years of reflection followed, and though I was not able to implement many principles of Deming's philosophy, the course led to a radical change in my attitude toward people. The single biggest realization I had was that most people want to do good work. My job was to let them do it. Most of what I had done as a manager was to kill the intrinsic motivation that people already had to do good work. I had to start trusting and delegating and having confidence in their intelligence and integrity. The essence of the philosophy was to learn from my people.

"This new approach didn't immediately solve my problems, but it started me down the right road. In fact, it was very tough at first and almost seemed like it was worse for a while. The fear of lost control was almost unbearable. I might have reverted back to my old self if I hadn't kept reminding myself of how miserable I had been.

"By the time we joined the ERAST program and started developing the Pathfinder, I had wrestled with my worst demons and felt like I was not only a different man, but a better manager. What's more, I had finally begun to be a leader and was leading my division in a transformation that enabled me to draw full value from all the brains of my workforce.

"I learned to search for the right balance in everything. I learned that finding the right balance between systems and people is critical to being a good project manager, but more importantly, I realized that people matter the most since they make the systems work. The key is collaboration through communication and trust. When I occasionally speak at schools, teachers sometimes ask me what, if anything, I would change about education. I always stress that 'I would encourage people to cooperate because that is the way the real world works. The hardest thing for people to learn in the real world is to work together.'"

It would appear that Ray does indeed practice what he preaches. Dougal Maclise sums up his unique style by saying, "Whether one meets the optimist developer, the experienced builder, the inquisitive engineer, or the energetic cowboy, one always immediately feels that each one of his personalities is an authentic and sincere person. His genuine spirit is contagious. You simply cannot *not* follow Ray."

Flight Party

After the Pathfinder's successful solar-powered, remotely piloted 14-hour flight to an altitude of 71,530 feet above Kauai in July 1997, the team had cause to celebrate. As Jennifer Baer-Riedhart declared, "Pathfinder's performance to date has exceeded our wildest expectations. Our team performed without flaw and way ahead of schedule. I am proud to be part of a world-class team led by AeroVironment and supported by our Hawaiian counterparts. We have set a very high standard for others in our ERAST team to follow."

Ray Morgan was looking to reward his team and his Hawaiian friends by throwing a big bash:

> "After a successful flight test, it's a tradition to throw a party. The project manager buys the refreshments, usually a couple of kegs of beer, and that is how you pay back your team. After Pathfinder set the world altitude record on July 7, 1997, we decided to throw a different kind of party. We invited everyone we could, our community of friends and supporters, and it turned out to be one of the biggest bashes they'd ever seen on the island.
>
> "We held the party in a park, and we had flyers printed up and sent out special invitations. AeroVironment had t-shirts made that said 'Thank You' in Hawaiian. I had NASA stickers and ERAST stickers to give to people. There was singing and hula dancing. Dave Nekomoto brought a karaoke machine. The reigning Miss Hawaii even showed up and sang for us.
>
> "People who worked with us from the Pacific Missile Range Facility were there, and they brought anyone from the base who wanted to come—electricians, telephone repairmen, even janitors. They never had a celebration like this before and were glad to help out with things like cooking. Even teachers, school kids, and community college students came.

"The party started at three o'clock in the afternoon and didn't end until well past midnight. Ostensibly, it was to celebrate the altitude record, but it was also just to say thank you to the community for all the help they gave us. The most memorable thing about the party for me was how happy they were that we had done this for them. By the time we left, every Kauaian knew about Pathfinder and what we were trying to accomplish—and, more importantly, they were behind us one hundred percent. So we wanted everyone to feel like they were part of the team. And they did. A lot of factors contributed to our success in the skies above Kauai. One very important factor was that the people of Kauai felt invested in our success and wanted to do whatever they could to help us reach our goals. Whatever advancements derive from our work on Pathfinder, the support of the Kauaians who helped make it possible must never be forgotten.

"Cynics will look at our public relations activities on Kauai and say that all we did was woo the natives in order to get what we wanted from them. For those inclined to see the world this way, you can bet that they make little distinction between a friend and an asset. The way I see it, we had friends on the island; if they were assets, too, that's beside the point.

"None of us can do much alone. People are the most important part of any operation, and it is only with the help of others that we do great things. We enjoyed sharing our accomplishments with everyone who wanted to be part of the team. Bottom line, the world record belonged to all of us."

4

Transferring Harbor Cranes: Delivering a Bold Idea Through Meticulous Preparations and Quick Responsiveness

by Alexander Laufer, Zvi Ziklik, and Jeffrey Russell

The Entrepreneurial Phase

In 1996, following a comprehensive program to streamline the Israeli ports, four large harbor cranes were designated for relocation: two cranes (weighing 400 tons each) from Haifa Port to Hakishon Port and two cranes (weighing 250 tons each) from Hakishon to Haifa. All of the cranes were about 40 meters high. The client, the Ports Authority, issued a public tender for the overland transfer of these giant cranes. The tender requirements were based on the vast knowledge accumulated by the Ports Authority and by local Israeli contractors as well as on their past experience in overland transfers.

The relocation activity was described in detail in the tender. The first stage was to involve disassembling each crane into approximately 70 transportable parts that would be transported overland on giant trucks, while taking into account the limitations of the existing roads and bridges along the way. Before beginning the land transportation project, meticulous coordination was required between the contractor and the Israel National Roads Company (reinforcement of bridges and construction of bypasses), the Police department (coordination of traffic and parking), the Electric Corporation (disconnection of power lines), the Ports Authority management (timing, prevention of inter- ference with ongoing activity, staging areas, and so on), other relevant authorities, and so forth.

After the arrival of the crane parts at their destination, the reas- sembly of each crane was to begin, including reconditioning/replacing all of the parts that could no longer be used after their disassembly. A thorough inspection of the cranes and their components by the Belgian crane manufacturer, as well as inspections by the safety and licensing agencies, would be required for approval of the cranes' return to service. Only after these inspections were completed would the cranes receive licensing and authorization to operate again.

Six companies specializing in the execution of similar works acquired the tender documents. The client estimated the time period for the relocation of each crane to be about three months, or about one year for the entire operation. Based on data from previous proj- ects, the client expected the relocation cost of each crane to range between $3.5 and $4 million and, therefore, reserved a budget of approximately $16 million for the relocation of the four cranes. The expectations of the client regarding price were based on the cost of past projects and were known to all of the leading and experienced crane relocation companies.

One of the six companies participating in the tender was Mifram, a private family-owned company. Since its establishment in 1962, the firm had developed expertise ranging over a broad industrial spec- trum, including the design, manufacture, and transportation of heavy equipment and the construction of unique structures and industrial plants. In addition, Mifram had an impressive track record of devel- oping and producing new and innovative industrial products.

Ofer Klein, the CEO of Mifram, appointed a think tank to identify possible alternatives to the usual method of relocation. As he explains:

"This was going to be a competition in a world of equals. All of the other competitors were familiar with the overland method of transfer and capable of doing it efficiently, so the differences in prices between the bids were expected to be small and the profitability minimal, if at all. I understood immediately that if we wanted to win and also make a profit from this large tender, then we had to find a solution that was different from the conventional solution. To have an advantage in the competition, we had to change the game."

Ofer's brother and vice president of production, Amos Klein, was appointed as head of the think tank. He describes his innovative idea:

"On a visit I made several years ago to the oil fields in the North Sea, I saw large barges towing a huge drilling rig in the open sea. I proposed to the team that we try to adopt a similar method in our case as well. The team began to examine this original and challenging idea, which, to the best of my knowledge, had not yet been tried elsewhere in the world for these kinds of tall cranes that have a very high center of gravity and a very narrow base and can be destabilized rather easily. The idea was to transfer the crane from the quay directly onto a giant barge (roll-in), transport it by sea using a special tugboat to tow the barge, and unload the crane by transferring it from the barge to the quay (roll-out) on the tracks that are already installed at the destination port. The team began investigating the feasibility of the proposed solution. After a week of inquiries with several external experts, the team reached the conclusion that the solution seemed feasible. Mifram's management gave the 'go-ahead' to invest in further examination of this unique solution."

Amos reflects on the financial risk involved:

"I estimated the cost of preparing such an offer at approximately $300,000, which would go down the drain if we failed to win the tender. I preferred to wait until I was convinced that the proposed method was indeed feasible. We decided to risk $50,000 in preliminary tests, as a kind of go/no-go test."

The decision was also made to bring Yitzhak, a marine engineer, on board. Amos underscores the importance of this decision:

"At this early stage, it seemed critical to cope with marine-related issues, such as the wave pattern in the eastern basin of the Mediterranean and its effect on the barge's stability, the intensity and direction of the ocean currents, knowledge of the civil and military activity in the Israeli ports, and so on. We came to the conclusion that a marine engineer who was familiar with the subject should be added to the team immediately to help prepare the tender."

Ofer further elaborates on the process:

"With the help of Yitzhak, we located several companies that specialize in the transportation of oil drilling equipment in the North Sea. We sent each of those companies a letter of intent, in which we requested full cooperation in the preparation of the tender, without yet revealing any details about the specific tender. Several European companies expressed interest in the matter and asked for additional technical details before giving their final consent, but we did not yet have those technical details.

"In parallel, we focused on identifying experts in the relevant areas, such as a meteorologist, maritime insurance and legal experts, a marine structural designer, and so forth. These consultants were asked to perform initial reviews of the proposed idea and give their feedback. Only after a fortnight of intensive examinations, during which it became clear that the chances of successfully executing this innovative idea were good, did we decide to move on to the next stage, namely to prepare a proposal."

Yitzhak, who was in charge of coordinating the activities of all the designers and consultants, outlines the planned approach:

"The main challenge when dealing with a loaded barge in the open seas is to prevent the cargo, especially that with irregular dimensions, from rolling with the waves. The barge is equipped with a special computer-controlled gyro system, which activates 12 pumps that pump seawater into the various tanks on the barge in order to balance it. Using an appropriate algorithm and based on previous rolling patterns, the computer, which is programmed in advance according to the various scenarios, can successfully predict the intensity and direction of the next roll and balance the barge in time accordingly."

In addition, the tugboat's cable system must create a continuous and uniform pull, with maximum neutralization of various forces that result from the independent and separate motion on the sea of the connected tugboat and barge. After approaching several European companies, the appropriate equipment was located in an Italian company specializing in towing marine vessels and large-scale marine projects. The costs for the tugboat and the barge, capable of carrying a load of some 3,000 tons, were estimated at $150,000 a day, with workdays counted from the day of the vessels' departure from the Italian port until their return. Most importantly, any backup capacity of alternative equipment that might be required in case of malfunction was typically difficult to obtain in the existing market.

Finally, a special cart would be needed to transport the crane from its location on the track on one quay onto the barge and from the barge to the quay at the destination port. The initial calculations done by the designers revealed that the quay was not built to withstand heavy local loads such as that expected to be created by the crane's weight upon being transferred to the quay over the wheels of the cart. Hence, a multi-wheeled cart was required to minimize the local load on each wheel. This kind of a cart was located in Germany. It had 1,200 wheels, each of which was computer-controlled so as to inflate or deflate in order to maintain leveling of the cart. The cost of the cart was approximately $30,000 a day, with workdays counted from the day of the ship's departure from the German port until its return.

A representative of the Italian contractor, who was responsible for supplying the barge and the tugboat, also joined the team. His experience in the marine transportation of irregular cargo contributed significantly to pricing of the proposal and identification of the project's potential risks.

Despite all these preparations, the client was not even aware of the possibility that transfer could be done any other way than by land, as was customary. Thus, no accommodations were made for this option as part of the tender documents. All of the technical and contractual documents were designed to deal only with the overland solution. As Ofer explains:

> "We had executed many projects for this client, and we were well aware of his sensitivity to changes in the tender conditions. We were concerned that proposing a solution so different from the tender conditions might lead to our immediate disqualification, so we decided to seek legal advice on the contractual aspects of our unusual proposal. We were advised that the client would find it difficult to object to our innovative solution, assuming that proper technical support and attractive cost estimates were provided."

Because the proposed solution was so innovative, the success of the bid depended on total compartmentalization of its preparation process and on meticulously safeguarding against any leakage of information about the proposed method. Any premature disclosure of information could have been devastating for Mifram, because the client might have rejected the method out of hand. Therefore, each of the participants in the proposal preparation process was required to sign a confidentiality agreement, which included severe sanctions against anyone who might breach it.

Likewise, Mifram took all possible steps to prevent leaks of information about the plan to the competition in order to ward off attempts by any other companies to adopt the same idea. As Ofer emphasizes:

> "It was very important for us to know whether or not the competitors had uncovered our intentions. We invested great efforts in trying to identify any approaches made by the competitors to large contractors and suppliers in Israel and abroad. Since many of our competitors also resort to 'business intelligence' for large contracts, we went one step further. We established an additional team, separate from the other team, which prepared a proposal for the land transportation option, and in a controlled manner we released information about the work of this team."

One last decision remained prior to submitting the proposal: the tender price. This decision turned out to be the most difficult one. The "conventional" price of the overland solution was about $4 million per crane, whereas the estimated cost of the marine alternative was only about $1 million per crane. Ofer deliberated between his natural desire to maximize his profits and to quote a price closer to the "conventional" $4 million, and his fear of putting himself at increased risk vis-a-vis the client, who might, if the price difference was too small, prefer the proven and safe solution over the never-before-tried proposal. The fear of a future lawsuit due to excessive profits was also a significant consideration.

Ofer shares his final considerations:

> "I realized that we were not like a typical contractor submitting a bid to a client; rather, we were like an entrepreneur. We identified an opportunity, we developed a new idea to address it, we were confident that we knew how to convert our idea into successful results, and now we were trying to sell our idea and our confidence to an investor. Since this 'investor' is a public entity and thus its primary concern is to minimize risks, the

price should be very attractive, so that the public entity would not have a choice but to 'invest' in our idea. I felt that developing the new idea was crucial to our success, but selling it would probably be our most challenging hurdle.

"So, finally I decided to give the sum of $2 million as the tender price for the relocation of each crane. This price guaranteed a fair profit, covered all our risks, and was very attractive to the client. We also added an accompanying letter to our proposal in which we provided reassurance that despite the low bid price, we would meet all of the tender conditions, including safety, as well as a commitment to shorten the relocation time for each crane from three months to only one month. It was, undoubtedly, a most attractive proposal for both client and bidder."

Upon opening the bids, the Tenders Committee saw that five of the six proposals indeed were within the estimated range, and that Mifram's surprising bid was approximately fifty percent lower. Amos recalls:

"Several days later, Ofer and I were summoned by the Tenders Committee. The Chairman of the Committee informed us that after an in-depth examination, it had been concluded that the method we were proposing was unreasonable. The Committee decided to reject it out of hand, exercising its contractual right not to prefer the least expensive bid in this case."

But Mifram had already anticipated this reaction, as Ofer describes:

"We were prepared for such a scenario, and we were not ready to give up. Following the Tenders Committee's notification, we met and brainstormed with the company's legal advisors. It was clear to us that the client, as a public entity, was not entitled to so hastily reject an offer that was significantly cheaper than all the other contenders. The Ports Authority would have to explain to the High Court of Justice their rejection of a bid that met all of the tender conditions and that was submitted by a proven contractor."

At this critical point in time, Mifram decided to concentrate its efforts on the legal arguments vis-a-vis the Ports Authority management rather than on the engineering/technical arguments vis-a-vis the Tenders Committee. This approach proved to be successful. The Authority's legal advisor recommended to the Tenders Committee members that at this stage, they refrain from rejecting the bid out of hand, and instead request additional clarifications regarding the proposal. The Tenders Committee notified Mifram that after reconsidering all of the arguments, it had decided to grant the bidder a hearing before the client's senior legal and technical team in order to present it with the proposed solution.

The entire technical consulting team that had helped prepare the proposal was summoned for the hearing, and the Italian marine contractor was flown in for the occasion. As expected, the Ports Authority's professionals opened the meeting by expressing their grave concern about potential damage to the cranes, which according to the manufacturer's definition were not suited to be tossed around by the waves. Ofer responded by way of example:

> "I understood the point that seemed critical to the client and chose to respond immediately. I got up and placed the full cup of coffee I had in my hand on the tray and then I carefully lifted the tray. The drink in the cup did not move. I explained to the client that this was exactly the essence of the action we would be taking: The cranes would appear to be on solid ground all the time. This tangible demonstration 'broke the ice,' and from this point onward, our proposal was not treated as fanciful and illogical again."

At the end of the hearing, the Ports Authority's chief engineer concluded that if the crane manufacturer was willing to take the risk upon itself and approve the marine transfer, then he, the client, would remove his objections. Indeed, in the absence of the maritime risk, the proposed method seemed preferable in all other respects. The client, therefore, agreed to give Mifram a one-week extension during which it was required to submit additional technical data, including certificates from the crane manufacturer and other drawings and calculations guaranteeing that all risks to the cranes and quays had been taken into account and that the transfer of the cranes by sea would not affect their performance or void the manufacturer's warranty.

In Yitzhak's estimation, these terms were quite reasonable: "The client's requirements seemed logical to me. I, too, would have done the same, especially in light of the fact that this adventuresome idea had never been tried before." But there was much to be done in that one-week grace period granted by the client.

Ofer was also sympathetic to the client's concerns:

"I understood that the client was willing to listen to us and that it was now up to only us to land the job. It was important to us to make it clear to the crane manufacturer that our primary task was to guarantee the crane's perfect stability throughout the entire process, as if it were on solid ground rather than on the sea. It had to be ascertained that the crane would not actually be affected by any change during its marine transfer, specifically that the extent of jolting would be in accordance with the Belgian manufacturer's guidelines and would not in any case exceed the permitted limit for land activity. We planned to conform to all of the manufacturer's requirements, including reinforcing and securing the crane on the barge during the sea voyage, and to build in safety factors that were three times higher than the calculated requirements for overland transport."

A series of meetings in Belgium with the crane manufacturer's technical and administrative team was scheduled in order to obtain approval for the proposed plan. The meetings lasted two days and ended successfully, with the crane manufacturer convinced about the safety of the marine transfer. They agreed to send the client a letter specifying that in light of the material presented, there was no apparent reason to prevent the marine transfer of the cranes, and confirming that the warranties on the cranes would not be void following such a move.

As an entrepreneur aiming to improve his chances of "selling his idea," Ofer decided at this stage not to limit his attention to the engineering issues. He chose to mount a parallel campaign with the Haifa and HaKishon port managements, for whom the shutdown of the cranes' operation would have had a critical impact on operations. The possibility of considerably shortening the duration of crane downtime and concentrating the work during the holiday season, when the workload in the ports would be significantly reduced, was an attractive prospect for the port managers. After hearing the persuasive arguments, they relayed their impressions and recommendations to the Tenders Committee accordingly.

All of the required documents, including the letter from the Belgian manufacturer, were presented to the Ports Authority's chief engineer, who was entrusted with the task of making the final decision on whether or not to approve the method. Ofer recalls:

> "Before we entered the meeting with the Committee, the chief engineer summoned me to a one-on-one meeting. He indicated to me that this was his last project before retiring from the Ports Authority and that failure of the project would cast a long shadow over his entire career: 'I believe in the method you are proposing and I expect your personal commitment to its success. I ask that you do not disappoint me.' The engineer's sincere words moved me, and I made a commitment to him to make every effort to ensure that the project succeeds."

It should be stressed that although Ofer and Amos might have been taking a real risk, they were also going to benefit directly, whereas the chief engineer was a public servant who did not stand to gain any direct benefits from taking such risks. Beyond his personal concerns about putting his career on the line, the chief engineer's willingness to support the plan was praiseworthy for another reason as well. At that time, the Ports Authority was about to issue a large tender for the supply of new cranes, and the Belgian manufacturer, who was coveting that tender, would have probably complied with any request made by the Authority's engineer. In all likelihood, even the slightest hint on the part of the chief engineer would have sufficed for the Belgian manufacturer to reject Mifram's request out of hand.

The Ports Authority's chief engineer proceeded to inform the Tenders Committee that after reviewing all of the documents he had received, he was now ready to approve the transfer method suggested by Mifram. About a month later, the Tenders Committee issued an approval of Mifram as the winning contractor.

The Risk Reduction Phase

Upon receiving the official notification about being awarded the job, Amos took the role of project manager:

> "While it was not clear when the actual transportation would start and we assumed we had about two months for detailed preparations, it was very clear, all along, that this project had only two possible outcomes: a complete success or a complete failure. Partial success would be a disaster for the client and for us. Accordingly, the overall objective of all our preparatory activities was also very clear: Reduce risk and eliminate it to the greatest extent possible.
>
> "Although the specific task at hand was completely outside my area of expertise, I had already acquired rich experience in leading 'out-of-the-box' projects. This experience guided me in selecting the execution strategy—meticulous preparations coupled with enhanced redundancies—and was also very handy in quickly identifying the right experts, a few of them from

abroad, as well as in adopting an appropriate decision-making process. In some cases, I relied almost blindly on the input of the experts, but in most cases, either because of the subject or the expert, I decided to seek a second opinion.

"For some aspects, we followed the typical design engineering patterns of information collection, analysis, and design. For other, more complicated aspects, the design was preceded by brainstorming meetings, where extreme scenarios were examined. We examined even very extreme scenarios, such as the capsizing of the crane on the quay during the overland transfer, which might damage anchored ships and shut down the quay for an extended period of time. For other aspects, where knowledge was completely missing, we started by testing our models in sophisticated labs. For example, the Faculty of Aeronautics at the Technion, the Israel Institute of Technology, was commissioned to test a computer model of the crane/barge system in a wind tunnel on a dynamic platform in order to calculate the forces expected to act on the crane during the sea voyage, with the swaying of the waves, and to determine the required harnessing."

There were many other issues that had to be addressed by Amos and his team in order to minimize risk. For example, a powerful magnetic surface was mounted on the front of the overland vehicle, which was equipped with a drive system that included about 1,200 wheels to minimize the load on the quay. The magnet was designed to prevent punctured wheels by collecting all of the sharp metal objects, such as nails and screws, scattered along the route. Another safety issue was preventing the barge from swaying dangerously due to the transfer of the crane from the quay to the barge and back. A steel bridge was designed and manufactured to connect the quay to the center of the barge to stabilize it and keep the crane's load uniformly distributed over the barge surface when loading or unloading it. Finally, the thickness of the tension cables had to be two and a half times that required by the calculations in order to satisfy Lloyd's, the maritime insurance company, whose job it was to approve the harnessing of the crane to the barge before each departure from port.

In order to provide immediate solutions for any mishap related to the critical issue of harnessing the crane to the barge during the sea voyage, Amos decided to triple the amount of designated equipment (such as welding apparatuses, generators, cranes, cables, and so on). Indeed, for all critical systems, including the number of wheels (1,200) and the capacity of the barge (3,000 tons), the safety requirements embraced were much higher than those dictated by the direct calculations. Extremely rigorous tests were also conducted, as Amos illustrated: "I decided to invite an expert in ship building and asked him to examine the tugboat and the barge very thoroughly, as if I was about to purchase this equipment." Moreover, work crews were reinforced, and an additional backup crew was added to each shift.

While still refining the "hardware" side of the mission, Amos started focusing on the people side of it as well. A project manager was specially appointed to take care of all the administrative issues on site, including hot meals, lavatories and showers on the barge, transportation, fueling, and daily changes of work clothes. Amos even decided to purchase new tools and clothing labeled with the name of the project so as to enhance the identification of the workers with the project.

The project workforce included 190 workers, comprised of 120 Mifram employees, 40 foreign workers (tugboat and barge operational crews), and 30 employees of local subcontractors (heavy equipment operators, welders, and maintenance crews). Strong emphasis was placed on selecting the right people for key positions, such as foremen, team leaders, and equipment operators. In more than a few cases, the best available people in the market were hired at a premium cost.

Special attention was given to the development of an accelerated, but comprehensive, training program for the different trades.

Accurate, reduced-size models of the crane, the barge, and the cart, including electrical motors, were built to train the workers and drill them on the loading and unloading processes, with an emphasis on safety. An extremely detailed plan, with about 300 specific activities, was prepared for each sea voyage. Important procedures were not only described in words, but were also drawn on large sheets of paper in order to ensure that all concerned would understand them and adhere to them. Various safety checklists were also prepared and played a central part in the training sessions, later being distributed to all key functionaries.

While Amos was leading the preparatory activities, his brother, Ofer, had developed better ties with the Ports Authority's chief engineer. As Ofer explained:

> "From the moment we received the notice to proceed, I took it upon myself to gain and maintain the trust of the chief engineer. Therefore, all relevant information that was available to us was forwarded freely and transparently to the chief engineer. I felt that this went a long way toward strengthening the trust between the two of us. I really don't believe that the first surprise we encountered in this project had anything to do with the trust that had developed, but at the same time it definitely did not hurt."

That first surprise was an out-of-the-blue request from the Ports Authority to deliver two very large cranes—this time from Haifa to Ashdod. Both cranes weighed 1,100 tons each and stood about 85 meters high. Only a few minor changes were necessary to accommodate these two additional cranes. The most significant change was to prepare alternative mooring places along the way, because the distance between Haifa and Ashdod is about 130 kilometers, as opposed to the 7-kilometer distance between Haifa and Hakishon. This change would have only a marginal cost and time impact, and the formal contractual agreement with the Ports Authority was arranged quickly—a big boon for Mifram.

The Constant Vigilance Phase

The first sea voyage with one of the big cranes went flawlessly according to plan until the tugboat and the barge were about to enter the port of Ashdod. Without any advance warning to the captain, the tugboat was not allowed to enter the port, and it was left waiting at the end of the line. Because the barge must be constantly on the move to minimize oscillations, this delay was risky. Following a series of urgent phone calls to the Ashdod Port management, which took about thirty minutes, the tugboat was finally given permission to enter the port.

It turned out that the very recent addition of the two cranes from Haifa to Ashdod in the scope of the work had not been coordinated with the workers in Ashdod. A couple of hours later, representatives of the Ashdod Port's union and management were meeting to discuss the long-term development plans for the port. In the wake of the incident that had just occurred, they also made one short-term decision: to allow the tugboat to enter the port without any delay the next time it arrives.

By the time the crane was unloaded safely and placed in its new location in Ashdod, everybody was extremely pleased, both on the side of the client and the contractor. That is, except for Ofer:

> "The full success of the first relocation actually worried me a lot. I was afraid of the 'driver with one arm hanging out the window' syndrome. Over-complacency on the part of the workers might impair their alertness and readiness to cope with mishaps. I collected all of the workers and commended them on a job well done, while reiterating and warning about the high risk inherent in each relocation: 'Each delivery is a new task that depends to a great extent on factors over which we have limited control, and so we must not delude ourselves that the success of one relocation necessarily means success of the next.'"

One of the brothers, Amos or Ofer, was constantly with the workforce throughout the entire operation. They were closely involved in this 24/7 operation and worked on it in shifts, including weekends and holidays, staying together with the workers and even eating with them. As Ofer underscored:

> "This was our norm for all the special projects we carried out, and our people expected it. We believed that this way we can learn quickly about changes and react in a timely manner, and not less importantly, we can naturally infect the entire workforce with our passion and energy. We promised large bonuses to the workers, but we believed that the role model approach is a more effective motivator. Our work philosophy was that the workers should stay focused on their task, religiously adhering to their procedures, while they were expected to 'raise a flag' if they observed a change in their surroundings. It was the responsibility of the various managers to react quickly, to adjust the procedures, or to improvise a new solution."

In addition to this process of identifying changes, each step in the transfer of every crane was continuously documented and photographed from different angles (land, sea, and air) in order to identify any possible mishap in advance, to implement lessons from each voyage to the next, and to minimize risks. All of the execution stages, the processes implemented, and the work and equipment invested were documented in a detailed logbook in order to draw immediate lessons from one relocation to the next.

Prior to each sea voyage, all vessels and designated equipment were meticulously inspected according to an inspection guidelines document ("Readiness for Towing"), prepared by the marine engineer in collaboration with the captain of the tugboat. This included, among other things, a thorough inspection of harnessing and connections between the crane and the barge, the qualifications of the professional crew, and the validity of the licenses and certificates for all of the auxiliary equipment.

All planning aside, Ofer was realistic about expecting the unexpected: "Although we were quite confident that we had prepared ourselves meticulously in the best way possible for this unique and risky operation, we were still sure that we would encounter surprises. So we had to be constantly vigilant."

And there was, indeed, no lack of surprises. Amos shares one of the emergencies they had to cope with:

"On the morning before Yom Kippur, the holiest and most solemn day of the year for the Jews, the barge was in Haifa Port with the second crane destined for Ashdod Port on it. It was obvious to me that we would not make it in time to unload the crane before Yom Kippur and return to port in time. Due to the shortage of mooring place at Haifa Port, we were instructed to sail the barge to the shallow waters of Hakishon Port and let it wait there until the end of the holiday, with the crane on it."

Waiting in HaKishon Port for 48 hours would require "sinking" the loaded barge until close to the sea bed in order to increase its stability. After all of the arrangements were completed, however, the marine engineer recalled a past incident in which a loaded tanker had capsized in Hakishon Port under similar circumstances due to "suction forces" that the muddy soil of the port had exerted on the bottom of the ship.

Ofer and Amos realized that they could not afford to take any chances and must change the previous decision. They went ahead and requested approval, after all, to moor in the Haifa Port for 48 hours. This change in plans on the eve of the holiday, when all of the approving entities were already off duty, was practically impossible. The port master refused to approve the request. There was indeed a problem, because the designated quay was completely full of passenger ships that were anchored in Israel for the duration of the holiday.

In the final hour, arrangements were made for mooring of the loaded barge in the Haifa Port, conditional upon Mifram's agreement to bear the cost of moving and coordinating the mooring of several ships on the quay. Only Ofer's personal involvement and intensive action vis-a-vis the person responsible for the moorings in the port yielded this last-minute solution.

Following the holiday, the voyage to Ashdod continued, though many small disturbances were encountered along the way. Despite their constant attention to meteorological conditions, with rerouting of the tugboat as deemed necessary, on this specific trip they had to cope with changes even after they had left the port in Haifa. They had not one, but two false starts when they were warned that the sea was expected to be squally. First, the tugboat captain decided to return and go back to Haifa, where they had to wait for the sea to quiet down, even though it delayed the trip by two days. During their second attempt, they were warned again of a squally sea, and this time the captain decided to moor in the alternative harborage in Hadera, which was prepared in advance for such an event. Amos recalls: "Due to the high waves, the barge could not maintain its stability, the head of the crane was making large circles in the air, and everything was noisy and squeaky. I have to admit it was quite scary. During those moments, prior to entering the harbor, we felt very thankful for the extra harnessing we had installed."

Besides the squally conditions at sea, the barge was getting jostled around even while moored in the port. Small military vessels that were accustomed to exiting and entering the ports at high speed created waves in their wake that jostled the barge, particularly during the critical periods when the crane was being loaded onto the barge until its final harnessing. Again, Ofer was proactive in meeting with the Navy commanders and was able to coordinate the movement of military vessels by day and night so that they would pass by the barge in a slow and controlled manner.

However, they had to cope with major mishaps as well. During the second transfer, a severe malfunction occurred that compromised human life and threatened to shut down the entire project. One night, while attaching the crane's harnessing cables to the barge, a foreign ship hit the harnessing cable that connected the barge to the quay and disconnected it. This caused the barge to roll heavily, to the extent that it was feared that it would crash against the quay and cause the crane to collapse onto adjacent vessels. The event was apparently caused by the failure of the port management to inform the captain of the foreign ship that the crane was being loaded onto the barge.

An alternative harnessing cable had to be transferred immediately from the barge to the quay and attached to the mooring installation on the shore. The tugboat captain and a Mifram portable crane operator saved the day by using the portable crane, which by chance was on the quay with its arm open and ready to load equipment onto the barge, to secure the end of the cable and pull it to the quay. Their resourcefulness not only saved the operation, but also prevented a major disaster.

A debriefing was performed shortly after the completion of each relocation operation, with the lessons used immediately as a basis for analysis and planning of the next transport. The lessons from the laceration of the cable by the foreign ship were implemented in the subsequent loading by using observers and enhanced lighting to secure the entire loading area. The method of securing the barge to the quay was also changed to prevent damage to the cables by any random ship.

Finally, closer coordination with the port authorities was also executed prior to each transport. Amos did not mince words on this point: "Up until that event, we had been very nice to the client and to the Haifa Port management. When we understood the severity of the event and its implications, as well as the magnitude of the client's neglect, we immediately said, 'No More Mr. Nice Guy.'"

Not all of the problems were weather- or coordination-related. Some were financially driven, such as when the Italian contractor's representative approached Ofer and demanded advance cash payment prior to the transport. This was contrary to the agreement, which stipulated that payment would be made after each relocation via bank transfer to the Italians' bank account. Ofer was stunned by their request: "The Italians' demand astonished me. We had already completed two successful marine transfers and had paid the Italians what they were due without any problem. Even if I had wanted to pay, I could not have done it at that moment because all the banks are closed at night and it was impossible to raise the required amount of money in cash."

The Italians decided to stage a "strike" and deliberately slowed down the execution process, giving "work safety" as the reason. This time, transporting the crane using the overland vehicle took about 5 hours instead of only 45 minutes, as in previous cases. Only after harsh talks between Ofer and the tugboat captain did the latter agree to instruct the crew to return to normal work pace.

But the standoff was not over yet:

> "After this relocation was completed, the tugboat captain haphazardly informed me that he had received orders from the mother company in Italy 'to drop everything and set sail that same night' for Africa, where his urgent presence was required in order to extricate a ship, an offer that apparently presented an excellent business opportunity for the Italians."

The captain was instructed by his employer to explain the termination of work with Mifram by saying that towing of the barge was dangerous and that according to maritime law, he could not be forced to take the risk. The captain seemed embarrassed in light of the special relationship that had developed between himself and Ofer, but he felt obliged to obey the instructions of his superiors in the company. The captain suggested that Ofer speak directly with the CEO of the Italian company and inform him that he intended to involve the Italian embassy in Israel and the Haifa Port management in order to prevent the tugboat from leaving the country.

Ofer asked the Haifa Port authorities not to approve the tugboat's exit from the port. At the same time, he instructed his workers to take possession of all the tugboat's and barge's loading and mooring equipment, without which the tugboat could not execute its task in Africa.

The threats and actions taken were effective, and eventually a different tugboat was sent from Italy to Africa to execute the other mission.

The crane relocation project was successfully completed. The entire project took only about four weeks and was cause for celebration by all parties. The client saved about 50 percent of his budget (direct cost) and additional sums due to the shorter shutdown time of the cranes and the quays. The contractor made a higher profit than he had originally planned because of the significant expansion of the work at a relatively low marginal cost. Last, but not least, the workers received high premiums for their outstanding performance.

Both Ofer and Amos agree that their rich experiences with "out-of-the-box" projects, their company's flat organizational structure, the quality of the people they recruited and developed throughout the years, and the norm of working closely with their staff in the field contributed to the success of the project. Regarding the flat organizational structure, they pointed out that when the heads of the organization are also the heads of the project, their ability to make decisions and quickly implement them is enhanced. Even more importantly, it enables them to tailor their decisions to the context, for example, to hire a consultant and, if needed, to pay him twice the going rate. Amos adds to this list boldness and systematic planning, while Ofer adds building trust and leadership, in particular leading the client. Finally, both Amos and Ofer agree that the most crucial weapon they brought to a dynamic environment was the fact that they complemented each other and created a dynamic harmony.

5

A Successful Downsizing: Developing a Culture of Trust and Responsibility

by Alexander Laufer, Dan Ward, and Alistair Cockburn

My Engineering Staff Shrunk from 80 to 12

Judy Stokley recalls the challenges she faced when she took over as program director of the Advanced Medium Range Air-to-Air Missile (AMRAAM) at Eglin Air Force Base in Florida:

> "Talk about a difficult start. The program was rife with problems when I arrived, not the least of which was the mandated drawdown plan that had not been met. The Air Force had issued a mandate to draw down the workforce, and everyone on the program knew about it—civil servants, military personnel, and support contractors. A lot of these people had been on the program for the full 20 years it had existed, and many thought they were going to stay there until they retired.

> "The program director before me had not been able to face letting people go. 'I would rather retire than let that many people go,' he had said, and that's exactly what he did—so there was a perception in the program office that perhaps we would be able to 'escape' compliance with the directive."

Judy called a meeting of all 200 workers who were assigned to the AMRAAM program in order to explain the drawdown plan. It was a daunting task to tell them that in less than a year, more than half of them would no longer be working in the program office. She tried to make it clear that she did not intend to just pass out pink slips, and she reassured them that they would receive assistance in finding new jobs. The initial reaction was dead silence. After the meeting ended, people rushed to gather around her, competing for her attention to convince her that their particular positions were indispensable.

> "It was neither pleasant nor easy. On a personal level, I had never experienced anything like it before. I had to deal with disgruntled people whispering behind my back when I walked past them. It was the first time in my life that I had experienced being disliked and gossiped about, and let me tell you, there is no pleasure in knowing that you are being blamed for other people's pain. One thing that I worried about was that somebody in the program office might take that frustration to an extreme. By that, I mean walk into the office with a gun and start shooting people. All you have to do is watch the evening news to realize that it would be foolish to write such things off as impossible."

In order to defuse the tension, Judy provided them with an outlet to express their frustration. She held monthly meetings where she gave everyone note cards to anonymously write down complaints or recommendations. The cards were deposited in a box at the end of the meeting. Every constructive recommendation—no matter how mundane—was actually implemented, and a report was given each time to explain what had been done to address the concerns expressed at the last meeting. The process moved forward, and the program office team was reduced to just 68 by the end of the fiscal year.

George Sudan, AMRAAM's chief engineer, was among the few people in the program who supported Judy's efforts:

"I was glad when Judy arrived at AMRAAM. She seemed to understand that acquisition reform—*real* reform—entailed something more significant than the cosmetic changes I had seen thus far. Still, I wondered whether anyone, no matter how dedicated a leader, could change the status quo and bring about serious reform. In the end, she proved that acquisition reform doesn't have to be a pipe dream. After the six-month process was completed, my engineering staff had shrunk from 80 to 12."

Likewise, Dennis Mallik, AMRAAM's chief financial officer, recalls:

"We talked about acquisition reform in the AMRAAM program office for some time before Judy took over as program director. In the early 1990s, her predecessor asked me to do a cost study on how to save money. I did it and produced a report, but he told me to take that report, lock it up inside my desk drawer, and make sure it stayed there until our base commander either transferred or retired.

"When Judy became program director, I understood immediately that it was time to open up my desk drawer and dust off that report. Her reaction was very different than her predecessor's. 'Why, we've got to get this information out to people,' she said. To many of us who had given up hope that real reform was possible, we knew that we had seen the dawn of a new day."

No one needed a study to see that the AMRAAM program was spending too much money. There were five separate simulation models checking the performance of the missile, including two contractors (Hughes and Raytheon) with their own simulation models, the Navy with its model, and two independent simulations conducted at Eglin Air Force Base. The government simulations might have been necessary during the research and development stage, but the need for that much expensive redundancy had to be called into question after the production phase started. The contractors were the ones who needed the data, and they were already getting that at their own facilities.

Sometimes it might appear that government engineers are too busy telling the contractors how to do their job rather than doing their own. George Sudan, AMRAAM's chief engineer, claims:

> "We don't do engineering very well in the government anymore, but we do have a lot of people who like to dabble in it. Engineers need to get out of the meddling business and into the specifications and verification business, but that requires the support of management.

> "Unfortunately, the attitude of management at AMRAAM was that: 'You can't trust these dirty contractors. They're all out to take advantage of you.' They expected us to line up with the contractor as though it were a basketball game. Here's their radio frequency guy, so we've got to have a radio frequency guy. Here's their software guy, so we've got to have a software guy. If he fakes left, you fake left. For our part on the government side, we were harassing our 'opponents' all the time. 'Let me see your documents. Let me review this. Let me see how you did that.'"

AMRAAM was the largest program on Eglin Air Force Base, with various stakeholders receiving AMRAAM money each year and viewing that as their right. Thus, the reforms being introduced would be expected to have a tremendous impact on a number of parties involved.

Judy Stokley personally experienced the weight of what was at stake, starting with a call one day that the base commander at Eglin wanted to see her:

> "Some of my people got wind of what was coming and warned me that the base commander was furious about not being funded for this, that, and the other thing. He had apparently already complained about me through his chain of command.

"I heard that he had gone all the way to my bosses in Washington, where he was told, 'We pay her to execute efficient and effective programs. We don't pay her to shore up work forces at the product centers.' After that, he had to figure out how to deal with me on his own, so he demanded a face-to-face meeting.

"In the Air Force, it's a big deal to meet with a base commander, especially when it occurs in a public forum. By the time I arrived at his big, beautiful conference room, people were already seated all around the table. Suddenly, the commander flung open the door to his private office and strode into the conference room, red in the face and with eyes bulging. He sat down without speaking, making it clear that he felt no need to be civil."

Throughout the meeting in his conference room, he attacked every word out of Judy's mouth with caustic remarks along the lines of how contractors are out there making millions off the government and how he didn't have any use for industry. Still, she remained courteous.

Judy understood that many people in the government, especially in the Department of Defense, have a problem with the idea that a contractor should make a profit:

"They think that they need to go to the negotiating table having gotten the contractor down so low on his cost that if he has one problem, he's going to be in the red. I always shock them when I remark, 'Sure, I want him to make a profit, and I want to help him make it.' To me, the worst thing in the world is to do business with a contractor in the red. That way, he can't get out ahead of the problems and can't invest in my products.

"At the end of the briefing, I said, 'I will proceed as planned with this program. Thank you very much for your attention today and all the time you have given me.'"

Partnership

The downsizing was painful, both for many people in the base as well as for Judy herself. Although she was authorized by the Pentagon to proceed with the downsizing and knew fully well how to achieve it, she also knew that downsizing alone was a necessary, but insufficient, condition for lasting success. She believed that without a radical change in the culture of the organization, involving a shift from control to trust and responsibility, her mission would not be truly accomplished.

So Judy took it upon herself to change the project culture. However, it would prove to be an arduous and complicated task to create a relationship of trust, mutual support, and teamwork between the government and the contractors. Acquisition reform was difficult to grasp for many people involved with AMRAAM, and Judy struggled to sell it both to government and industry. Not long after she announced the drawdown plan in the program office, she hosted a meeting with several of the key members of Hughes and Raytheon, the two contractors building the missile.

> "I wanted to talk with them about our 'partnership,' what was wrong with it, and what we were going to do to improve it. To make my point, I brought a copy of the 'spec tree' that governed the program at the time. The document was hundreds of pages thick, and it illustrated all that was wrong with AMRAAM. Over the years, people had added endless low-level specs, and it was a disaster. I don't think anyone could make sense of it.

> "If something needed to be changed for any reason, like for instance if a part went obsolete or there was a problem with a vendor, then the contractor had to submit an Engineering Change Proposal and the government had to approve it. The contractor documented every change in parts, down to the lowest-level nut, bolt, or screw, and sent those change proposals all day long. The government paid the contractor to make

the changes or else they didn't get done. I used to say, 'If I want my contractor to flush the toilet in Tucson, I have to write him a contract letter and pay him to do it.'"

Judy wanted to change that mindset and get the contractors to develop what she referred to as a "heart and soul" relationship with their products. She was striving to create a win-win situation for both sides by taking an unwieldy spec tree and writing a good, simple set of performance specifications that the contractor could control, while paying a fair price for the product on the government side.

"Coming together in a partnership meant more than just saying, 'Starting Monday, we're a team.' I told my counterparts on the contractor side: 'I'm going to help you pay for everything, I'm going to help you make a decent profit, and you are going to make sure that we have a good product out there.'

"I laid all this out at the meeting I held with the contractors. All of a sudden, Raytheon's chief engineer stood up and spoke across the room to his vice president: 'Boss, I've got to make sure that before you agree to this, you understand what she's saying. Because if you do, I don't think there's any way you'll agree to it.'

"Everyone looked at him, and then back at me. To say that things got tense is putting it mildly. 'Today,' he continued, 'if we change something here, the government pays; but what she's telling you is that with this deal, if we change something, we pay.'"

This was a perfect expression of what was holding them back. They couldn't see opportunity; they could only see risk. It was indicative of the way in which they had managed their business for years. They were used to doing things a certain way, and change—regardless of how necessary—made them jittery.

"'Oh man, we don't want any part of this,' said the Raytheon vice president. I realized that I wasn't going to convince him to embrace reform if he fundamentally didn't want to change. They were so cynical about working with the government that they had a hard time believing I could offer any kind of deal that would be good for them. The best I could hope for was that he would go along with it until he saw that the reforms worked. He could only see where we had been, and he feared the problems that could befall us if we wavered from that."

As it turned out, Chuck Anderson, the head of the AMRAAM program at Hughes, had a past experience with Judy and was much closer to her management philosophy than his superiors, even prior to her initiation of the drawdown:

> "Back when Judy Stokley was Deputy Program Director, we had a problem—a big problem—with the control section of the missile. It was a design issue, and it was our problem. We at Hughes needed to fix it. It was only my second week on the job, and I went to Eglin Air Force Base to discuss the issue.
>
> "I walked straight into the program director's office and said, 'We're going to fix the missiles, and we're going to do it at our company's expense.' That was a $3-million decision. His mouth hung open in disbelief. My company wasn't obligated to do a darn thing, but that's not the way I thought we should do business."

Chuck believed that his company had a responsibility to take care of its customers and live up to its agreements. Judy saw that, and when she took over as the program director, she understood that she had a teammate ready and willing to reform a troubled program.

Realizing the huge impact that Chuck would have on the success of the change, she recounts:

> "Fortunately, it was a different story with the Hughes vice president, Chuck Anderson. Chuck not only knew where we had been, but he could also see where we might go and what we

could become. I was fortunate to have someone like him on the industry side.

"When Raytheon and Hughes merged, Chuck stayed with the program and the Raytheon vice president left to tend other patches of status quo. The merger created lots of other issues to deal with, but the fact that we had the right person in place on the contractor's side and a meeting of the minds was a tremendous help in implementing the needed reforms."

Chuck Anderson recalls the crucial meeting when Judy's team came out to Tucson to work with them on staffing and initially proposed drawing down the workforce to as low as 30 positions. He knew that he could not get the job done with so few people and warned that the program would not be the same in that case. They went through the staffing requirements, position by position, but still could not come to an agreement.

"Finally, Judy and I went into my office, apart from everyone else, and she said, 'Chuck, tell me what you need to do this job.' I told her, 'I think I can do it with about a hundred people.' At the time we had around 400 people working on AMRAAM, so we would still need to displace a significant number of people. We shook hands on the number.

"When we rejoined the group, Judy announced that we would keep 100 people on the program. I remember the look in my team's eyes. They knew that many of the people who had worked on the program for years would lose their jobs and that the rest of them would have to figure out how to get the job done with one-quarter of the former workforce. They also knew that a handshake was our only assurance that our customer was going to live up to the agreement. 'Look, we have to trust the customer on this,' I said to them. 'We have to trust that they understand what kind of risk we're taking in signing up for this.'"

Chuck was no stranger to taking risks:

> "I decided that we were going to open our books to the Air Force, prompting a swift visit from the Raytheon corporate police. They came to my office and told me that I was breaking the rules. 'That's confidential data! You're not allowed to show that kind of data to the government.'
>
> "I told them, 'Go to hell,' literally, and then threw them out of my office."

It wasn't the first time he had been told that he had no authority to make an agreement with a customer:

> "They'd try to tell me, 'That has to go to Lexington' (home to Raytheon's corporate headquarters). Anything over a dollar had to go to Lexington for approval. As such, I was on report a lot.
>
> "At the time I entered into this agreement with Judy, I still had a Hughes badge on. I actually had to get Raytheon's chief operating officer to approve it. How did I get it done? I said we could pull it off, and I was believable. My prior track record probably had something to do with it, too. The bottom line was that I had run successful programs all of my career, and it's hard to argue with success. Beyond all that, we definitely benefited by being in Tucson, Arizona—a long way from Lexington."

When it became obvious to Chuck that Judy was trying to seize the merger between Raytheon and Hughes as a catalyst for real reform, he knew that the outcome would be worth the risk:

> "The biggest reform of all was getting government out of the way to allow the contractor to do the job of designing and building better missiles. We called it Total System Performance Responsibility, or TSPR. Officially, this meant that the contractor would accept responsibility to do what was necessary and sufficient to develop, deliver, warrant, and support missiles that would be affordable, combat capable, and readily available. In

layman's terms, it meant that the government would trust the contractor to decide when the product successfully met performance requirements. This was a unique approach in government contracting. In fact, it was exactly the opposite of what government employees and contractors were used to doing."

One welcome change of TSPR would be to eliminate the long waits required for government approval on simple spec changes: "I had to have a whole bureaucracy in place just to substitute a round capacitor for a square one on a circuit board. As ridiculous as it may seem, changing a capacitor required a four-month approval process up to that point."

But as Chuck knew all too well, change doesn't always come easy: "With this merger, I would come under more scrutiny by my corporate office. All my freedom to make decisions and 'do what's right' would disappear if I didn't make reasonable profits. This was a new way of doing business, and I had to sell it to my people."

And a hard sell it was. Tom Gillman, the contracting officer for Raytheon, recalls:

> "Judy Stokley's intentions were good, no doubt, but I had been burned in the past by people with good intentions. Good people in the government have made commitments to me as a contractor that they have been unable to fulfill. Likewise, I have made commitments to the government that I have been unable to fulfill. In both cases, it hasn't been for lack of trying.

> "I have to admit, I was skeptical that the government was capable of living up to the commitment they made. Try telling your bosses, 'I'm going to do several hundred million dollars worth of business on a handshake. Don't worry, I trust my customer and they trust me—so you should trust both of us.' Most contractual relationships in this industry revolve around legalistic interpretations of big, thick documents called contracts. Usually, whoever has the best lawyer wins.

"One thing that Judy did to win my trust was to eliminate the bureaucracy on their side. A large staff on the customer's side is disruptive to work. We had to be staffed in such a way as to take care of our customers, and so we had a lot of hand-holders. I used to have one person in my organization for every person that the government was going to assign to a project, plus the people to do the work. The bigger their bureaucracy, the more feeding it took. Suddenly, we didn't have to put as much into care and feeding, and that freed us up to pay more attention to building missiles. That went a long way in proving that the commitment was for real."

Several key people on Judy's team came up with original steps aimed at enhancing the understanding and acceptance of the new culture. Following the meeting where Chuck and Judy made their handshake agreement, a "mirror exercise" was conducted, with a facilitator asking each side—government and contractor—to make one list of its most important issues and another list of what it thought was the other side's most important issues. When the two sides shared their information, it became immediately apparent that there was little trust between them.

Dennis Mallik, AMRAAM's chief financial officer, describes the sense of mutual distrust:

"The contractor's side thought that the government wanted the product for the lowest price, and they thought that the government team was willing to suck our company dry if that was what it took to get a low price. On the government side, some of the team thought that the contractor only cared about a big profit and didn't care about quality. One thing was clear from the process. Everyone needed to work to dispel these toxic stereotypes, or else we were never going to be an effective team."

Dennis decided to apply his own experience to solving the problem and put together a presentation for the contractor's financial managers and program managers:

> "I had worked for a contractor for 12 years before I entered the government. I believed that the contractor's people would do the best job they could for us. What I didn't understand was how little they understood us. It occurred to me that if I educated the contractor about government program planning and budgeting, I might be able to help the situation."

He learned quite a bit from that visit:

> "They explained that Raytheon had gone deep into debt to buy Hughes Aircraft. Profit wasn't their main concern; it was cash flow. They thought that all I had to do was ask for money today, and it would be available tomorrow, so I helped them to understand that I had a two-year delay before I could get anything written into the budget. One of the things that we worked on was figuring out how I could improve cash flow on the program."

The visit also netted him a better rapport with his contractor counterparts: "We continued to meet face-to-face once every couple of months, and we kept in close contact the rest of the time, with frequent emails and telephone calls. I went out to Raytheon and asked for everything I thought I needed to know—and they gave it to me."

As Dennis explains, open communication between the government and the contractor was not the norm on other Air Force projects:

> "When some of the people working on other programs came by to ask me for advice, they were stunned to learn how open my relationship was with Raytheon. They had been told that they couldn't ask their contractors for information, but they saw that I didn't operate that way. 'You'll be surprised by how much better you do once you get to know the people you're working with,' I explained."

In another attempt to promote the new culture in AMRAAM, Col. Wendy Massielo, contracting officer for the U.S. Air Force, came up with the idea of a coffee mug with the slogan, "TSPR Is *Not* a CLIN," as a way of helping to embed this change in philosophy in people's minds:

> "In the government, our traditional way of operating is to ask, 'Well, what does that cost?' no matter what 'that' is. The way we account for each of these costs on a contract is through a line item: a Contract Line Item Number (CLIN). People were trying to apply that same CLIN approach to understanding what we were doing on AMRAAM.

> "I found that I had to answer the same question all the time: How much was this Total System Performance Responsibility going to cost? Many people from both the government and the contractor were at a loss to understand what TSPR meant. I wanted people to stop thinking of it as a line item, as a number, and instead look at it as a philosophy. When you embrace the TSPR concept, it means so much more than the cost of delivering a missile. Cradle to grave responsibility, that's what we were trying to instill in the contractor."

Jerry Worsham, chief of logistics for the U.S. Air Force, describes the waste involved in the process prior to implementing the new TSPR approach:

> "Certain roles that were traditionally performed by the government now made sense for the contractor to do, and one of those was the repair of damaged missiles. The way it worked was that damaged missiles still under warranty were sent to the contractor's facility in Tucson, while those with an expired warranty went to government depots for repair.

"The more depots you have, the more expenses they incur for the program because every location has to have spare parts in inventory, plus management and maintenance facilities. It made sense that if you could combine those depots, you could streamline the operation and save money. We looked at what it would cost for the one location at Tucson to do all the depot work, and the cost savings were substantial—approximately $10 million worth of savings in spare parts alone.

"Some of the depots resisted giving up their work to the contractor. As soon as I started talking about the contractor having total system responsibility for the life of the missile, they only saw that to mean jobs flowing from a military depot to a contractor facility."

In addition to repairing the missiles, one of the other things slated for reform was sustainment engineering:

"Certain elements of the missile had a history of breaking, which compromised reliability. Who better to keep the engineering up-to-date than the contractor who designed, built, and knew the missile better than anybody else?

"The way I saw it, I was there to try to make the most of taxpayer dollars. They thought that I was there to shut down jobs. Each time I talked with someone who was stubbornly opposed to reform, I became more convinced of the need for reform. It was a difficult task at times, but it was necessary work."

Increasing the responsibility on the contractor also enhanced its sense of ownership. Brock McCaman, program manager at Raytheon, demonstrates how being innovative and initiating change also allowed it to save money:

"Traditionally, when a missile arrived at our depot, the clock started ticking, and we had exactly 60 days to do whatever was necessary to repair the missile and make it available for shipment again.

"When Judy came to us and said, 'Here's my budget,' our collective response was, 'Yikes!' We realized immediately that we couldn't keep repairing missiles the way we always had—the money wasn't there.

"This is the conclusion I came to: Let me decide what to work on and how to work on it, and I can provide you with more missiles per month than I can with 'turn-around time.' We said to Judy, 'Want to save money?—then let's forget about turn-around time,' and she agreed. Now we're measured on field availability. Because of this, we can take the contract for less money and deliver more missiles.

"For example, sometimes a missile is returned so broken that it isn't worth repairing, what we call 'beyond economical repair.' From a customer's point of view, there's no such thing as beyond economical repair. Everything is economical if you've already paid the contractor to do it. Suppose that I receive one missile that's smashed up. After that, I receive five others that just need simple repairs. Because the clock is ticking on each unit, I have to throw all kinds of people and resources to get that first, smashed-up missile fixed so that we can send it out before the 60-day deadline. Give me the flexibility to push that one aside and work on those other five missiles, and I can get them out with the same amount of energy and for the same cost as the single missile that needs more work.

"Here is another way we're saving money on repairs: Before TSPR, we had to tell the government about every nut, bolt, and screw we replaced on a missile, how much it cost, who worked on it, and how many hours it took to repair the unit from the day it came in until the day it went out—and we were required to file reports with all that data. Today, we send them a bill once a month for a fraction of the cost of what we were doing before, and we get the missiles back into the field sooner. This way of contracting works better for us, for the government, for the taxpayer, and especially for the war fighter."

Constancy of Purpose

Jon Westphal, an engineer with the U.S. Air Force, differentiates between roles and describes his role as an "enabler":

> "The government is not in the manufacturing business; the contractor is. Judy Stokley and George Sudan were adamant about this. 'Let them do their job. We'll work with them to provide insight—not direction, not oversight.'
>
> "The best way to do that was to be on site, working side-by-side and supporting open communication between the contractor and the government. That was the role of an 'enabler,' and that was what I did."

The enablers had to have a broad background because they were not experts in any one field per se, but rather dealt with everyone— contracts people, finance staff, business reps, program managers, and engineers. They knew enough across the board to communicate with people and get them in touch with whoever was needed to help solve their problems. Probably more important than anything else, the contractors had to feel comfortable that the enablers understood what they were talking about.

> "The first thing I had to do was try to convince the contractor that even though I was from the government, I was there to help in whatever capacity I could. The contractor's employees wondered how safe it was to tell this government guy anything and how much they should keep secret. I had to reassure them that whatever we talked about would remain confidential until

we had identified the potential impact of a problem and created a plan to overcome it. Once I got past their initial suspicions about me, it was easier to forge relationships because more and more people understood my role.

"About nine months after I started going out to the contractor's site in Tucson, I needed to check something with the director of operations. I walked down to his office, where there were five or six engineers standing outside waiting in line. I walked up to the front of the line and was about to stick my head in the office and ask my question, when the guys in line jumped on me, 'Hey, what do you think you're doing?' I said, 'Look guys, I'm just going to ask Rick a quick question.' They objected, 'Come on now, there's a line here.' I said, 'Yeah, but I'm the customer.' And they said, 'You're an enabler. Get in the back of the line.' Right then, I knew that I had been genuinely accepted!"

For Brock McCaman, program manager at Raytheon, it took some time to get comfortable with the notion of a government representative being an asset rather than a liability:

"The government thought the enablers were absolutely necessary, but I was skeptical at first about the whole idea of using them. These guys had complete exposure to all our dirty laundry. And I don't care how good you are; you still have some dirty laundry hanging around. I figured that this would be just another bunch of government guys watching over us, reporting every little thing.

"It turned out I was wrong, and that's because AMRAAM became an altogether different program under Judy Stokley. Before TSPR, government reps would get big points for sniffing out problems in our organization. Now reporting problems was no longer considered as good behavior because it violated trust.

> "Each enabler had different strengths, and yet they never tried to give us contract direction. There were times during meetings when I would turn to one of them and say, 'Hey, what do you think about this?' And he would come back with some real jewels.
>
> "At one point down the road, we had a program-wide discussion about whether or not to continue using the enablers. I said, 'Are you kidding? They're too valuable not to have around.'"

One of the things that Judy wanted to do was establish a long-term pricing agreement with the contractors so that their vendors, many of whom are small businesses, would not be forced to provide certified cost or pricing data every year. Operating under verbal approval for Price Based Acquisition (PBA) from her boss in Washington, she pitched the plan to Hughes and Raytheon before the merger as one of the benefits of reforming their old way of doing business. Then a month before they were supposed to award the contract to Raytheon as the sole source provider, her boss in the Office of the Secretary of Defense told her that they would not be allowed to go forward with PBA, claiming that a lot of people in the political system weren't happy about the merger.

> "I was crushed. I got the call on my cell phone as I was leaving Eglin. She went on to tell me that PBA was a 'dead issue.' She said, 'Don't come to Washington to try and revisit this.' I was so upset that I had to stop driving, and I pulled off the road. That was probably as down as I have ever been about my job.
>
> "But I pulled myself together that weekend, and I called Chuck Anderson at home on Sunday. 'Chuck, I can't deliver on Price Based Acquisition,' I said. 'I'm sorry, I thought I could do it, but I can't. I can't get approval for it.' 'Well Judy, if that's the way it is, I guess that's the way it is,' he said. 'Let's have a video conference on Monday, and get everybody together to figure out what to do.'

"On Monday, when we brought the team leaders together for the video conference, I explained the situation. At first there was a lot of venting, and then Tom Gillman, the contracting officer, spoke up: 'I never thought the Price Based Acquisition mattered anyway. We have to get cost data from all the same vendors on our other programs, so unless the entire department goes Price Based, it really doesn't help us that much.'

"I still remember that Friday night after the phone call and how I felt like driving off the road. I thought so much depended on getting Price Based Acquisition. Part of the hurt was that I thought it would damage the business, but the other part was that I took it too personally. I had gotten too full of myself. I was focused on implementing all these great reforms and strategies, and I expected every part of the process to fall into place. I came to understand that my pride had been hurt because I had promised people something I couldn't do. I was embarrassed— but, more importantly, it was all perfectly workable."

"I learned something extremely valuable from this teamwork," explains Judy. "When you've got a strong team, they will figure out how to overcome the little barriers that pop up along the way. By the second year, there were no barriers anymore. They did miraculous things, things no one would have believed they could do when we first started working together. Anytime we had a problem, they had it worked out before I even knew it was a problem."

Tom Gillman, the contracting officer for Raytheon, highlights the importance of trust in his working relationship with Dennis Mallik on the Air Force side of the AMRAAM team:

"The fact that Dennis invited me to his internal budget meetings and wasn't afraid to publicly display the openness that existed between the Air Force and Raytheon was not only remarkable, it was unprecedented in government-contractor relationships. I had been part of trusting relationships with my government counterparts before, but these were one-to-one relationships that we kept quiet, lest our leadership get wind of them and scold us for setting such a dangerous example for others.

"It was the trust to be able to share with your counterpart what is really going on rather than some version that's been smoothed over by your leadership. It was the trust that your counterpart is going to listen to you thoughtfully and try to help you come up with a solution, but never use it against you. Because I wanted to honor this trust, I never used any of the data that I saw at these meetings for business purposes at Raytheon outside of the AMRAAM program.

"Dennis never told me I couldn't, but I understood why I was there. He regarded me as a member of 'his' team as much as anybody who was in the room wearing a government badge. He asked me only once, 'Do you see anything limiting our abilities to get the job done?' After that, whenever I saw anything that could impact the AMRAAM program, it was expected that I would speak up and not wait to be asked for my input. It was all about our abilities to get the job done. I have to emphasize that word again: *our*."

Sustaining a major cultural change may require constant maintenance. Chuck Anderson describes a practice that he instituted to sustain change:

"All of my team members, approximately 80 of us, met for half a day off-site at a hotel. We did this every month. We rented a ballroom, and the whole purpose of that meeting, every month, was constancy of purpose. It was to get everybody aligned—or brainwashed, as some said.

"My message was: 'Let's do what's right. Let's make sure that we deliver on time, make sure that the design is right, make sure that we meet every requirement. Our customer will help us in every way possible, and then by definition we'll succeed and we'll meet our financial targets.'

"During our open discussions, members of my team brought up examples of how the government wasn't living up to their end of the deal: 'I still have to do this.' 'I've got to write a report for these guys.' That sort of thing. 'There are probably always going to be problems,' I said, 'but we've got to have faith in the leadership there. They are committed to this, so let's try to work through it.'"

Ultimately, most of Chuck's team members had faith in him as a leader, and the ones who did not "get it" were eliminated from the team: "I was the one whose job was on the line if we screwed up, if it didn't work out—and I did my best to make it clear that I knew we were doing the right thing."

"But, you can't do it on your own. That's why I made sure to surround myself with a team of effective leaders. I'm talking about six or seven people, all hand-selected by me. I knew every one of them. You need to have real leaders on your team when you're doing something like we set out to do on AMRAAM. These were people willing to make decisions, take risks, get on with it, and not study a problem to death.

"We've got so many smart people in this business who can't bring themselves to make decisions because they're afraid of failing. I selected people who could make swift decisions if that's what was required. And that's what they did, proving themselves time and time again."

Tom Gillman, the contracting officer for Raytheon, concurs:

"All programs have problems. In the normal mode of government contracting, everybody runs to the contract and says, 'What does it say on paper?' Not us. The first thing we did was ask what the best thing was for the war fighter. Once we determined that, then we decided on the best way to solve the problem, given our resources.

"When people asked me about the impact of TSPR, I used to say that it was like buying a Sony TV. They say that Sony technicians never turn the televisions on when they put them together. Because of their quality control system, they know that they're going to work. What the government tried to instill in us was that same kind of pride in our work."

Tom recounts a story of how his people were doing just that:

"For example, on a particular piece of missile hardware that had to work only 90 percent of the time, it was determined that failure occurred less than one percent of the time. Contractually, they were not required to resolve that one percent, but instead, they decided that it was the right thing to do to see if they could figure out what was happening.

"We locked some engineers in the lab for six months and had them duplicate that failure. They determined that with a simple modification of the missile, we could eliminate it. We ended up spending a couple of million dollars to fix 5,000 missiles that weren't under warranty. We could have hidden behind the specifications. Nobody paid us to do the extra work, but it was the right thing to do for the war fighter, and that typifies what this kind of business relationship can offer."

In the end, the AMRAAM program received the DOD Life Cycle Cost Reduction Award. The average unit procurement cost for the program decreased from more than $750,000 to under $400,000, saving the Air Force and Navy $150 million over the course of four years.

6

A Peaceful Evacuation: Building a Multi-Project Battalion by Leading Upward

by Alexander Laufer, Zvi Ziklik, and Dora Cohenca-Zall

The Turbulent Birth of the Unilateral Disengagement

Israeli Prime Minister Ariel Sharon shocked the entire political spectrum on December 18, 2003, when he announced:

> "...if in a few months the Palestinians still continue to disregard their part in implementing the Road Map, then Israel will initiate the unilateral security step of disengagement from the Palestinians... The Disengagement Plan will include... a change in the deployment of settlements, which will reduce as much as possible the number of Israelis located in the heart of the Palestinian population... This reduction of friction will require the extremely difficult step of changing the deployment of some of the settlements..."

Then, on February 3, 2004, Sharon clarified that the disengagement would primarily be from the Gaza Strip: "It is my intention to carry out an evacuation—sorry, a relocation—of settlements that cause us problems and of places that we will not hold on to anyway in a final settlement, like the Gaza settlements."

Sharon, who was one of the settlement movement's staunchest allies, outraged and alienated many of his right-wing nationalist supporters, while eliciting startled disbelief from his left-wing opponents in Israel. He had been elected on the mandate to protect the settlements, which he described as being "no different from Tel Aviv." He applauded the strategic value of Jewish communities such as Netzarim in the Gaza area, declaring that "the fate of Netzarim is the fate of Jerusalem."

The disengagement plan was indeed divisive. Failing to gain the support of several senior ministers, Sharon agreed that his party would hold a referendum on the plan in advance of a vote by the Israeli Cabinet. Most polls showed approximately 55 percent of party members supporting the plan before the referendum, which was held on May 2, 2004. In the end, more than 60 percent of the voters cast their ballot against the disengagement plan.

Sharon announced that he accepted the referendum results and would take time to consider his steps. However, he and his government largely ignored the results and approved an amended disengagement plan on June 6, 2004. The plan was approved with a 14–7 majority, but only after two ministers were dismissed from the cabinet. The plan that the cabinet approved called for a complete disengagement from the Palestinians in the Gaza Strip, including the relocation of all 21 Jewish settlements there, and a limited relocation of four settlements in northern Samaria. Consequent to passing the plan, two additional ministers resigned, leaving the government with a minority in the Parliament, which forced Sharon to later establish a National Unity government. Opponents of the plan and some other ministers called on Sharon to hold a national referendum in order to prove that he had a mandate, which he refused to do.

Polls consistently showed support for the plan in the 55–60 percent range and opposition running around 30–35 percent. However, the people who opposed the plan were much more active in voicing their opinion. For example, on July 25, 2004, the "Human Chain," a rally of close to 100,000 people, joined forces to protest against the plan and demand a national referendum. The protestors formed a human chain over a distance of 90 km, from the Gaza Strip to the Western Wall in Jerusalem. A couple of months later, about 100,000 people marched in cities throughout Israel to protest the plan under the slogan "100 cities support the settlements in the Gaza Strip."

On September 14, the Israeli cabinet approved a plan to compensate settlers for leaving the Gaza Strip. The compensation plan used a formula based on location, house size, and number of family members, among other factors. The total cost of the compensation package, as approved by the Parliament, for the 8,000 settlers was about $870 million.

On October 11, at the opening of the Parliament winter session, Sharon outlined his plan to start legislation for the disengagement process at the beginning of November. After several rounds of votes and ensuing upheaval in the government over the following six months, the Parliament rejected a bill to delay the implementation of the disengagement plan on March 28, 2005. In June, the Israeli High Court of Justice rejected the appeal of the settlers against the government.

The Systematic Preparations of the Israeli Defense Forces

It was widely expected that the evacuation from the Gaza Strip, which was part of a unilateral withdrawal without any peace treaty, and which involved 8,000 settlers, most of whom were affiliated with right-wing parties, would be met with strong resistance. The traumatic evacuation of Israeli settlements from Sinai 25 years earlier, and in particular the evacuation of the city of Yamit, as agreed upon in the peace treaty with Egypt, is remembered as one of the most sensitive and divisive events in the history of Israel. Even then, when the evacuation was carried out as part of a peace treaty and most of the settlers were willing to leave peacefully, a violent confrontation still took place between a small minority of the settlers and the soldiers who were sent to evacuate them.

The evacuation from the Gaza Strip was sure to be even more traumatic, despite the government's declaration of the evacuation as a national mission. At the beginning, it was unclear whether the evacuation would be carried out by the police or the Israeli Defense Forces (IDF), both of which were reluctant to take responsibility for the mission. The police leadership was simply worried that it lacked sufficient manpower to carry it out. The IDF claimed that its forces were trained to protect the country from its enemies, not to evacuate citizens from their homes. Also, the IDF was worried that the lack of public consensus would not only render the accomplishment of this mission more difficult but might eventually affect its ability to carry out its normal tasks. Eventually, the government decided that the IDF would be responsible for the evacuation with assistance from the police.

At the same time, a parallel civil administrative body was established and tasked with developing both temporary and permanent accommodations for the evacuees while maintaining their community structure; finding and developing new employment opportunities for them; providing psychological assistance to adults and youths; and facilitating the transfer of compensation packages. Unfortunately, the majority of the settlers was firm in the belief that the evacuation would not take place and thus for a long time refused to interact with this new organization.

In late October 2004, the Israeli Parliament formally approved the government's decision. Major General Dan Harel, head of the Southern Command, was put in charge of the mission. He formed a small think tank that began examining the meaning of the decision, including the operational implications for the day after. He invited Lieutenant Colonel Daniel, the chief psychologist of the Southern

Command, to join his small think tank, telling him: "You psychologists have a rare opportunity this time to take front stage and professionally lead a complex military operation."

Daniel conducted searches to locate relevant information on the topic of evacuation to learn from the experience of the past. The two sources that seemed to be most relevant were the evacuation of the French civilian settlements from Algiers in the 1950s and the evacuation of the city of Yamit, which had been the largest Israeli settlement in Sinai. In both cases, it turned out that no preliminary preparations for the evacuations had been carried out, and it became clear that they were not suitable models for the current project. As Daniel commented, "We were forced to act upon our own healthy intuition."

In that spirit, Daniel gathered together the IDF's psychologists one day in November 2004 for a "day of thinking together," with the objective of expressing and listening to their different opinions about the potential problems expected in the evacuation project—an attempt to batten down the hatches. The key question identified during the meeting was how to execute the mission according to the government's guidelines while ensuring that the damage incurred during the evacuation itself, as well as the day after, would be minimal.

Daniel recalls:

> "Due to the complex situation, we were concerned that the emotional burden on the soldiers would be too heavy. On the one hand, over-determination can lead to uncontrolled exertion of force. On the other hand, over-sensitivity might land the soldiers in situations in which they are not able to exert force at all. Our success will be measured by the ability to help people find the correct balance between determination and sensitivity. Following the assembly, I coined the clear and catchy slogan 'with determination and sensitivity,' which became the vision of the entire disengagement."

Many other key issues were identified during the meeting, and following the meeting Daniel distributed a document to the various military entities summarizing the critical aspects of the disengagement project from the psychologists' point of view. The next step involved the establishment of a team of leading psychologists who would help the commanding officers of the various units to combine the operational aspects of the disengagement project with its "softer" aspects.

The IDF's psychology group continued with preparations for the various scenarios, finding that often the greatest concerns were not about the anticipated intensity of the settlers' physical resistance, but rather about the soldiers' ability to withstand heart-rending scenarios that might affect them emotionally and thus compromise their performance. Daniel gave a good analysis of the problem from the military perspective:

> "It seemed to us that it was very important to reinforce the mental capacity of the evacuators, which constituted a critical tier in building the individual's strength as part of the whole. After several weeks of deliberating between several alternatives, we found that the most appropriate solution, from the perspectives of both the evacuees and the evacuators, was to use large concentrated masses of soldiers as an effective means of psychological warfare."

On the one hand, concentrating a large force of soldiers opposite the evacuees might weaken their will and ability to resist. On the other hand, a larger group of evacuating soldiers might minimize the probability of individual deviations on the part of the soldiers.

Thus, the IDF operational plans attempted to amass a huge force. The plan called for the IDF and the Israeli police to amass a force of about 42,000 troops on the ground plus a backup force of 13,000. The 55,000 soldiers would be divided into six circles, each of which would have a different function. The first circle was designated to be inside the settlement responsible for the evacuation. The other five circles would be responsible for supporting the first circle, for stopping protestors from disrupting the process, and for responding to Palestinian terrorist activities should they occur during the disengagement.

The soldiers operating inside the settlements, who would be performing the most difficult task of evacuating the settlers, would be unarmed and under strict orders not to use violence unless violence was used against them. Thus, they would be allowed to remove the people physically, but not to use violence against them. Due to the need to concentrate so many troops, the army decided that not only combat units would take part in the evacuation, but also soldiers and commanders from rear units and various staff entities.

It was decided that women would be evacuated only by female soldiers or policewomen, so the increased presence of women in the evacuation force was required. The IDF recognized that the task of the female soldiers was likely to be more challenging than that of the men. First, because it was decided that female soldiers who had children would not take part in the evacuation, it was expected that most participants would be rather young and therefore possibly more fragile. Second, as a result of this decision, they would simply be outnumbered by the female population among the settlers. The female soldiers would also have to cope with various unique requirements, especially regarding evacuating mothers and their children. For example, it was strictly forbidden for the female soldiers to separate the children from their mother in such a way that the mother would not see her children or that the children would not see their mother. It was thus clear to the IDF that an additional effort must be invested in the preparation of the female soldiers.

During the first months of 2005, the group of psychologists continued in their efforts to expand and refine the guidelines for the evacuation, often through workshops that prepared the evacuators through practice and at the same time served as a lab for the psychologists. In these workshops, the participants were trained to evacuate children and families from their homes and to cope with the possibility of evacuation under fire and violence on the part of the settlers. Various scenarios that were expected to take place during the evacuation were practiced, and role playing in which the participants played both the evacuators and the evacuees was performed. It was found that playing the role of the evacuees was effective in helping them to exhibit greater sensitivity and better embrace the required new culture "with determination and sensitivity."

The Fight for the Makeup of the Battalion

It was late April 2005 when Yaron, a Lieutenant Colonel in the Israeli Air Force, was summoned by his commanding officer and asked whether he wanted to volunteer for the evacuation operation as the commander of a battalion. At the time, Yaron led a design engineering unit in the Air Force, though earlier in his career he served as a deputy battalion commander in the Paratroopers.

Yaron, who perceived it as a personal challenge, immediately responded favorably and one week later was informed that the Air Force Commander had approved his appointment.

On May 10, the Brigade Commander convened a forum where Yaron first learned that his manpower would be coming from three very large Air Force dispatching bases, each one hosting a large variety of units. He also learned that the forces designed to take part in the evacuation would be composed of two divisions, each made up of two brigades, which were in turn comprised of three battalions each. His battalion would be one of the three battalions of the Air Force's Blue Brigade.

When Yaron learned that he would have to build his battalion from scratch, he got to work immediately. The battalion would eventually be composed of 700 people, including 3 evacuating companies and 1 company serving the day-to-day needs of the battalion. Each evacuating company included four platoons, and each platoon was composed of two squads. According to the plan developed by the

IDF, it would be the responsibility of the individual squad, composed of a commander, 12 male soldiers, 4 female soldiers, and 1 policeman, to approach each house and evacuate its inhabitants.

The battalion staff included officers and senior NCOs from a variety of Air Force positions: staff personnel, mechanics, engineers, pilots, anti-aircraft personnel, and so on. Although the process of placing people at the different levels of the battalion (squads, platoons, and companies) was being implemented, Yaron encouraged the battalion's company commanders to initiate ongoing meetings with their soldiers. Because they all continued to serve in their dispatching units in their original capacities, these meetings took place twice a week in various formats whenever the soldiers had time off from their ongoing activities.

Yaron describes the commonly held assumptions by the top commanders of the Blue Brigade regarding their mission:

"First, it was assumed that while our task as evacuators might be difficult, all of the hard decisions had already been made by the government and the IDF Southern Command. Second, it was assumed that our only task leading up to the actual evacuation was to build and prepare the three new battalions. Third, it was assumed that by following the training and operational guidelines prepared by the Southern Command and its psychologists, we would be able to prepare the new battalions without encountering too many difficulties or surprises. The difficulties and surprises, it was assumed, would emerge only once the evacuation had been started. Unfortunately, the upcoming events forced me to rethink the validity of each of these three assumptions."

The first surprise encountered by Yaron was that of the behavior among some top officers in the Air Force. On May 17, 2005, he was invited to give a presentation about the mission to the officers of the Blue Brigade. One of those officers did not like what he heard, so he reacted by sending a lengthy email to a Brigadier General, one of the top leaders in the Air Force, complaining about Yaron's choice of words and overall attitude to the evacuation mission. Among other things, the officer said: "The fact that we are IDF officers in the first circle is not a source of pride, as can be deduced from the battalion commander's words, but a constraint due to a shortage of police troops." He also rejected the statement that the evacuation is a "highly valued mission," claiming that "it might be deduced that the expulsion of Jews from their homes has become a highly valued mission."

Yaron was shocked by the email message:

> "I was convinced that my lecture was very appropriate and the feedback I received directly following the meeting was very positive. I began to realize the complexity of the mission and the way in which the message that I am trying to impart might be misunderstood because of the listener's perception. Most importantly, we are expecting our soldiers to be 'determined and sensitive,' yet here I was not being sensitive enough. Still, I was disturbed by the fact that the Brigadier general, who conveyed the message to me, was not interested in understanding my point of view, and it caused me to start reflecting on the commitment of some of my superiors."

Unfortunately, soon enough Yaron was surprised by the behavior of other top officers in the Air Force, this time the commanders of the dispatching units. Yaron found that the quality and motivation of certain staff being assigned to the mission fell far short of meeting his needs, primarily because of the poor selection process adopted by some of the dispatchers. Yaron made immediate inquiries with the commanders of the dispatching units, who were mostly colonels, through face-to-face meetings, telephone calls, and email communications. Although he found that a few of them acted the way he expected by identifying the most suitable people and encouraging them to volunteer, the majority did not do so, either because they were not convinced that the evacuation was a crucial mission or simply because they did not want to detract from their ongoing operations by spending energy on it.

Major David, who served as one of the squad leaders in the battalion, describes the process of allocating soldiers as random and unstructured:

> "Though some of the soldiers volunteered for the mission, most did not. Only in a small proportion of cases was the process defined according to any criteria. Most of the soldiers, who were chosen largely by drawing lots or by the commanders' arbitrary decisions, did not want to participate in the evacuation mission. The 'fish in the net' syndrome very aptly describes their situation, and they invested a great deal of energy in attempts to be relieved from duty. It was not uncommon to hear 'Why me?' 'What am I doing here?' 'How can I get out of this?'"

Likewise, it did not take long for Major Ilan, one of the company commanders recruited to the battalion, to conclude: "The more I understood the task and the more familiar I became with the people who were put at my disposal, the more concerned I became about the company's ability to execute this problematic mission. I kept asking myself how I could execute the mission with career soldiers who lacked suitable motivation and skills."

Yaron concluded that training the soldiers who he had on hand would not be enough for a successful mission and decided that he must first make an effort to persuade the commanders of the dispatching units to send him their most suitable recruits. He asked his company commanders and platoon commanders to immediately identify those people who were unsuitable for the mission and act to have them removed from the battalion. Yaron then approached the commanders of the dispatching units demanding more qualified people. The responses were disappointing, so Yaron requested an immediate meeting with a Brigadier general and reported to him that: "Without the personal involvement and commitment to the mission on the part of the commanders of the dispatching units, we have no chance of succeeding." During that meeting, the Brigadier general gave Yaron his personal cell phone number and his permission to call him whenever Yaron saw fit. Yaron's reaction was that: "I finally felt direct openness and communication between the senior commander and his subordinates. It was a very good feeling."

The next day, the Brigadier general sent an important email message to the Air Force's senior commanders in which he instructed them to give the battalion's tasks "priority and total preference over any other task required by any other entity." The impact of this email was quite significant. This time the response from the dispatching units was more favorable, and the battalion was able to replace many of the unsuitable soldiers.

While attempting to change the composition of the manpower of his battalion by managing his superiors, Yaron and his commanders were also focusing on all the routine operations required to prepare the new battalion. The officers continued with practice simulations of possible evacuation scenarios, using training kits and teams of instructors to boost the knowledge and self-confidence of both the troops and the commanders.

First Lieutenant Benjamin, who served as a squad leader in Major Ilan's company, describes some of the preparations being made by the company:

> "We are practicing a great variety of situations—how to remove a crying child from a house, how to separate a mother from her infant son, how to treat people who are eating their last breakfast at home. We are trying to formulate prepared responses but are heading toward the unknown, knowing there will be things that we will have to deal with in the field."

One of the platoon meetings included an exercise in which each soldier was asked to describe the most serious event that he thought might take place during the evacuation. The other soldiers were asked to respond to the speaker and to assess the probability that his concerns would come true. According to Major David, "This discussion contributed to the coordination of expectations in the platoon. Each person had to open up and speak freely about his fears and concerns, which constituted another step in the internalization process."

The battalion's group of commanders gradually came together through joint dinners, tours of the Gaza Strip settlements to familiarize themselves with the arena, and meetings in an open and free atmosphere where everyone was invited to listen and voice their thoughts and opinions. All of these contributed to raising the morale and fostering a sense of belonging among the battalion's commanders. On May 31, 2005, all of the battalion's soldiers and commanders gathered for the first time at a resort in Ashkelon for a special event: the formal establishment of the battalion. The event's primary objective was to introduce the soldiers to the battalion's various commanders and functions.

A few days later, the company commanders conducted a preliminary tour in the Elei Sinai area. The objective of the tour was to become more closely acquainted with the settlement, which was assigned to the battalion for evacuation. During the tour, a surprising encounter took place between the battalion's commanders and two of the settlers. As Yaron describes:

> "During the tour, two scowling settlers approached us. One introduced himself as the settlement's security coordinator, and the other one was Arik Harpaz, the father of a girl who had been murdered by terrorists along with her friend two years earlier in the settlement. He seemed angry and emotional and refused to shake my hand: 'I am not willing to shake the hand of an enemy who is coming to evict me from land that is saturated with Liron's blood and from her room that is full of memories. I cannot understand how you are willing as IDF soldiers to evict Jews from their land.'"

Yaron tried to communicate with him, but to no avail. At some stage, the father revealed a gun that was tucked in his belt and said, "I don't know how I will act during the evacuation. I prefer to give up my private gun for fear that I will do something foolish."

The icy conversation "defrosted" a bit when Yaron and Arik shared memories from their military past and together visited the memorial that Arik had erected at the site of his daughter's and her friend's murder. At the end of this emotional meeting, the men shook hands with a feeling that there was a place for some hope. Yet, two seemingly contradictory comments that Arik made just before they parted were cause for concern.

His first comment was: "I admit that the political level 'duped' us by sending the army rather than the police. We will never raise a hand against soldiers. When the evacuating troops come to us, my family and I will hold a ceremony at Liron's memorial following which we will quietly evacuate the settlement."

His second comment was: "I want you to tell your soldiers that we are not the enemy... I understand that you received an order to evacuate... I expect you not to bring soldiers here who come to this mission with joy and enthusiasm. Such soldiers must not be here; otherwise, there will be violence."

Yaron recalls:

> "This was the first time I fully understood the meaning of 'with determination and sensitivity,' even though I've used the term countless times during the last month. It struck me like a lightning bolt. Suddenly I understood it all. In each house, behind each door, my people may find an 'Arik'—someone who does not want to raise a hand against a soldier, and at the same time, someone who might use his gun if he perceives the soldiers as being too enthusiastic. The leader of the squad is the only person who can ensure that at each encounter, at each door, there will not be any misunderstanding, and that the squad will be able to cope in the event that there is such a misunderstanding. Only following the encounter with Arik did I really comprehend its meaning for us. Most importantly, I realized how difficult it is to train people to exhibit this behavior in the kind of chaotic situations that we were anticipating. It is nearly

impossible to develop the capability for such balanced behavior in two months or even in two years. For these situations, you simply need people with proven leadership capabilities whose skills and attitudes have been developed through a lengthy process of selection, training, and experience."

Yaron explained that he could have a successful operation with soldiers of average quality, but not with squad leaders of average quality:

"For my battalion, at the current stage, the key to achieving a peaceful evacuation is the leaders of the squads. I have 24 squads in my battalion, and the success of the evacuation is dependent on the quality of the leadership of each one. They should be able to quickly 'read' each new situation and demonstrate the appropriate response to accommodate both the evacuees in front of them and their own squad behind them. Each one of these squad leaders should be capable of functioning like an independent project manager for each new house they are about to evacuate. I realized that although everybody views me as the commander of a battalion, I would be functioning primarily as the head of a multi-project organization during the evacuation itself."

Given that anticipated role, Yaron immediately started focusing on recruiting the best possible junior commanders, the squad leaders. He started another campaign, this time asking to replace many of the senior NCOs who currently headed his squads with experienced officers, and he asked for Captains and preferably Majors. One more time, the first responses from the top commanders were disappointing. Yet, Yaron persisted and was eventually able to communicate directly with the Air Force Commander, a Major general, and to get his complete support for his request. Toward the end of June 2005, about six weeks after the May 10 meeting with the Commander of the Blue Brigade, Yaron finally felt satisfied with the makeup of his battalion and was ready to focus on the training.

The Speedy Implementation of the Evacuation

The training, which took place primarily according to platoons or squads, was conducted only twice a week, because most soldiers continued with their regular activities at their dispatching bases. On June 28, the first exercise of the entire battalion took place. The objectives of the training were to enhance acquaintance and team-building, as well as to hold lectures and simulations on negotiations and communications. The soldiers were divided up into squads, with one squad simulating the evacuators and the other playing the role of the evacuees. Every half an hour, the squads switched roles. A film was shown, which documented the moving encounter with Arik Harpaz. At the end of the exercise, Yaron gave the participants a formal letter of appointment to the battalion and a book with a personal inscription.

On July 1, six weeks before the evacuation date, the battalion commanders and their spouses gathered at Yaron's house for an evening of acquaintance and team-building. Two days later, an R&R day was organized for all of the battalion's soldiers. All soldiers and commanders were scheduled to leave their dispatching bases on July 25 for six weeks.

At that point, Yaron found himself attempting to fulfill a variety of roles. For his superiors in the Blue Brigade, he was a member of the planning team; for the commanders in his battalion, he was the facilitator of planning and training; for his soldiers (who are not used to field conditions), he was the chief supplier, making sure that when they arrive in late July, their clothing, boots, field accommodations, and food supply will be appropriate; for some of the Air Force commanders of the dispatching units, on whom he was now dependent for the supplies, he was the persistent nagger; whereas for the settlers, he was the government.

Prior to the onset of the evacuation, the soldiers had to cope with a string of demonstrations. This time the demonstrations had a very clear operational aim: to stop the disengagement by getting tens of thousands of people into the settlements to make it impossible to remove the settlers. The first and the most crucial event took place in the small Israeli village of Kfar Maimon, just outside the Gaza Strip, on July 19, 2005. About 20,000 Israeli soldiers and police troops formed a massive human wall to prevent the 40,000 protesters from penetrating into the Gaza Strip. For three days, the tense standoff continued, after which the protesters finally left.

No violence erupted over the course of those three days, but it was tough for most of the soldiers, as one of them describes it:

> "They called us from home, without any early warning, when we did not expect it... we were not prepared to cope with the mundane difficulties of this task, just standing, sitting, eating, sleeping... it was hot and we were not used to the improvised hygiene conditions in the field... and most importantly, we did not fully understand our task until it was over."

Another soldier reported:

> "The platoon commander briefed us and announced that we were part of the 'sixth circle.' We were not familiar with this terminology, and in any case we did not know what it was about. We were surprised, since we were prepared for evacuating people from homes and not for blocking demonstrations. I had grown accustomed in recent days to tasks that were unclear until the moment of their execution, and we called this phenomenon 'the kingdom of uncertainty.'"

On July 27, all of the brigade soldiers were taken for a concentrated training exercise that was defined as the final training in preparation for the onset of the disengagement operation. The exercise was planned to last three weeks and was supposed to simulate the entire course of the evacuation itself, which was also scheduled to last three weeks. All of the troops were supposed to remain in the field without leave throughout the whole exercise.

The commanders of the platoons and the squads practiced behaviors under harsh conditions and various scenarios, such as the abduction of soldiers by settlers, the breaching of houses in which settlers are holed up, negotiations with evacuees, and the encircling of areas using a closed human chain. Daily seminars were held in the field on various issues, with lectures by legal experts, psychologists, and sociologists. The troops also watched professional actors perform simulations of different evacuation scenarios after having received professional guidance from negotiation experts.

On August 3, Yaron's battalion was rushed to a demonstration similar to that of Kfar Maimon but smaller in scope. The battalion was deployed along the roads as a living chain together with police and border police troops. On the next day, the battalion was rushed to yet another demonstration. Although the Gaza Strip had been officially closed to nonresidents since July 13, and although the IDF and the police were largely successful in blocking the attempts to get through, there were an estimated several thousand youth who were able to infiltrate into the Gaza Strip prior to and following the closure.

Following the failed attempt to flood the settlements with tens of thousands of people through the Kfar Maimon demonstration, messages reached the IDF that some families in the Gaza Strip were willing to be evacuated from their homes voluntarily, provided they received a formal request from the State. The IDF decided to postpone the compulsory evacuation by two days and to carry out an interim operation (code name "giving brothers a hand") whose objective was to convince the settlers to evacuate their homes voluntarily. The operation turned out to be successful. IDF officers helped the settlers who chose to evacuate by packing their belongings and carrying them. The voluntary evacuation continued after midnight on August 17 for settlers who requested a time extension to pack their belongings. Afterward, some of the evacuated settlers called the commanders who had participated in the evacuation and thanked them for the sensitivity that had accompanied the process.

Despite the peaceful nature of the voluntary evacuation, Yaron still had his doubts about what was to come:

"Following the success of the voluntary evacuation, some people thought that the rest of the evacuation would also be very smooth. I was not so confident. I could not easily dismiss other possible outcomes. A few days earlier, I had met with the Deputy Commander of my Brigade, a Colonel who had been in charge of the evacuation of settlers from the Gilad Farm, an unauthorized outpost in the West Bank, several years ago. He described the thorough preparations that his troops had undergone, the difficulties they had encountered, and the lessons he had learned. I was fully aware that in the Gilad Farm case, the settlers had been ready to fight, violently if necessary. Yet, I could not forget the numbers. During the first day of the operation, there were already 140 wounded soldiers, none very seriously, but nevertheless wounded. Although my battalion was not going to face unauthorized settlements, we had no idea how many of the illegal infiltrators might have come from places like the Gilad Farm. We could not forget that what we saw as an evacuation, the residents of the settlements saw as an expulsion. Thus, I made all my commanders aware of the need to stay vigilant."

The day of the onset of the forced evacuation finally arrived on August 17. The entire country was tense. The radio and TV news broadcasts went live, and media representatives from Israel and abroad were everywhere. Major David recalls:

"It was a heavy feeling of responsibility—an entire nation had its eyes on us. The words of one of the settlers especially became engraved in my head: 'everyone, evacuators and evacuees, must leave here with a scar so that we never forget what happened here.' At the beginning, I felt that this attitude was in sharp contrast to our approach that no one should leave even with a small scratch. But then I realized that we were focusing only on the immediate physical damage, while the settler was referring to the long-term psychological consequences. Now I believe that we were both right."

Yaron recounts:

"We began passing between the houses, listening to families... the settlement was in a state of great sadness, families sat on the ground like in mourning and wept. The scene was not easy, but we tried to exhibit a lot of patience. I went around monitoring closely a few of the more difficult cases throughout the day and felt very proud of my people. I felt that the squad and platoon leaders were well prepared and really did not need my intervention."

The first day of evacuation went by quite peacefully. At the end of the day, all of the settlers gathered in the settlement's synagogue for one last prayer. It was a difficult sight, with evacuators and evacuees crying bitterly as one. The national hymn closed the ceremony, and everyone boarded the buses in an orderly fashion. Last-minute searches were performed before leaving the settlement.

At the end of each day, Yaron met with his commanders for a debriefing session to discuss the difficulties they had encountered during the day and the solutions they had implemented, to draw conclusions, and to prepare for the next day. Overall, it was widely agreed upon that they were meeting with less violence than expected. Although most residents had eventually agreed to be escorted out by the soldiers, there were some cases in which the troops had to enter the houses and carry out the family members one by one, four soldiers to a person at times, with the settlers screaming and sobbing.

The overall sequence by which the settlements were evacuated was based on the "small wins" principle, according to which the IDF progressed from the easy targets to the difficult ones. In a few settlements, outside Yaron's "jurisdiction," the infiltrators clashed violently with the soldiers. The worst confrontation took place on the roof of the Kefar Darom synagogue. After hours of talks, police officers were hoisted by crane onto the roof, where they were attacked by dozens of youths. About a dozen policemen had to be hospitalized after acid was thrown at them. Police arrested dozens of teenagers.

On August 22, the last settlement, Netzarim, was evacuated. This officially marked the end of the 35-year-long presence of Israeli settlers in the Gaza Strip. The evacuation of the settlement was successfully accomplished within one week instead of the allocated three weeks. Yaron's superiors, both at the brigade and the division levels, were pleased with the performance of his battalion.

Yaron recounts a moving moment:

> "On the last day of our mission, we arrived at Elei Sinai to evacuate the last settlement. I went to Arik Harpaz's home. The stone from his daughter's memorial and the olive tree planted alongside it had spent the last few days in Arik's trailer, waiting to leave Gaza with him at any moment. Arik hugged me and commended us on the way we had acted in his personal case. I realized then that throughout the last several months, I had been preoccupied with the important role of leadership on our side—leadership at the national, Air Force, battalion, and squad levels. I had completely missed the crucial role of the leadership of the settlers. We had fought a tactical war: the evacuation of the settlers from the Gaza Strip. The IDF is stronger, and so we won the war. However, at the same time, we had been fighting a more difficult war and a more important, strategic one: making sure that the evacuation would be completed peacefully so that as a nation, we would emerge from it stronger. In this war, we both won."

7

Exploring Space: Shaping Culture by Exploiting Location

by Alexander Laufer, Edward Hoffman, and Don Cohen

"Good Enough" Is Good Enough

The core science group that proposed the NASA Advanced Composition Explorer mission, or ACE, had worked together on other NASA missions and had even built instruments together. Two members of the group were from the Johns Hopkins Applied Physics Laboratory (APL), and they were quite experienced building the type of spacecraft that they thought they needed, so the group proposed using a spacecraft built by APL. The initial unsolicited proposal of the group was not accepted, but it raised their visibility. When an opportunity came along to propose a new mission five years later, they proposed ACE as an Explorer-class mission to be run out of NASA's Goddard Space Flight Center. Patience paid off, and in 1991 their proposal was selected for funding.

Dr. Edward Stone, principal investigator at the California Institute of Technology (Caltech), recalls: "When it came down to who would be the leader of our group, all eyes fell on me. I was the Project Scientist on Voyager, a high-profile NASA mission, and I was considered a known quantity by the Agency. People knew how I did things and how I managed science. They also knew that Voyager had been going well."

The group has grown, and the challenge on ACE was working with 20 different science institutions spread out across the United States and parts of Europe. Even the distance between the two primary players—Dr. Stone and Don Margolies, the project manager from Goddard Space Flight Center—was more than 2,500 miles. Don describes how they addressed this problem:

> "Dr. Stone and I set up a schedule to talk with each other on the phone every week. In the early stages of the project, much of what was about to unfold was still up in the air. You might say the spacecraft itself was about the only thing not in the air. I thought it was crucial to the success of the project that Dr. Stone know everything that was going on—and if something happened that involved the development of the instruments, he could be on it right away. Even if it was just to say that the weather was nice in California and there was nothing much happening here at Goddard, we always kept the appointment."

Don Margolies found very early that he had to address the money issue: "Before we had been confirmed, we looked at our budget and it looked as though we were going to exceed our total resources by $22 million. The word came back from NASA Headquarters that they wouldn't allow us to continue with that kind of overrun." Don describes his dilemma:

> "I had the choice of spreading the money among all the players or focusing on the elements that posed the greatest risks on the project. I responded by putting the bulk of the money into trying to identify the key risks in the development of the science instruments and mitigating these to the best extent that we could at the earliest stage possible. To do this, I had to hold back spacecraft development at APL, which was not a popular decision, and APL did not like it at all."

The greatest uncertainty on a science mission is in the development of the instruments, and of the nine on ACE, five were new. Don describes the risk involved in his decision:

"In holding APL back by three to six months, I knew I could be shooting myself in the foot if they were not able to recover. But I believed that even with a slow start, APL would be able to catch up. You're never right 100 percent of the time. Still, you have to go with your judgment. Experience counted for a lot here, and as it turned out, they were able to catch up."

However, Don understood that money issues still had to be addressed in a more comprehensive and profound way: "What I set out to do was to establish a mutual agreement with everyone that 'good enough' is good enough. Set your requirements and stick to those requirements. Once you meet the requirements, spend no additional money to make it better."

So Don asked everyone to identify what his or her de-scopes would be if necessary, when each would have to be taken, and how much each would save. Scientists in every area—instruments, spacecraft, ground operation, integration, and testing—were forced to go back and ask themselves, "How much can I save if I take out a circuit board? Will I lose any performance by doing that, and if so, how much?"

Don explains his rationale for the de-scoping:

"ACE was part of the Explorer program, and at the time, the Explorer program budget was one big pot of money, and if one mission sucked up most of the funding, the other projects would have to work with what was left. Thus, I wanted Headquarters to make a commitment to us in writing that they would give us stable funding. The way to seal the agreement was to assure them that we were able to control the program and not run over cost. The only way to do that was to say what we would do if we got in trouble. We were willing to commit to a fixed price if they would guarantee stable funding."

Don discussed the whole thing with Dr. Stone, who was in favor of having a de-scope plan: "I knew that if we were going to get the scientists to buy-in on 'stopping at good enough,' it had to be Stone who sold it to them. Without his help, I dare say ACE would have been a much different project, and we probably would not have been confirmed."

Dr. Stone gave Don his total support:

> "Some of the scientists felt that we should not have to make any compromises on requirements. Scientists prefer to draw a large circle around their requirements because they know somewhere in there is what they need, and it is easiest just to draw the circle large—meaning enough mass, enough power, enough whatever, because then you can say, 'I know that's going to do it.' That's fine, if you can afford anything you want, but it's probably not the way to optimize the mission."

Don describes how the de-scope plan was carried out:

> "As we were defining the de-scopes on the payload side, we looked at each and every instrument and its capability, and we found considerable overlap in terms of the capability of many instruments. We said: 'All right, starting from scratch, what would be the impact if any single instrument failed? Is there another instrument that can provide similar data? What if two of them failed in different combinations?' Realizing the amount of redundancy we had, it looked to me like we could tolerate some failures in the payload and still have a successful mission."

ACE was classified as a C mission. NASA classified missions in terms of A, B, C, and D, which was all about the level of risk involved. Class-A missions were on the order of the Space Shuttle, where failure would mean a national catastrophe, so everything was done in order to make it 100 percent reliable. Class-B missions had a slightly lower profile, and risk was a little more acceptable. Class-C missions were less expensive to begin with, and even higher risk could be afforded. Class-D missions were reliable and cheap projects, such as small satellite rockets.

With all the redundancy in our instrument suite, I started to think that maybe we could get away with dual-classifying ourselves. If we could get away with flying a set of Class-D instruments, this would simplify our job tremendously. Could we go to a lower level of reliability testing, for example, and still meet the ultimate mission requirements? We determined that the answer was "yes."

Headquarters agreed. They looked at all the redundancy and said, "Yes, it made sense to dual-classify ourselves." You may fly a Class-D instrument suite on this Class-C spacecraft. Most importantly, we were able to commit to a fixed price, and Headquarters was willing to guarantee stable funding.

Nurturing the Culture of Location

In the meantime, on the other side of the continent, at the California Institute of Technology, Dr. Stone selected Allan Frandsen to serve as the payload manager. Allan recalls his first meeting with Dr. Stone:

> "During my interview when I was applying for the job of payload manager on ACE, Dr. Stone said, 'Al, give me an idea of your management style.' It was a question that I had not considered before. I thought about it for a few seconds and then answered, 'Well, the first descriptive term that comes to mind is the word tranquility.'
>
> Ironically enough, that seemed to startle him. So I added, 'I guess what I mean is that if the situation is tranquil and the project is running smoothly, then I've anticipated all the problems and taken necessary actions to head them off.'
>
> He then asked, 'Have you ever reached this state?'
>
> 'No,' I admitted, 'but I strive for it.'

Tranquility is probably an overstatement, but in running a project, I have always tried to anticipate problems. To lead a project effectively, one has to establish and maintain the flexibility to take appropriate actions when needed."

Allan gives us insight into what he considers to be the 'ABCs of project management': "If I had to write down the ABCs of project management, 'A' would signify *anticipate*.

Of course, a good project manager already knows, at least in general terms, what is supposed to happen next—but all too often it doesn't. So what are the alternatives? Are there sensible work-arounds? What can I do now to lay the groundwork or facilitate matters should something go wrong? These and other questions make up the ongoing process of anticipation. And because it is an ongoing process, the "A" in the ABCs of project management could just as well stand for "anticipate...anticipate...anticipate."

Another crucial ingredient for project success is identifying and recruiting the best people to do the job. With the right team in place, the manager's job is likely to have fewer day-to-day problems, as well as being less stressful than it otherwise would have been. So it is well worth the effort up front to carve out the time and generate the enthusiasm to *build* a good team, the "B" in the ABCs of project management.

Once a project is up and running, a manager needs to establish and monitor channels of information flow in order to foster communication between participants. Take the time to *communicate* upward, downward, and sideways, which is the "C" in the ABCs of project management.

Now there is also an "s" at the end of the ABCs of project management. Does that have any significance? Well, I would say that despite your best-laid plans, the situation can turn to manure in a hurry if a personnel matter arises. So another important part of a manager's job is to *sustain* this prized team you have recruited."

Indeed, in a dynamic environment, sustaining the team might be a challenge, at times even for the head of the team, as Dr. Stone came to realize:

> "About the time that I was interviewing Al, I had been asked to become director of JPL. Obviously, I would not be able to spend a lot of my time on ACE, but I thought that I could still be an effective PI. Whether I would be able to continue as the ACE PI was not my decision, however. It was up to NASA Headquarters. I asked, "Do you want me to step down?"

The answer was, "No, we want you as PI."

At the time that Dr. Stone was relocating from Caltach to JPL, Allan Frandsen was also moving, but in the opposite direction. Allan explains that it is all about the culture of location:

> "When I accepted Dr. Stone's offer to head up the ACE payload development, I handed off my responsibilities as chief engineer in NASA's Jet Propulsion Laboratory (JPL) science division and moved to an office at the Caltech campus.

> "Although Caltech is only seven miles from JPL, there is a noticeable cultural difference between the two institutions. From my vantage point, Caltech was the perfect place for a relatively small, low-cost ($50 million) payload like ours to flourish. Short of choosing the wrong people or having inadequate resources, nothing will torpedo a project quicker, I think, than the wrong operating environment."

Allan's core team was small, with just three others besides himself plus an administrative assistant. They were responsible for developing all nine of the scientific instruments and for making sure that they remained on schedule and within budget. Allan preferred keeping his small permanent team and recruiting additional technical expertise from JPL as needed. For these JPL technical specialists, being given a temporary task in support of ACE was both a new challenge for honing their skills as well as a refreshing assignment in a new operating environment. Although this approach was not always welcomed by the JPL managers, who understandably had other priorities and responsibilities, it succeeded as long as the specialists' absence from JPL assignments could be worked around and the arrangement was mutually beneficial.

The timing was fortuitous because the project came along at a point when the upper management at JPL was yearning for closer working-level relationships with Caltech. Not everyone liked what Allan had in mind, because no staffing arrangement exactly like what he was trying to put in place had ever been tried before. However, by the time it was announced that Dr. Stone was to become the next JPL director, any remaining resistance to the idea of enmeshing JPL staff in a campus research group seemed to fade.

Allan elaborates on the criteria for selecting his team members:

> "In searching for the right talent at JPL to staff the ACE project, I was concerned about getting people who were too imbued with the JPL way, too hidebound from big projects. After working on big projects for years and years, one can get to the point where you can't think any other way, and that's not what was required for this job. Flexibility was more important than sheer brain power, so I was looking for people who were a little bit out of the mainstream. The way I saw it, they would be getting an opportunity to spread their wings and be innovative.

> "Because my team members would be working primarily with scientists and instrument developers scattered across 20 universities and labs, I needed to find the right mix of talents and attitude—people who could flourish in a university environment. Some people want to go in a familiar direction, often the one of least resistance. Their whole career has been about following the rules, and they feel comfortable doing that. Following rules is fine, but you have to know when the rules need to

be bent, tailored, or even broken, especially on an R&D project designed and executed within a university environment where most rules are flexible and processes generally adaptable to circumstances. So I sought out people at JPL who would not be afraid to deviate from the rules."

Although solid foundations for good relationships were being put into place between the payload team and the scientists on the West coast, relationships were not quite so harmonious on the East coast. This was especially true between Johns Hopkins Applied Physics Laboratory (APL) and NASA. As Don Margolies so aptly puts it: "If Goddard said the sky was blue, APL would say it was pink."

Mary Chiu, program manager for spacecraft development at Johns Hopkins Applied Physics Laboratory, describes one example of the tension between the two organizations:

"We thought everything was settled, until some people at Goddard suggested that we use a different data handling format. With all the really neat things being done on other spacecraft, they asked, why were we getting this 'old fashioned' data handling system? For my team at APL, the people building the spacecraft, this was no small matter. To change to a different data handling system would have required a major restructuring of the spacecraft's design.

"But when NASA wants to know why you can't do something, the last thing you want to do is ignore them. Their position was that newer data handling systems provided a reprogrammable system, meaning that if one instrument shut down you could send more data to the other instruments. I tried to explain the ramifications of such a change and the fact that we had not intended the system to be reprogrammable.

"We went round and round about it until finally I said 'Okay, if you want to give us a change order, fine,' but I made it clear that they couldn't change the requirements this radically and still maintain the original cost and schedule. This was met with several comments intimating that the people on my team were not a 'can-do' group, which upset many of us. As it turned out, the flap about the data handling system passed quickly enough, and we ended up sticking with the original system."

John Thurber, observatory manager at Goddard Space Flight Center, recalls that it took a long time to develop a good rapport with Mary Chiu and her team:

"Early in the program, while I was visiting APL, I took an opportunity to visit some of the subsystem leads. Mary Chiu did not want me talking to her leads without her being there, and when she found out I had done that she got very upset. Next time I went out there, my visitor's badge had been pulled. There was no problem getting me reinstated, but it sent a strong message as to how she ran her program. It was a good six months later before I felt I could say, "Hi Mary. How are you doing? Let's go have a cup of coffee."

John describes how another dispute between NASA and APL finally led to a peaceful reconciliation:

"I needed more detailed accounting data than we were getting from the standard government form the contractors had to fill out each month so that we could tell how much money subsystems had spent. One of the things I was concerned about was that APL had recently lost a large contract with the Navy, and I noticed that new people were jumping onto ACE, presumably charging to the project.

"Mary assured me that wasn't the case, but the accounting sheets we were getting didn't provide specific enough information to verify it. I asked her for more detailed accounting data, and she kept saying, 'It's going to cost me more money on the contract if I have to go to a special accounting system.' We went around about that for a few turns, and then, finally, I gave up asking.

"To my surprise, one day she just handed me a brown envelope and said, 'Here are my internal sheets. Why don't I just give them to you? Is this adequate?' I looked them over, and they had everything I needed. 'This works,' I said.

"After that, we developed a much better rapport. Every month I got a brown envelope from her, and everything worked out fine. I got what I needed, and she never caught any more grief from me about who was charging to the program."

Don Margolies compares the different attitudes of APL and NASA:

"APL is a proud organization. If you ask them to describe the way they like to work under contract, they will tell you, 'Give us the requirements, give us the money, and get out of the way and leave us alone.' But NASA's way of doing business is considerably different from APL's. We say to our contractors, 'We'll give you the money, but we're not going to leave you alone. We expect to be partners with you.'"

Despite their differences, however, the geographical proximity between the two organizations enabled frequent meetings and communication. Don underscores the value of location to project success:

"Fortunately, the distance between Goddard and APL is only about 20 minutes by car. Let me tell you, when they talk about 'location, location, location,' they don't just mean real estate. Having that kind of proximity to each other made all the difference in the world toward cultivating a partnership between our organizations. My being able to get out to APL in a few minutes and Mary coming over to Goddard went a long way toward establishing a trustful relationship.

"I held staff meetings at Goddard every week. Mary was always invited, and she attended most weeks. I also held monthly meetings at APL, and I brought my Goddard team with me. Each of Mary's subsystem leads stood up and gave a status report on their subsystems. People weren't afraid to say what was happening or to make mistakes because they understood that our working philosophy was just to fix mistakes and move on. My staff would then get up and talk about the status of the instruments, ground system development, and so forth. I don't know how to put the value of those meetings into dollars and cents, but I can't think of anything we did on the project that was more valuable.

"I'm not sure that the relationship between APL and Goddard, between Mary and myself even, was ever 100 percent harmonious—but then, is that what you want... total harmony? A little friction is good for a project. We at least reached a point where it seemed that when one of us said something, the other one could take it to the bank."

Frank Snow, ground system and flight operations manager at Goddard Space Flight Center, confirms Don's conclusions regarding the importance of proximity and face-to-face communication:

"It occurred to me that the Flight Operations team, which I managed, should get involved in the data analysis after launch, something that was usually the sole responsibility of the science teams. My Flight Ops team knew the ground system we were using inside and out, and I thought that they should, at the very least, train the people out at Caltech on how to use it. So I offered our help.

"One of the coinvestigators at Caltech, however, was terribly suspicious of the Goddard project office. Almost any help we offered to make his life easier was, he believed, a ruse to take control of his instrument. As appreciation for my offer, he sent me a blistering email that basically said, in 300 words no less, 'Hell no!' At that point, I decided to fly across the country to Caltech to talk with him. Maybe I'd have better luck in a face-to-face meeting.

"I went there and listened to his concerns, empathized with him, and then reassured him that no one in the project office was trying to take anything away from him or from Caltech. In fact, if they were agreeable, we were actually interested in expanding Caltech's responsibilities to include flight operations. Moreover, I told him that I would put it into the operational plan to move the total operations of the spacecraft over to Caltech after launch.

"He never formally acknowledged it, but I think he saw that what we were offering was not such a bad idea after all. He allowed the Flight Ops team to come to Caltech and provide training in the ground system. Whenever he asked for help, we sent someone immediately and we made it clear that we were willing to do so at the drop of a hat.

"Clearly, face-to-face communication went a long way toward dispelling his suspicions about my intentions. I don't recall after this ever getting another 300-word email from him of the 'no-thank-you-and-please-go-away' variety. As a matter of fact, I think I can even say that this was the beginning of a fruitful relationship, which lasted for the rest of the project."

A Gentle Touch

One of the key persons in an engineering and technology project is the systems engineer. Despite the need for the two systems engineers from APL and Caltech to work tightly together, they initially found it extremely difficult to agree on appropriate work methods.

Gerald Murphy, payload systems engineer at the California Institute of Technology, describes his relationship with Judi von Mehlem, his counterpart at APL:

"ACE was my first experience with finding cultural differences between institutions that actually manifested themselves in heated differences of opinion at the engineering level. Initially, Judi von Mehlem and I tried to pretend that our differences didn't exist or that they would magically go away, but there were a number of times where our differences came to a head.

"Being the systems engineer for payload was nothing like Judi's job on the spacecraft side. At APL, Judi could say, 'Okay, everybody has to test hardware to 12.5 g's,' but I had to tailor specifications to each of the instruments. Each university or institution where an instrument came from had a different culture, and each had its own way of doing things. It was close to impossible to get uniform compliance across all of the subsystems.

"Although our relationship started out rocky, Judi and I worked hard at building good communication. For me, earning Judy's respect on technical issues became a challenge that I found motivating. On numerous occasions she challenged my opinions, and I had to go back and sharpen my pencil and come back with sound reasoning and a better technical argument.

"Judi and I are both headstrong and intelligent—and used to winning arguments. Here we were, two equals sort of battling each other. I think it took us the better part of the first year to realize that this was dumb. We had to ask, 'Why are we battling each other when we're both trying to get the job done?' It took a while to understand one another's point of view, but we found a way to work through things and resolve our differences. I'm making this sound easy—it wasn't.

"Vibration specification was a good example where APL wanted to do it one way and we wanted to do it another. APL had a specification that they wanted us to use to qualify all instrument boxes. Their specification was based on their institutional precedents, which we felt were overly conservative in the area of vibration test levels. Our environmental test program for the payload was less conservative, and—we thought—more appropriate. We knew how delicate the payload sensors were, so we specified a lower vibration test to avoid damage.

"'Well, you don't really have to worry about the payload,' we said, but they thought they did. When we couldn't come to an agreement, Goddard had to intervene. They told Judi, 'You don't have to worry about the payload. If something in the payload breaks, it's not going to be your fault; it is payload's fault, and they have to deal with it.'

"ACE challenged me intellectually, but this is also what made the project so rewarding. What I think we learned was this: the fact that I did things this way, and Judy did them that way, and Goddard did them yet another way did not mean that any of our ways was the one true way. Even though we might argue about things and agree to disagree, we earned each other's respect, and we didn't make our differences personal."

The Caltech team was faced with a different challenge in its work with the scientists and instrument developers. Allan Frandsen describes the challenge and the unique way in which his team approached it:

"One aspect of my job as payload manager involved keeping track of what the different science teams were working on and offering help where it was needed. At first it seemed as though many of the scientists, or their technical staff, weren't certain about how safe it was to confide in us.

"The challenge to my team was getting these science groups to regard us as partners or as people who could help them, rather than what they seemed to expect us to be—a troop of requirements enforcers. There were 9 instruments and 20 co-investigators on ACE working at various universities and a few government labs across the United States, in addition to labs in Switzerland and Germany.

"At one university in particular, there was a designer who held things very close to his chest. At first, we could barely get him to acknowledge that we were in the room with him, until we arranged to help him solve a power supply problem. His boss, a coinvestigator, recognized the contribution we had made and figured that we might be able to help solve a sensor head problem as well.

"There was no pressure, so we waited for him to approach us—and when he did, we didn't press him to let us get more involved. It was that kind of gentle touch, which eventually changed peoples' perceptions about our role on the project.

"A lot of it just came down to working hard with the coinvestigators at solving development problems and building their trust in the process. When you spend days and nights with people, and you suffer with them, they begin to realize that you're on the same team. They also knew that we could bring precious outside resources to bear in addressing special problems.

"I enjoyed telling people about how my payload team adapted the spirit, if not the letter, of NASA practices to fit the university environment. Understand, we still had to meet our requirements and satisfy the Goddard project office. I can recall my visiting reliability and quality assurance manager walking down the hall at one university with his arm over a technician's shoulder, asking, 'How's it going? What's happening here?'

"All the time, that technician never realized that this was part of a work-process audit. The word 'audit' can put a terrified look on people's faces, but again, a gentle touch paid off by keeping everyone working together toward the same goal: delivery of a performing payload, on time and within budget."

Gerald Murphy illustrates what a tall order that was for ACE, where they needed to produce five instruments that were either entirely new or considerably modified from earlier models:

> "The biggest challenge in managing scientific instrument development, or any new technology development for that matter, is trying to get the project completed on schedule for the money you have. Few project managers accomplish that, despite what they might tell you.
>
> "It just doesn't happen, and it's easy to understand why—technology development doesn't have a predictable path. You haven't built this thing before, so how the heck do you know how much it's going to cost? And besides, you can't foresee all the problems you'll run up against. You know the result you want, and you declare success when you are 'close enough.' In short, the job must be dynamically managed.
>
> "Some of our problems early in the project derived from not understanding exactly what the instruments were intended to do—that is, what was going to be 'good enough,' and not knowing what we could do to help the university teams build them. We in the payload management office took the approach of asking each team, 'What do you need in order to get your job done, and how can we make that happen?'
>
> "To address these concerns, we decided to have implementation reviews. I had never been on a project before where this was done, but it turned out to be the single most valuable review we had from the point of view of project success. Typically, reviews are design-focused. In point of fact, many of a project's problems are not caused by design flaws—they are caused by implementation flaws. In our case, even if an instrument had a good 'design,' its implementation needed to be executed smoothly.
>
> "When I use the word 'implementation,' I mean it in the broadest sense—implementation of the design and manufacture of the instrument. And I don't just mean taking a look at schedules

and money. I also mean looking to see if you have the right team—a team that is assembled in such a way that the lines of responsibility make sense, and interfaces that are clear and easily defined. Do you have margin for error? What are the technical risks and what is your plan to deal with them? Who is responsible for what? How many engineers do you have on the job, and do they have the right experience?

"For the ACE payload, we traveled around to each instrument developer. The process was labor intensive because we camped out onsite for three days. We sat around the table together, listened to presentations, and figured out how we were going to get the instrument built and delivered. We found the holes and looked for ways to plug them—together. We tried to be efficient, but not to be overly optimistic and fool ourselves.

"The size and composition of the review teams were tailored to the places we went. The teams were usually made up of between five and eight people, with a balance across the different disciplines, including the payload group. It was always tricky putting together just the right team, but we managed to find the expertise that we needed. For example, let's say that we knew a team was having a problem making their detector meet launch load requirements. We would grab somebody from JPL who could solve that in a week instead of letting the instrument team spin their wheels for six months. In addition, we would typically bring people from Goddard who were good at understanding resources and estimating actual costs.

"The point of the implementation review was to prevent problems from occurring later by trying to get our arms around the planning from the start. The implementation review happened only once at each site, but the timing had to be just right. If it occurred too early, it was not beneficial; on the other hand, if it was too late, you would already be buried in trying to solve the problems of the day instead of being ahead of the wave."

Implementation reviews accomplished one other thing: They set the tone for the management of the project and established a team relationship. Dr. Stone, the principal investigator at Caltech, reminds us of Allan Frandsen's interview when he was applying for the job of payload manager and how he had used the word "tranquility" to describe his management style:

> "Al showed remarkably good judgment in dealing with the instrument teams. The thing was not to try and oversee what they were doing. These were all people who had built instruments before. They weren't going to pay attention to somebody telling them to do things they knew were unnecessary. Having dealt with NASA before, their tendency right away was to think that someone coming from JPL would try to oversee what they were doing, demand a lot of paperwork, prescribe rules to be followed, and expect things done a certain way.

> "Obviously that wasn't Al's style. The way Al ran the payload office was to try and be helpful to the instrument teams, and that is how I interpreted what he said about his management style being one that strived for tranquility. I wouldn't have used that term myself, but what it indicated to me was that he wanted to work *with* people rather than to direct them."

When "Good Enough" Is Not Good Enough

Dr. Stone stresses the need for collaboration until the very end:

> "After environmental testing was fully completed on ACE, the scientists wanted to take off all the instruments for recalibration. But meanwhile, APL wanted them to stay on the spacecraft. Because of the way the instruments were mounted on the ACE spacecraft, they should have been relatively easy to

remove and reinstall. It comes back to 'What's good enough?' The question was 'How much does taking off the instruments increase risk?' In my view, not calibrating them properly increases risk as well—the risk of not getting good science.

"As the project manager, Don had the ultimate responsibility to decide what risks to take, but I wanted him to understand the importance of recalibration for the scientists, and this came down to explaining what I considered to be the broad view of the issue. Reintegration, while it was certainly a doable task, would be no small matter for Mary Chiu and APL. There were real engineering issues. The job of the project manager was to balance the interests of the engineers and the scientists so that we ended up with an optimal system. I was going to stick my neck out and guarantee Don that the instruments would be back on time for reintegration, but I recognized that it was still his decision to make."

Don Margolies explains his decision and his considerations:

"If approved, it would have been the first time on any NASA project that I know of when all the instruments on an observatory came off for rework or calibration after the full range of environmental tests and then were reintegrated at the launch center without the benefit of an observatory environmental retest.

"Several people on the project thought I was crazy. Why do it? We had gone through our environmental test programs successfully and everything seemed to be operational. If it's not broken, don't fix it, right? Normally, I would take the pragmatic approach: 'Your instruments are working, and good enough is good enough.' On the other hand, we had more than adequate slack in the schedule, and we were coming in $30 million under budget—amazing, I know. We were in a position to ask, 'What can we do to make the science better?'

"Given that we had the schedule, given that we had the money, one answer to the question was better calibration. For those who had only completed marginal calibration prior to testing, the alternative was to calibrate again in orbit. Calibration in orbit takes time, and it's not as precise as on the ground. So there really was a net benefit to the science by doing this. If the scientists had the opportunity to tweak and calibrate their instruments on the ground, they would most likely get better science in space. In order to provide a proper return on the $100 million NASA investment, ACE, an Office of Space Science mission, had to perform on all cylinders, so to speak.

"But how do you know the risk is low enough to put an instrument back on without retesting it under vibration? That was the question my management put to me. When I approached them about this, they didn't mince words. 'Don, you are crazy,' they told me. But I knew I was going to hear this, and I was prepared to explain. Ultimately, I was able to get management to buy off on the decision, but not without first undergoing an independent review of our plans.

"There were still other stakeholders whom I had to convince, and the one I was most concerned about was Mary Chiu because it was APL's responsibility to reintegrate the instruments. We talked about it exhaustively, especially in terms of what the impact would be on her team. Mary was a key part of the planning process, and getting her buy-in, albeit a reluctant buy-in, was a major precondition for going through with it. Clearly, I wouldn't have agreed to this had the APL team said it was an impossible risk.

"And so it all worked out in the end. The orderly return of the instruments didn't happen exactly as we had planned, but due to the skill and dedication of the APL team, we reintegrated the instruments at the launch site. It happened because people were willing to work with one another to make it happen."

Frank Snow, the ground system and flight operations manager at Goddard Space Flight Center, sums up the overall feeling about working on ACE:

> "Though I've long since moved on to other projects, I still get reports probably on a monthly basis from both the ground system team and the scientists. I read them because I'm still curious about how the mission is going. I'm happy that the ground system is working so well and the scientists are getting lots of good data.
>
> "But when I think back on ACE, my memories aren't of the technical sort. They're of the fun I had working with such excellent people, people who had a passion for their jobs. And that is the word I like to use. They all displayed 'passion,' no matter what the job. It's always fun working with people like that, and I enjoyed it very much."

The ACE spacecraft is currently operating in an orbit, which lies between the sun and the Earth at a distance of some 1.5 million km from the latter. The spacecraft is still in generally good condition and has enough fuel to maintain its orbit until the year 2024.

8

Building a Dairy Plant: Accelerating Speed Through Splitting and Harmonizing

by Alexander Laufer, Jeffrey Russell, and Dora
Cohenca-Zall

Shifting from Park to Drive

Tnuva Food Industries Ltd., a 70-year-old company and one of the ten largest industrial companies in Israel, initiated a major project that called for switching to a new "specialized dairy" organizational structure. No longer would five small, local dairies each produce and market all of its dairy products to the local buyers. Rather, three large, modern dairies would be built, each with its own production specialty, relying on logistics centers for distribution. One of these three new dairies was slated to specialize in cup products (cottage cheese, yogurt, and so on). That dairy would replace three veteran dairies around the country, in Jerusalem, Haifa, and Tel Aviv, which would then be closed down.

The new dairy, at Alon Tavor, was slated to be the largest dairy in the Middle East and among the largest ones in Europe. The constructed facilities for the factory, including the buildings, systems, and infrastructure, would cover about 60,000 square meters. The equipment was linked together by more than 80 kilometers of stainless steel pipe and 7,000 automated valves, all on a 130,000-square-meter site at the foot of Mt. Tavor, approximately 12 kilometers from Nazareth.

Following a thorough selection process, Zvika, the head of one of the branches of a large project management company, was hired by Tnuva to lead the planning and construction of its new dairy. During his first months on the job, in the fall of 1999, Zvika discovered that the equipment and processes design was still in its infancy, and that Tnuva's contractual obligation to provide the construction designers with the basic data needed to begin designing the structures in three months would not be fulfilled:

> "In order to design the product flow in the plant, from the finished products to packaging and storage, and to produce and install the basic equipment, a German company, GEA, was chosen in the beginning of 1998. The results of the basic equipment design were meant to be the basis for the construction planners in designing the physical structure of the various buildings in the plant, systems, and supplies."

However, it was a complex project, and as such it suffered from a multitude of technological and organizational problems. It also suffered from the physical and cultural distance between the professionals leading the project at Tnuva in Israel and their counterparts at GEA in Germany. Benjamin, Zvika's counterpart who served as the project manager for equipment and processes, felt helpless: "I understood the needs of the construction team, but the GEA engineers from Germany were still at the very beginning of designing the equipment layout, and we couldn't get any information from them."

Zvika describes the typical engineering and construction work required for dairy plants:

> "In designing and building a complex dairy plant, two main groups of engineers are engaged: equipment and processes and construction. The equipment and processes group is responsible for designing the production and transportation equipment and arranging it in the optimal way. All the equipment

and processes engineering was done outside Israel, mostly in Germany. The construction group is responsible for the building design and its systems, including air conditioning, refrigeration, electricity, communications, water, sewer, and drainage, as well as for outdoor plot development, including roads and landscaping. The construction engineers and architects were almost all local."

Beyond all of the logistical problems encountered in getting the project off the ground, the primary source of the prolonged delay was the feeling among many key people within Tnuva that it was not time to converge, that is, to switch from planning to implementation. Although the CEO of the dairy division, Ofer, kept demanding strict adherence to the agreed-upon schedule, the ongoing fights between technology, marketing, and operations made it difficult to see that they even all belonged to the same division. Moreover, judging by the constant stream of changes they were requesting from GEA, it seems that they had not accepted the decision made by the division months earlier to freeze the defined scope and requirements of the project. To make matters worse, a few people seemed to be simply enjoying this period of planning the "dairy of dreams," which, among other things, included learning from the best examples worldwide and necessarily entailed taking quite a few trips abroad.

Despite the lack of information from the German designers, Zvika thought that it was time to move ahead. He felt that the prolonged delay in the beginning of the design and engineering of the facilities was unhealthy for the project, and in a way even legitimized the delay. Moreover, he was of the opinion that starting before all open issues are resolved is the best way to ensure their speedy resolution. Thus, with the consent of Tnuva, he started forming the design engineering team. For the most part, he selected people that he knew from his own past experience to be competent, trustful, and, most of all, responsive. In the interests of enhancing responsiveness, Zvika primarily recruited designers with offices in the northern part of Israel so that frequent visits to the site would not be a problem. During the negotiations, Tnuva went along with Zvika and kept the price level fair and often favorable to the designers, thereby enabling them to demand a particularly high quality of service.

The process of forming the design engineering team served as a crucial trigger for highlighting fundamental issues. For example, it became evident to everybody that some of the most basic decisions, such as the location of the various buildings on the plot, had not been finalized. The architect wanted to position the production building so that the milk arrival area, with its vast piping and many silos that projected high above the building, would face north, and the main entrance of the plant would face south, with a "clean" view free of piping and storage tanks. However, the manufacturing division recommended the opposite solution, arguing that allowing the milk trucks access to loading and unloading on the southern side would facilitate the material flow through the plant.

Ofer, the CEO of the dairy division, and his team of senior managers came to the conclusion that the beauty of the plant would truly come through via the "forest" of piping and giant stainless steel tanks in the front of the plant, which define the plant's reason for existing. In the end, the milk arrival area was placed in the south—a decision that actually determined the positioning of the production building and was supposed to open the door for the rest of the design work to proceed.

However, despite the time that had gone by, it seemed that too many functionaries at Tnuva still did not feel the pressure to move forward. For example, the managers were still unable to reach a decision as to the placement of the energy center. The debate was around whether the energy center should be placed near the entrance, south of the production building, which would provide a shorter distance for the piping (and save a loss of energy through that piping). On the other hand, the strong winds on the southern side might cause the ash coming out of the chimneys to blow toward the area where the milk would be delivered, thus contaminating the main side of the production building. This decision was critical, because it affected the placement of all the other structures in the dairy plant. Yet, the debate went on and on without any clear closure.

By March 2000, it was clear that GEA was not even ready with the preliminary equipment plans. Without these plans, it would be difficult to proceed with the design of the facilities, because the equipment setup is what determines the final dimensions and requirements of the facilities in such terms as weight, column placement, area size, and plumbing.

By that time, Zvika had to accept the painful conclusion that the only two key people who were really concerned about the constantly delayed timetable were Ofer and Zvika himself:

> "More than once, I felt that three separate plants were being designed: one by Tnuva, one by GEA, and one by my team. There were more than a few people, both at Tnuva and at GEA, who had not embraced any sense of urgency; rather, they felt that the constant delays and the stalemates were just unavoidable. It was my experience that this state of affairs is very unhealthy, and at times a project simply cannot recover from these delays. I felt that maintaining momentum was the key, and I worked hard to find ways to advance the project."

Zvika realized that attempting to proceed through the typical process—that is, to start the design and actual construction only after all major decisions regarding equipment are finalized—would be wrong. As he explained:

> "I understood that we had to start construction as soon as possible, even before GEA had submitted its equipment layout. Why? First, we were late, and an early start, at least with some activities, would enhance our chances of overcoming at least some of the delay and thus open the possibility of finishing the entire project on time. However, there was another, less obvious, reason. I came to the conclusion that without taking a

radical step, the project was simply not ready to shift gears from park to drive. Unfortunately, too many people at Tnuva were still sending GEA changes regarding project requirements, and this at the time that GEA was supposed to be done with its planning, at least the preliminary planning."

Zvika strongly believed that the only way to stop this endless planning and preparation phase was by action, so at the end of March 2000, he requested a meeting in Ofer's office. Tnuva's equipment and process people strongly recommended that the design and construction of the facilities not be allowed to start for at least six more months. By that time, so they claimed, Zvika's team would have all the needed information from GEA. Zvika was prepared with his response: "Accepting a decision to wait six months will amount to making a decision to wait 12 months. Due to the upcoming winter in November, if the earthwork and foundations are not begun immediately, then we will have to wait until the ground is dry around March 2001. Thus, I strongly recommend that we start the earthwork no later than May 2000."

Zvika was able to surprise them all. However, the key is that Ofer was convinced. The project could not wait one full year, and he was ready to bear the consequences of starting construction prior to finalizing the equipment planning. At last, the project was about to shift gears from park to drive.

Gaining Independence

When the series of intense meetings regarding the earthmoving work was over, it was time to review the entire picture, and the results were quite alarming. Apparently, many functionaries at Tnuva were still bound to the idea of a state-of-the-art-driven dairy. Many visits were carried out in other leading dairy production plants and design offices throughout the world as part of the ambitious project scope, which led in the end to an additional 10,000 square meters of future construction and equipment, along with a deviation of more than 20 million dollars from the approved budget of 160 million dollars.

In light of this situation, Ofer declared a state of crisis at the beginning of July 2000. He summoned his entire executive team and the leadership of the project and instructed them to make radical changes in the project scope in order to cut the cost back to the original budget. Ofer's instructions were unequivocal: "To cut costs, we must be willing to examine everything, make the spaces smaller, lower the standards, recycle current equipment in place of purchasing new ones, put off investing in new fields, and the like. My decision obligates everyone to go back to the drawing board."

For six weeks, the project scope was re-evaluated and was then presented to Ofer with a significant physical reduction in the middle of August 2000. Ofer approved the plan changes and the new budget, and the project was now back on track, with a strong emphasis on cost savings.

However, the project maintained its "cost-driven" orientation only for a short period of time. Toward the end of 2000, Tnuva learned that Strauss, its greatest rival, was about to embark on a new cottage cheese line in its new dairy. This new development represented a threat to Tnuva's domination in the cup products field, and it seriously worried Tnuva's management. The new guideline to the project team was issued very soon and was very sharp: Make every possible effort to expedite the completion of the Alon Tavor dairy. Now the project had become "schedule-driven." At every meeting, Ofer stressed that the project had to be completed within 36 months. He further emphasized to all involved parties what the consequences for Tnuva would be, even at a strategic level, if the schedule was not maintained.

Although this new development was clearly a possible source of difficulties for the project, Zvika viewed it differently. He saw it as crucial leverage for finally making real progress. Now, with this timetable pressure, he could try to decouple the construction component of the project from the equipment and processes component that was lagging behind. Decoupling is always costly, but now he knew that he would be armed with a strong incentive to justify the added cost: meeting the expedited timetable.

Benjamin, the project manager for equipment and processes, did not have a choice but to agree:

> "I was between a rock and a hard place. Zvika was rightfully putting pressure to get immediate data about the loads and equipment placement. On the other hand, the processing engineers and some of the key people in Tnuva had not yet agreed even on the basic operations of the plant. It was clear to me that the data Zvika was looking for was critical to start planning the building, but at that stage, I couldn't help him."

One of the key unknowns preventing the design of the structure from proceeding was the weight of the permanent and portable equipment on the floor. During meetings with the processing engineers, Zvika and his team were able to identify a number of areas in which the loads required were extremely heavy. The common load in many industrial structures is about one ton per square meter. In most areas of the production hall of the dairy, however, the required load was much higher—two to three tons per square meter. Supporting these types of loads is very expensive and requires a scrupulous design of the skeleton system, including foundations, columns, beams, and floors.

Zvika recalls:

> "I asked them to indicate these areas on the plans and to confirm that this distribution of loads was final. They were reluctant to confirm. Their design was not final. Following several meetings with no closure regarding the distribution of the loads, I realized that there was no other choice. If we wanted to make any progress in the design of the structure, we must be willing to pay for redundancy. I, therefore, recommended to Tnuva that

all floors in the production hall be designed for three tons per square meter. We then identified several other elements of the structure that required added redundancies. The cost of all the added redundancies was about half a million dollars. Once they were approved by Tnuva, we would be able to decouple the design of the structure from GEA, at least for a while."

Dror, who was the designated CEO of the dairy once operational, was supposed to be overseeing and assisting Zvika and Benjamin. As is customary in many companies, he also served as the overall project director. However, he was still tied to his previous job and could not give the dairy his full attention during the very critical first year. He was ready to go along with the program:

"In this case, the construction people led the design of the dairy plant, just the opposite of a common situation, in which the construction is led by the design constraints of the equipment layout. Since there wasn't enough time, I needed to agree to Zvika's recommendations, as I realized that his solution was the best we would find under the difficult circumstances at that time. Thus, we approved the added cost."

Now that the design engineers were working full speed on the design of the facilities, it was time to think about the next phase: construction. Tnuva wanted to proceed through the common way—that is, to issue a bid and sign a contract with one large construction firm. However, Zvika disagreed: "By adopting the typical approach of hiring one large contractor, we may find ourselves engulfed in an endless stream of paperwork and grievances. Instead of having difficulties only with one big supplier, GEA, we may find ourselves having to deal with two big and inflexible suppliers."

He further argued: "We should not kid ourselves. A huge, complex, schedule-driven project that suffers from limited cooperation with its equipment and process designers will undoubtedly have to cope with numerous delays and changes. We would do better to develop a construction organization that will allow us to cope with these changes by being adaptable and responsive."

Zvika therefore suggested to Tnuva to enlarge his contract and, on top of the design of the facilities and quality control inspection in the field, to assign him the overall responsibility for construction as well: "As the 'general contractor,' it would be my responsibility to issue work to many medium-sized contractors and to ensure their responsiveness. With this additional responsibility, I was going to take a great personal risk. However, I was sure that without it, the project would not meet its objectives."

Apparently, the prospects of experiencing bumpy progress one more time, like they had with GEA, convinced Tnuva to go along with Zvika, and his contract was enlarged accordingly. However, as Zvika and Tnuva soon learned, the relative freedom gained from GEA and from any future construction companies was not enough for ensuring speedy progress. Zvika had to gain freedom from Tnuva itself.

Following the decoupling from GEA, the construction designers were able to finalize the design of the foundation and to prepare the needed material for the bidding process. Tnuva has a set of clear procedures for the bidding process, according to which the central tender committee meets at Tnuva Headquarters in Tel Aviv once bi-weekly to discuss material received in the previous week. The foundations tender was treated by the committee in accordance with the formal procedures—that is, "by the book." This was followed by two weeks of negotiations with the different bidders, and only then a contractor was selected.

However, this process was far too long for a schedule-driven project. It was not too difficult to convince the committee to abandon the standard process, move it to the construction site, and streamline it. Yoram, the head of the construction division at Tnuva, was certified to represent the committee at the site, and together with Zvika, they were authorized to negotiate with prospective contractors. This step allowed Zvika and his team to significantly shorten the time necessary to choose contractors, and especially to have a decisive influence on which contractors were the most appropriate for each type of activity.

They chose contractors not only on the basis of price, but rather based on previous experience working with them and on their ability to commit to a schedule. Zvika was now fully independent and finally ready to move to the site and start construction.

Splitting and Harmonizing

In October 2000, Zvika was ready to recruit someone to staff the position of the "general contractor," the person who would serve as the overall manager of construction. He interviewed a number of good candidates for the position, yet Mike, a 69-year-old civil engineer, was the one who caught his attention. He had once worked at a different branch of Zvika's project management company and had vast experience working on large and complex projects. However, Zvika was concerned that Mike was rumored to have a "centralist" personality, with trouble accepting authority: "I was concerned that we wouldn't be able to work as a team. I was also worried about his ability to cope with the huge and complicated site at his age. While the other good candidates were more 'mainstream' types of managers, something inside me, my intuition if you will, told me that I must first test and see if I could work with Mike."

Accordingly, Zvika and Mike agreed to a mutual trial period of three months, during which they would try to devise the appropriate "division of labor" between the two of them. During that time, because of the slow and unpredictable flow of basic information from GEA, the design of the facility was not smooth and produced only small chunks of work. To maintain speed, Zvika was forced to split the project among a large number of contractors:

"While usually I might not like the added burden of coordinating between many contractors working on the same project, in this case we took advantage of the situation, since dividing up the work greatly increased the competition between the contractors. I used to compare the quick pace and agility of the 'monkeys' on-site versus the reliable, but inflexible, work of the 'elephants' at GEA."

At the peak of operations at the dairy plant, there were around 250 different contractors and suppliers in construction alone. For example, there were ten contractors simultaneously working on the concrete skeleton, another eight on the steel frame, six in stainless steel, and another four on electrical systems. Mike describes the work climate: "We very much encouraged competition between the different contractors. Each contractor who completed his work to our satisfaction immediately received another 'chunk of work.' I made sure to keep continuity in providing the contractors with work in order to avoid wasting equipment and manpower."

The contractors, who relied on Tnuva's financial stability, were not afraid to accelerate their pace of work and knew that all bills submitted would be approved and paid on time. Likewise, the client trusted Mike and his team and never appealed a bill that he had approved:

"In more than a few cases, Tnuva went above and beyond to help contractors who were in need. Thus, for example, if one of the contractors was having trouble with cash flow, Tnuva agreed, under my recommendation, to pay a one-time sum as a premium beyond the contract, which would allow the contractor to complete the work in the meantime. On a different occasion, one of the contractors was having difficulty paying his foreign workers, who were generally paid in cash. In order to help him, Tnuva took it upon itself to directly pay the workers."

At the end of the three-month trial period, there was no question in Zvika's mind as to whether Mike would be staying:

"Mike and I did not have to discuss whether or not he would stay on the job. We agreed that our strong cooperation had surprised us. We both knew that it was a great success for both of us, but more importantly, for the project. Mike was a man of extremes. He helped, in every possible way, the contractors that he considered to be good, while he did not hide his dislike toward those he considered inferior. When the manager of a certain contracting company came onsite in fancy clothing or in a Mercedes, it drove him crazy. As much as he could, he made sure that those contractors would not work again in his territory. Mike was a man of action and hated sitting at large meetings, which he viewed as an outrageous waste of time. He preferred to focus on helping the contractors on-site. He loved meeting and talking 'on the scaffolding' with work managers as well as with the 'simple' workers. The contractors loved him and trusted him blindfolded that he wouldn't hold back any effort to help them with anything."

Due to the accelerated schedule, the building skeleton was designed to be built with pre-fabricated concrete elements, which were made by specialized manufacturers, shipped to the site, and assembled there. To meet the compressed timetable, the order for the pre-fabricated elements was split between three separate manufacturers.

Zvika explains:

"The pre-fabricated elements that were designed for the production building were especially heavy, with the weight of each unit ranging from seven to twenty tons. Dividing up the manufacturing of the pre-fabricated elements between three suppliers sped up manufacturing but created a new problem. While each one of those contractors now needed to order a very expensive crane, none of them needed it continuously on-site, and the cost of moving a crane to and from the site was extremely expensive. In order to cut these costs, Zvika proposed that Tnuva rent the cranes. Tnuva agreed and signed a one-year rental contract with a crane supplier. This time frame provided all the on-site contractors with two large mobile cranes for the duration of construction. The constant presence of these cranes on-site not only significantly lowered the costs, but also sped up the rate of work, since the cranes were now available 24 hours a day."

Zvika emphasizes the importance of communication between everyone involved in the construction:

"At this stage, my strategy for accelerating construction was focused on better communication—that is, on developing a system which would enable the quick updating of changes, as well as on creating a climate which would facilitate sharing problems quickly and openly. To encourage the ongoing planning and coordination among all the design engineers, and to ensure that all designers in Israel and in Germany were working with the most up-to-date version of the plans, we put a unique intranet system in place. The system allowed everyone to view and use all the plans in the system in real time. That way, designers and managers, both on-site and at the various offices, could always be updated about any change that was made."

He went on to explain the significance of this system, particularly for designers at a distant location:

"In order to avoid the need for the common, yet expensive and inefficient, messenger services, an advanced workstation was installed on-site to produce blueprints. The blueprints were sent to the site via the intranet, and within minutes, all the necessary copies could be made and distributed to the many contractors on-site. In addition, the team of inspectors we had on-site carried out daily documentation of progress via digital cameras. The photos were distributed via the intranet network to all the designers and contractors in Israel and abroad. Receiving an up-to-date documentation of the situation on-site was very helpful, especially for foreign designers working abroad."

The construction site was even photographed once a month from the air. The most recent photographs were compared with the photographs from the previous month and sent to all managers at Tnuva and GEA. During most of the construction, GEA was still behind schedule, and because they were sure that construction on-site was also lagging behind, they were not making a special effort to overcome the delay. They were sure that the schedule reports sent by Zvika, showing extremely fast progress, just could not be accurate. By displaying the monthly progress in a clear and vivid way, Zvika was trying to call everybody's attention to the fast progress on-site, and especially to convince GEA that it was time to accelerate its pace of work.

Zvika sums up his team's approach:

"As much as we invested in 'high-tech' communication, I believe that the key was rather 'high-touch' communication and especially being 'close to the action' on-site. Therefore, all project meetings, from the beginning of the work to its end, took place on-site. For this purpose, Tnuva built a temporary, but comfortable and sophisticated, office building on-site. The designers of the facility met weekly there, and each of the meetings began with a tour of the site. These meetings were very effective, both for solving problems in real time and for building strong cooperation among the various design engineers."

As Zvika describes,

"The best example of how rich and frequent face-to-face communication can connect people and make them into a cohesive team was the daily meetings that Mike held with his team of inspectors. The team of inspectors was composed of twelve engineers who were carefully chosen by Mike and me, and their expected role was to continuously verify that the work was being performed according to the project design and specifications and the accepted standards."

Mike elaborates:

"Each one of the inspectors undertook a specific aspect of the project, and in that framework acted relatively independently, felt responsible for it, and was committed to its success. Each day the entire team gathered to analyze the contractors' performance, to share learning, and to prepare for the next day. The intensity of performance and the daily meetings created a 'team spirit,' extending to informal meetings, held even outside of work hours and including other family members, which contributed greatly to strengthening the connections made during work."

The most important contribution of the inspectors, however, was completely unexpected. As the project progressed, the commitment to project success, on the part of both the inspectors and the contractors, grew immensely. Gradually, most of the inspectors perceived their job as helping the contractor to produce quality work, as if they were his consultant or partner, rather than his policeman. Mike describes this transformation:

> "They have stopped seeing their role as 'a policeman who writes a ticket for violating the rules,' but rather as someone making sure that the contractor can accomplish the mission without violating the rules. I may have contributed a bit to the development of this unique and harmonious relationship between the inspectors and the contractors, but I have to admit that I did not attempt to bring it about and did not even see it coming."

Zvika believed that Mike was being far too modest:

> "I disagree with Mike. The harmonious relationship between the inspectors and the contractors was the direct result of Mike's behavior. He made his inspectors change their outlook and start to see the contractors as their customers. Then it was only natural to become more responsive to their customers, the contractors. Rather than wait until a problem developed and became visible and difficult to rectify, the inspectors together with the contractors solved problems as soon as they arose. Often they were able to prevent problems from happening at all. In this way, the unpleasant control function of the inspectors became a very productive joint problem-solving function.

I believe that the huge contribution of the dedicated work of the inspectors to the quality, efficiency, and speed of the work cannot be overestimated."

This feeling of cooperation and mutual respect was expressed in the "Holiday of Holidays" event. When Mike learned that in December of 2001, the holidays for the Jews (Chanuka), the Muslims (Eid al-Adha), and the Christians (Christmas) were set to fall during the same week, he decided that this was an excellent opportunity to celebrate and to say a loud and clear thank-you to all 500 workers on-site. He declared that pouring the second concrete ceiling, which had been done around the same time, and which was completed faster than expected, was a good enough reason to throw a joint party for all the workers. The event was nicely organized and was funded by Tnuva and the various contractors. Tnuva also funded a personal gift that was distributed to all of the workers. A nice printed card was attached with a message in three languages (Hebrew, Arabic, and English), in which Tnuva thanked the workers for their contribution and wished them a happy holiday. Outside catering was ordered, and nice tables with food and drink 'fit for a king' were set up and served personally to all the workers by the catering staff. All the contractors were asked to arrive that day in festive clothing, and the CEOs of all the companies as well as from Tnuva also attended. Workers and exceptional contractors received certificates of appreciation. This event aroused a lot of excitement for all involved and even received attention from the local media.

As time went on, the friction between GEA and Tnuva and the on-site construction team did not subside. GEA was very busy with other projects in Europe and chose to match the pace of their work to the premise that the construction team would not be able to complete and hand over the structures for equipment installation according to the planned schedule. Suddenly, they realized that their assumption was wrong. Construction was about to be completed, and GEA—still hopelessly behind schedule—was going to be held responsible for the delays.

Dror, CEO of the dairy, delivered a reality check and an ultimatum:

"In a stormy meeting that I had in January 2001 in Germany with GEA management, I complained about the great delay in design. I threatened that if the size of their design team was not going to be increased significantly and immediately, we would fine them for damages. I specifically referred to the milk basement, which GEA had promised to begin working on in March 2001. The CEO of GEA was astounded that I dared claim that the completed basement would be handed over to GEA in the beginning of March 2001, when two weeks earlier he had been informed by on-site delegates that the basement floor had just been poured. I immediately called Zvika and asked him to photograph the status of that day and send it to me by email. The photograph showed that during those two weeks, the basement foundation had been entirely completed. Zvika attached a daily work plan showing that the structure would be ready to be handed over to GEA by the beginning of March 2001. It seemed to me that my visit put GEA under great stress because their premise that the facility would be delayed had not stood up to the test of reality."

In March 2001, GEA installation teams, including about 35 people, arrived at the site. The disputes between GEA and Tnuva continued. This time, GEA needed Tnuva's approval for changes to already constructed facilities, such as cutting large openings in existing walls. These proposed alterations would be costly, both in terms of money and time, and this added friction was not helpful for progress on-site.

However, Mike was able to smooth things over. The fact that he was American and was fluent in many languages, including English and German, was a big advantage in this project, which involved working together with many foreign companies and experts from a wide variety of countries. As it turned out, speaking German became crucial when GEA arrived on the scene. Mike had cultivated an overall friendly working relationship with the GEA on-site manager. At the end of each workday, the two had the habit of meeting in the office to have a glass of whisky, when all the troubles of the day were brought up, issues that needed coordination were pinpointed, and a work plan for the following day was agreed upon. The two had a liking for "betting" on tasks that seemed impossible, and the loser had to pay for drinks that day. This informal relationship helped substantially in reducing the stress between the two sides.

Benjamin, the project manager for equipment and processes recalls: "Mike helped me a lot in dealing with the German contractors. He developed very unique ties with them, and they trusted him much more than they trusted the Tnuva people. He won their highest level of cooperation, and he was a great asset to the project."

Zvika agrees with Benjamin and adds:

> "The dairy project required me to make more than a few difficult decisions, which led me to take several out-of-the-ordinary actions. Looking back at the project, I think that the most unusual action, and the most successful one, was creating the role for the general contractor and recruiting Mike for the job. Mike and I are such different people, and yet, we were able to easily split the work between the two of us and to cooperate in the most harmonious way possible all the time. I believe the key was that Mike is a person who does what he says, a person you can easily trust. You can quickly gain his trust if you happen to belong to the camp of people who do what they say. Having Mike on the team allowed me to concentrate on planning and preparing for the next month and the next quarter, knowing that today and next week are being taken care of by him in the best possible way."

The project ended on time, with a small deviation in budget. Zvika and his team won much praise from the Tnuva management and from the operators themselves. They also received a letter of recognition and a premium for accomplishing a near-impossible mission.

Epilogue

Practices for Project Leadership

by Alexander Laufer

Successful project leadership is an ongoing process of learning. Thus, this book's content, format, and structure were designed with a clear purpose: to encourage an attitude of responsibility for one's own learning and to facilitate the learning process. This was also the main guideline for developing the following nine practices for project leadership.

The eight contextually rich and vivid cases should have provided you with enough direction to start the long journey from management to leadership. Leadership develops primarily through on-the-job experiences. However, experience alone without thoughtful reflection is meaningless. Moreover, effective reflection should be done in light of a theory or a model of the phenomenon at hand.

The *individual* practices should guide you in building your experience base, one practice at a time. The nine practices as *a whole* represent an overall model for project leadership, a model built on the basis of the actual behavior of successful practitioners. As such, this model can serve as an excellent tool for facilitating your ongoing thoughtful reflection.

First Practice: Embrace the "Living Order" Concept

About 2,500 years ago, Heraclitus, a Greek philosopher, argued that the only constant in our world is change. Today, the economic, social, and political challenges of globalization and the rapid technological innovations make this statement as true as ever. Indeed, Peter Vaill, an American professor of management, explains that the complex, turbulent, and changing environment faced by contemporary organizations renders the leadership of these organizations like navigating in "permanent white water."

In using the "permanent white water" metaphor, Vaill calls our attention to the fact that the external environment of contemporary projects is full of surprises, tends to produce novel problems, and is "messy" and ill-structured. However, it was the French Nobel Prize winner Henri Bergson who a century ago proposed a concept of order that today might help us to better see project reality. In his 1907 book *Creative Evolution*, Bergson claimed that there is no such thing as disorder, but rather two sorts of order: geometric order and living order. While in "geometric order" Bergson related to the traditional concept of order, in "living order" he referred to phenomena such as the creativity of an individual, a work of art, or the mess in my office.

As the cases in this book clearly demonstrate, all projects aim to reach a perfectly functioning product with geometric order. At the start, they may face great uncertainty—living order—that does not completely disappear over the entire course of the project. Gradually, some parts of the project approach geometric order, though in an era of "permanent white water," the project as a whole does not assume geometric order until late in its life.

In a 1977 *Harvard Business Review* article, professor Abraham Zaleznik of Harvard Business School was the first to pose the question, "Managers and leaders, are they different?" Zaleznik answered resoundingly in the affirmative. He further explained that one crucial difference between managers and leaders lies in the conceptions they hold of chaos and order. Leaders can tolerate chaos and lack of structure, and thus, they are ready to keep answers in suspense, whereas managers seek order and control. Zaleznik added that the instinctive move of the manager to prematurely impose order on chaos is more problematic to the organization than the direct impact of the chaos.

The project leaders throughout this book demonstrated that they did not rush to impose "geometric order" prematurely. They knew that their projects would inevitably be affected by one or more of the following:

- Changes resulting from the dynamic *environment*

- Surprises resulting from the unique and often innovative *tasks*

- Difficulties of coping with challenging *requirements* and radical *constraints*, as well as with sudden changes in these requirements and constraints

- Numerous *unexpected events* and *problems* subsequent to the above difficulties

- Difficulties of coping with these problems due to the unique, temporary, and evolving *project organization*, which is composed of heterogeneous units

These project leaders were clearly able to tolerate the "living order" in their projects, and you, the reader, must as well. Reflecting on the stories in this book should help you embrace Bergson's classification of two sorts of order. It should facilitate your ability to perceive reality as it is, to accept that you can't avoid "living order" in your projects and that you better expect and tolerate it. As a result, you will quickly understand and easily apply the practices to your own project.

Practice Two: Adjust Project Practices to the Specific Context

Malcolm Forbes, the publisher of *Forbes* magazine, made the following insightful observation: "What is strength in one context can be a weakness in another context. I'm persevering—you are stubborn. I am flexible—you are weak. I am practical—you are opportunistic... It depends on the context."

The current practice is a key practice that significantly affects all other practices. Indeed, the rationale behind the design of this book is to help the reader understand how successful project managers deviate from the common "one best way" approach and adjust their practices to the specific context of their project. Avoiding the "one best way" approach does not imply, however, that there are no "wrong ways," that "anything goes," or that you must always "start from scratch." There is always the need to strike a balance between relying on the accumulated knowledge of the organization, on the one hand, and enhancing the flexibility and creativity within each individual project on the other.

In contrast to the literature emphasizing standard, context-free practices, all of the project managers throughout this book spent a great deal of time adjusting their practices to the specific context of their project. At the same time, the four distinctly different types of projects in this book allow us to see that in projects sharing common characteristics and coping with similar challenges, the project managers used many practices in a like manner.

Let us compare, for example, the use of procedures in a product development project with their use in a repeated tasks project. In the JASSM project, Larry Lawson, the project manager for Lockheed Martin Corporation, was instructed to throw out all the military standards and was given the freedom to put together his own approach as long as it met the project's three key performance parameters. In sharp contrast, the team at the Pathfinder project was expected to strictly adhere to the extremely detailed flight procedures. Moreover, there was even an extremely rigorous process for preparing and refining these flight procedures.

We can also compare between the different ways in which planning was accomplished in one project involving product development and another project involving repeated tasks. In the Yad Vashem Museum project, the only way for the contractor's project manager to make progress was to frequently disregard the existing plans and instead embark on "planning by action" via well-prepared mockups. In contrast, the project manager of the harbor cranes transfer project prepared and followed an extremely detailed plan with about 300 specific activities for each sea voyage.

In all four cases, the project managers adjusted the practice to the situation. In the two product development projects, they adjusted the practice to be highly flexible and informal, and in the two repeated tasks projects they changed the practice to be highly rigid and formal.

Still, it is important to be aware that different contexts are found not only between projects, but also within projects. For example, the dairy project was forced to adapt to three distinct overriding strategies. It started with the development of a state-of-the-art-driven dairy, a "dairy of dreams" as they termed it. When they found that this strategy led to a huge growth in project scope and overall cost, they embraced a cost-driven orientation. Yet, when they learned that their domination in the cup products field was about to be threatened by their greatest rival, they switched one more time to a schedule-driven focus. Each change of strategy meant a change of context and was accompanied by an adjustment in project practices.

Following the change to a schedule-driven strategy, Zvika, the project manager, realized that the existing procedures for the bidding process would not allow them to accelerate construction. By convincing the committee to abandon the standard process, move it to the construction site, and streamline it, Zvika and his team were able to significantly shorten the time necessary to choose contractors to fulfill the new schedule-driven strategy.

Likewise, the ACE project went through changes in its major drivers. After starting under severe cost constraints, the project ended up being ahead of schedule and under budget in the final stages. Thus, Don Margolies, the ACE project manager, decided to reverse the previous practice of good enough is good enough, to good enough is *not* good enough by supporting the uncommon step of taking off the instruments for recalibration.

The classical model of project management, in which standards are developed for virtually all situations, expects the project manager to serve primarily as a controller: to ensure that team members adhere to the established standard. This role entails only a minimal requirement for judgment and no requirement for adaptation. In reality, the project manager must constantly engage in making sense of the ambiguous and changing situation, and he must adjust the common practices to the unique situation. This process requires a great deal of interpretation and judgment based on rich experience. Stories, such as those presented in this book that present a variety of contexts and solutions, are an excellent source for enriching your experience base.

Practice Three: Challenge the Status Quo

The most powerful developments in all eight projects took place as a result of the willingness of the project manager to challenge the status quo, usually several times throughout the life of the project. Challenging the status quo might significantly change the fate of the project and is the essence of project leadership.

Following are several examples of how our project managers challenged the status quo:

- In JASSM, Larry Lawson, the project manager for Lockheed Martin, tells how to cut costs drastically, the company took a risk and produced components of the missile at two small companies that had not previously been in the missile business. Rather, one had specialized in producing baseball bats and golf club shafts and the other in building surfboards.

- In Pathfinder, Jenny, the project manager for NASA, propelled and nurtured a unique organizational structure that was far from a traditional one. It was composed of four industry rivals, with NASA serving as an advisor and team member with limited authority.

- Judy Stokley, the project manager of AMRAAM, was authorized by the Pentagon to proceed with downsizing. However, she believed that without first introducing a far-reaching, unconventional change in the culture of the organization involving a shift from control to trust and responsibility, her mission would not be truly accomplished. So Judy took it upon herself to change the project's culture.

- In the evacuation case, Yaron, the battalion commander, was instructed by his superiors to start training his recruits, but he did not. Yaron was of the opinion that training the soldiers whom he had on hand would not enable him to complete the mission successfully. Thus, Yaron embarked on a long campaign, initially against the will of his superiors, to replace many of his recruits.

- In the final stages of ACE, Don Margolies, the project manager, supported the uncommon step of taking the instruments off the spacecraft for recalibration. This operation had never before been done at NASA and put him at odds with both his superiors and his team members.

- Zvika, the project manager of the dairy plant, was convinced that it was time to stop the endless planning and preparation phase of constructing the new dairy. Against the advice of the client's professional staff, he took it up with the head of the client's organization, where he was finally able to obtain the green light to move ahead.

Is there a fundamental characteristic that these project managers share that can explain their unconventional actions?

In a famous essay, Oxford philosopher Isaiah Berlin described two approaches to life using a simple parable about the fox and the hedgehog. The fox is a cunning and creative creature, able to devise a myriad of complex strategies for sneak attacks upon the hedgehog. The hedgehog is a painfully slow creature with a very simple daily agenda: searching for food and maintaining his home. Every day the fox waits for the hedgehog while planning to attack him. When the hedgehog senses the danger, he reacts in the same simple, but powerful, way every day: He rolls up into a perfect little ball with a sphere of sharp spikes pointing outward in all directions. Then the fox retreats while starting to plan his new line of attack for the next day. Each day this confrontation takes place, and despite the greater cunning of the fox, the hedgehog always wins.

Based on this parable, Berlin attempted to divide the world into two basic groups: foxes and hedgehogs. Foxes pursue *many ends at the same time, yet they do not integrate their thinking into one overall concept.* Hedgehogs, on the other hand, simplify a complex world into *a single overall concept that unifies and guides everything they do.*

In recent years, several prominent management scholars have discussed this parable while attempting to answer the following question: Do successful senior managers behave more like hedgehogs or like foxes? The debate regarding senior managers is still ongoing, but when it comes to successful project managers, I have found that they behave both like hedgehogs and foxes, though they place the hedgehog in the driver's seat.

Like the hedgehog, the project managers in all eight cases were guided by one overriding purpose: delivering successful results to the customer. They clearly felt a sense of ownership of the project, involving an intellectual and emotional bond with the mission that they were trying to accomplish. For these project managers, the project objectives were not simply the technical definitions of the customer's needs. Rather, for them, project objectives meant first of all project results, and they felt total personal accountability for those results. It also meant that they had the self-discipline required for placing all other objectives and opportunities secondary. It was almost as if they were programmed to follow an inner compass that was always pointing toward true north. However, if they could not reach this goal by following conventional methods, they responded by challenging the status quo. This kind of response requires strong willpower and courage.

It is important to note, however, that this very focus on delivering results to the customer was also responsible for keeping the frequency of challenging the status quo within limits. These experienced project managers knew very well that challenging the status quo comes with its own risks and costs. In each case, they had to dedicate special attention and energy to overcoming the natural resistance to change and to learning how to perform effectively once this resistance was overcome. This temporary disequilibrium in the project could have led to loss of momentum and progress, eventually hurting their ability to serve the customer. Since their primary focus was not on proving that they were heroes, but rather on delivering results to the customer, they were selective in employing this practice. Thus, their hedgehog's mentality with its overriding purpose guided them in selecting the right cases for challenging the status quo.

And now to the role of the fox. It is evident from the eight cases presented in the book that while it was the project managers' focused willpower that led them to challenge the status quo, the solutions to the problems they faced demanded a great deal of adaptability and creativity. That is precisely the time when the focused hedgehog calls on the creative fox for help. By embracing the behavior of both the hedgehog and the fox, you should also be able to successfully challenge the status quo when the need arises.

Practice Four: Do Your Utmost to Recruit the Right People

In 1911, Fredrick Taylor, the father of "scientific management," said: "In the past, man has been first. In the future, the system must be first." One hundred years later and the project managers of all eight projects beg to differ loud and clear.

For example, Ray Morgan, the Pathfinder project manager, learned that finding the right balance between systems and people is critical to being a good project manager, but more importantly, he realized that people matter the most because they make the systems work.

Terry Little, the JASSM program manager, describes his management philosophy by declaring: "McNamara, I am not." Here he refers to the limited impact he found in projects for the analytical approach of the Robert McNamara School of Management, where everything is quantifiable and based on models. Terry shares his own conclusion: "Projects move ahead because of the activities of people."

The underlying assumptions and demonstrated behavior of the project managers throughout the book can be summed up as follows: People are the make-or-break factor in projects. With the right people, almost anything is possible. With the wrong team, failure awaits. Thus, recruiting should be taken seriously, and considerable time should be spent finding and attracting, and at times fighting for, the right people. Even greater attention may have to be paid to the selection of the right project manager.

Indeed, Shimon, the Yad Vashem Museum project manager on behalf of the client, understood the pivotal role of selecting the general contractor. He took great pains to identify and recruit the most suitable project manager for the contractor's team by using an unconventional three-stage selection process based on multiple factors, not only the total cost of construction. After reviewing all of the proposals received, Shimon selected the company most likely to be awarded the job as contractor and then applied pressure on the director of the company to include his choice for project manager on their team. Shimon's efforts paid off, and his request was met by a positive response from the company.

Yaron, the battalion commander in the evacuation case, provides another example of the importance of finding the right people for the task at hand. When he realized that many of his squad leaders were not fit for the mission, he started a campaign to replace them and did not stop until he was able to reach the commander of the Israeli Air Force and recruit new squad leaders who were more suitable for the job.

Recruiting the right people does not have to mean recruiting the world's most talented "stars." Often this is simply not practical, and organizational politics might make it impossible for the project manager to steal away the best people within the organization because they're already involved in other critical projects or fiercely defended by other managers. What's important, as Brian Rutledge, the financial manager at JASSM, reminds us, is that *"you have to get the right people for the right job at the right time."*

Even if they could have recruited many stars, our project managers would not have attempted to do so because they knew that if everybody is a potential CEO, then it becomes too difficult to develop a cooperative environment. Indeed, while recruiting, they were constantly thinking about the team as a whole, making sure that the selected team members could work with each other as required by the unique context of the project. Thus, they selected people not only on the basis of their technical, functional, or problem-solving skills, but also on the basis of their interpersonal skills.

Allan Frandsen, a payload manager from the California Institute of Technology, looked for people who were a little bit out of the mainstream and could flourish in a university environment—people with the "right mix of talent and attitude," a flexible outlook, and high adaptability. Indeed, he considered flexibility to be even more important than sheer brain power.

At times, especially for large projects, the project manager must select a group of leaders for his or her team. Chuck Anderson from Raytheon explains that the "right" people he was searching for were real leaders who would be willing to make swift decisions and take risks without fear of failing.

Practice Five: Shape the Right Culture

Project culture is what holds the organization together, providing project members with a shared frame of reference, rules for behavior, and an understanding of the do's and don'ts of project life. When project members share the same culture, they develop a set of mutually accepted ideas of what is real in their constantly changing environment, what is important, and how to respond.

The Talmud says: *"We do not see things as they are. We see things as we are."* Cultural differences between project groups are often accompanied by divergent assumptions, values, and perceptions of reality that can have serious implications for project performance. As Don Margolies, the project manager of the NASA Advanced Composition Explorer (ACE) project, quips: "If Goddard (NASA) said the sky was blue, APL would say it was pink."

Unfortunately, these difficulties are not uncommon for projects. Project organization is temporary, with a finite end, and is typically composed of groups from different organizations, often with a range of cultures. The project organization evolves throughout the life of the project, where different groups join and leave the project as dictated by the unique nature of the specific project. The limited and relatively short life of most projects, and the typically different cultures and interests of the various groups composing the project, render shaping project culture—one culture for the whole team—very difficult. Zvika, the project manager of the Tnuva dairy plant, uses this vivid metaphor to illustrate the impact of working with different project cultures: "I used to compare the quick pace and agility of the "monkeys" on site versus the reliable, but inflexible, work of the "elephants" at GEA."

It is important to stress that even in permanent organizations, shaping culture is not easy and indeed requires leadership. Professor Edgar Schein of the MIT Sloan School of Management, who is generally credited with introducing the term "corporate culture," distinguishes between leadership and management by arguing that leadership creates and changes cultures, whereas management acts within a culture.

Indeed, the project managers in all eight cases in this book found that one of the key factors for project success was the need to shape the culture of their projects. Teamwork—mutual interdependence and mutual responsibility for project results—was one element of culture that was universally guided by the philosophy of "we're all in this together."

For example, the focus of the AMRAAM project was on shaping project culture, with an emphasis on teamwork, mutual trust, and responsibility for results. This change was successful as a result of the deep commitment and personal involvement of the two project leaders from the U.S. Air Force and from Raytheon. A more limited effort to improve teamwork and trust, but nevertheless a creative one, was introduced by Don Margolies, the NASA project manager of ACE. Don attempted to alleviate some of the problems that resulted from the cultural differences between APL and NASA Goddard by introducing frequent face-to-face meetings. Fortunately, the short distance between Goddard and APL went a long way toward establishing a trustful relationship and cultivating a partnership between the two organizations.

The cultural change in the Pathfinder project was also focused on collaboration, this time not between two organizations, but rather between the project team and the residents of the island of Kauai, who had a natural apprehension about outsiders. Ray Morgan, the AeroVironment project manager, explains how Dave Nekomoto served as their entrée into the community, smoothing the way for them in dealing with the local authorities. Still, they had to take a highly unconventional approach to "fitting in" and establishing a good rapport with the local residents: "Dave had—how shall I say it?—a thing for karaoke. So we sang with him. Yes, that's right, we sang." The "mandatory" karaoke parties held at Dave's place with the whole NASA and AeroVironment team helped to break the ice and form a crucial basis of trust with the people of Kauai. Once the locals felt invested in the team's success, they were ready and willing to do whatever they could to help AeroVironment reach its goals.

Project leaders need to shape their project culture not only to promote a "teamwork" culture, but also to ensure that the "right" culture fits their unique context. Making such a successful change is often dependent on having the right people and sometimes may be accomplished only by replacing some key people. For example, in the evacuation case, Yaron, the battalion commander, did not have any choice but to replace many of his squad leaders to be sure that his battalion would embrace the required attitude of "with determination and sensitivity."

However, even selecting the right people does not always bring about the desired cultural change. For example, Allan Frandsen's hand selection of his small team at the NASA Jet Propulsion Laboratory was still not enough to foster development of the right culture on the team, at least not fast enough. To accelerate this change, Allan moved the team from JPL to Caltech. Although Caltech is only seven miles from JPL, there is a noticeable cultural difference between the two institutions. Allan assumed that being surrounded by scientists and interacting with them on a daily basis in Caltech's research environment would help the new team to quickly develop an adaptive culture—a culture that allows, and at times may actually encourage, tailoring, bending, or even breaking the rules when necessary.

Another example of facilitating the desired cultural change can be found in the JASSM case. By being a failure-tolerant leader, Terry, the JASSM project manager, was able to develop a culture of autonomy, risk taking, learning, and innovation. Larry Lawson, Lockheed's project manager, describes Terry's reaction to the team's initial failure and how he used it to help shape this culture:

> "After months of working seven-day weeks, our first missile launch after the contract award failed... It was the defining moment for the program... Terry could have said, 'I don't trust you, and I want to have an independent technical review.' But that's not what he said... Instead, he asked me if I wanted some help. Teams are defined by how they react in adversity—and how their leaders react. The lessons learned by this team about how to respond to adversity enabled us to solve bigger challenges..."

Practice Six: Plan, Monitor, and Anticipate

Classically, planning and control are portrayed as the backbone of successful projects. According to this outlook, planning establishes the targets and the course of action for reaching them, while control ensures that the course of action is maintained and that the desired targets are indeed reached. Therefore, control involves measuring and evaluating performance and taking corrective action when performance deviates from plans.

The cases in this book demonstrate that in today's "permanent white water" environment, while planning and control are still central for project success, their scopes are significantly different. In general, they demonstrate that the planning time and the planning methods are strongly affected by the stability of the available information. For example, in the two product development projects, much of the information was missing or highly ambiguous and remained volatile throughout the life of the projects. Thus, only short-term plans were prepared, and a great deal of planning was accomplished through prototyping as part of "planning by action" (more on planning by action in "Practice Eight").

The change in the scope of project control has been even more radical. Classic concepts of project control were developed for stable environments in which it was expected that planning would be fairly accurate and implementation would largely adhere to the plan. Accordingly, the primary role of project control was to identify deviations from the plan and adjust execution to conform to the plan. Today, however, the central role for measuring and evaluating performance is to provide quick feedback necessary for further planning. The main purpose of project control is not to answer the question, "Why didn't your performance yesterday conform to the original plan?" but rather, "What kind of feedback can help you learn faster and perform better tomorrow?"

Under conditions of uncertainty, measuring and evaluating performance, which is classically regarded as project control, can serve only as a means to monitor performance. But by no means are these activities enough in order to provide project control. Project control, that is, ensuring project targets are reached, can be achieved only by applying all nine practices described in this Epilogue.

Successful project managers do not limit their monitoring to events occurring within the typical boundaries of their assigned role. These project managers know that in a dynamic environment, projects succeed only through the constant monitoring of performance and changes outside their formal boundaries. Terry Little, the U.S. Air Force project manager of JASSM, demonstrated this notion by taking a trip to visit one of the contractors' suppliers. Terry was aware that a government project manager does not normally visit the suppliers of a prime contractor. However, he was also aware that such a visit would allow him to anticipate problems even before they actually occurred, leaving sufficient time to attenuate and often eliminate their impact on the project.

The critical importance of anticipation has been demonstrated throughout this book. In particular, many of the most crucial "challenging the status quo" actions were initiated proactively by the project managers, primarily as a result of their constant engagement in ongoing deliberate anticipation. Deliberate anticipation entails focusing attention on identifying irregularities, as well as early signals of possible problems, and being flexible and ready to respond.

Allan Frandsen, the ACE payload project manager, concisely described his project management philosophy, with anticipation of problems topping the list as the most important role of the project manager:

> "To lead a project effectively, one has to establish and maintain the flexibility to take appropriate actions when needed. If I had to write down the ABCs of project management, 'A' would signify anticipate. Of course, a good project manager already knows, at least in general terms, what is supposed to happen next—but all too often it doesn't. So what are the alternatives? Are there sensible workarounds? What can I do now to lay the groundwork or facilitate matters should something go wrong? These and other questions make up the ongoing process of anticipation. And because it is an ongoing process, the 'A' in the ABCs of project management could just as well stand for 'anticipate... anticipate... anticipate.'"

Practice Seven: Use Face-to-Face Communication as the Primary Communication Mode

Because a project functions as an *ad hoc* temporary and evolving organization, composed of people affiliated with different organizations, communication serves as the glue that binds together all parts of the organization. When the project suffers from high uncertainty, the role played by project communication is even more crucial.

The project managers in this book employed a great variety of communication mediums, covering a wide spectrum from high tech to high touch. In the following example, Zvika, the project manager of the dairy plant, explained some of the unique features of the high-tech communication systems that he developed for his construction site:

> "...an advanced work station was installed on site to produce blueprints. The blueprints were sent to the site via the intranet, and within minutes, all the necessary copies could be made and distributed to the many contractors on site. In addition, the team of inspectors we had on site carried out daily documentation of progress via digital cameras. The photos were distributed via the intranet network to all the designers and contractors in Israel as well as abroad. Receiving an up-to-date documentation of the situation on site was helpful, especially for the foreign designers working abroad."

However, Zvika goes on to describe another component of the communication system that he used on site:

> "As much as we invested in 'high-tech' communication, I believe that the key was rather 'high-touch' communication... all project meetings, from the beginning of the work to its end, took place on site. The designers of the facility met weekly there, and each of the meetings began with a tour of the site. These meetings were very effective, both for solving problems

in real time and for building strong cooperation among the various design engineers."

Indeed, face-to-face communication is repeatedly shown to be a powerful tool, particularly for novel and ambiguous issues and when building social bonding and trust is crucial. Its strength lies in the fact that it provides timely and personalized feedback by using multiple channels of communications, including eye contact, body language, and facial expressions, which can convey a deeper and more convincing message than any other form of communication. Furthermore, face-to-face interaction provides a valuable opportunity for ongoing responsiveness. By seeing how others are responding to a verbal message even before it is complete, the speaker can alter it midstream and provide necessary clarification. When interaction takes place in a group setting, the number of verbal and nonverbal "conversations" that can be conducted simultaneously is almost impossible to replicate with any other media. Thus, face-to-face communication is the best medium for quick resolution of ambiguity and for building a strong foundation of trust.

Although face-to-face communication is often expensive, its significance and popularity were stressed in each one of the eight projects. For example, when returning from a visit to Raytheon for a series of face-to-face meetings, Dennis Mallik, the U.S. Air Force chief financial officer of AMRAAM, found that his colleagues at home were stunned with the kind of information he was able to get from the contractor. Then, Dennis reminded them, "You'll be surprised by how much better you do once you get to know the people you're working with."

In recent years, scarcity of attention has become the key challenge for effective project communication. Herbert Simon, the Nobel prize-winning economist, provides a succinct description of this challenge: "What information consumes is rather obvious: It consumes the attention of its recipients. Hence, a wealth of information creates a poverty of attention."

Frank Snow, the ground system and flight operations manager at Goddard Space Flight Center, discovered the power of face-to-face communication when he attempted to offer help to another member of his team, who was terribly suspicious of the Goddard project office. This researcher at Caltech, who was located about 2,300 miles away, responded to Frank's offer by sending him a blistering email that basically said, "Hell no!" Frank decided to fly across the country to Caltech to talk with the researcher. Frank summed up the results of his trip:

> "Clearly, face-to-face communication went a long way toward dispelling his suspicions about my intentions. I don't recall after this ever getting another 300-word email from him of the 'no-thank-you-and-please-go-away' variety. As a matter of fact, I think I can even say that this was the beginning of a fruitful relationship that lasted for the rest of the project."

There is no doubt that Frank succeeded because he was willing to listen patiently to his host's concerns. Yet, Frank was also able to ensure that his host would listen to him because he was able to capture his host's attention.

Practice Eight: Be Action-Oriented and Focus on Results

What is the most important leg of a tripod? The missing one!

Successful project management stands on the following three legs: *people, information, and action.* Yet, *action* is regularly ignored.

Lucy Suchman opens her book, *Plans and Situated Actions: The Problem of Human-machine Communication*, with a comparison between the different navigation methods employed by the European and the Trukese navigator:

"The European navigator begins with a plan—a course—that he has charted according to certain universal principles, and he carries out his voyage by relating his every move to that plan. His effort throughout his voyage is directed to remaining 'on course.' If unexpected events occur, he must first alter the plan, then respond accordingly. The Trukese navigator begins with an objective rather than a plan. He sets off toward the objective and responds to conditions as they arise in an *ad-hoc* fashion. He utilizes information provided by the wind, the waves, the tide and current, the fauna, the stars, the clouds, the sound of the water on the side of the boat, and he steers accordingly. His effort is directed to doing whatever is necessary to reach the objective. If asked, he can point to his objective at any moment, but he cannot describe his course."

Suchman, whose research focus was on "purposeful action," concludes that while the European navigator exemplifies the prevailing scientific models of purposeful action, she believes that ignoring the Trukese navigator is a serious mistake. The project managers in this book concur.

Conceivably, for navigation, neither method is superior to the other. The differences between these two methods might simply reflect different styles of thinking and acting. Yet, from the cases in the book, it is clear that for managing projects, the differences between the two reflect much more than just styles of thinking and acting.

The European method is most suitable when uncertainty regarding the task, environment, and constraints is low, as in an established production process ("geometric order"). However, the Trukese method is more suitable when uncertainty is high and the situation is novel and confusing, such as in the development of a new product using an immature technology or while coping with a disruptive technology ("living order"). The projects in the book employ a mix of these two methods, but there is clearly a greater use of the Trukese method in the early phases of most cases.

The comparison between the working styles of the two navigators highlights the three key components of the current practice:

- Planning by action
- Management by hands-on engagement
- Focus on results

Following are three short examples from the eight cases that demonstrate these components.

Planning by Action

In JASSM, Larry Lawson, the project manager for Lockheed Martin, highlights the use of prototyping by one of their suppliers for the development of the missile. The first prototype they built took a long time, but the end product did not measure up. Still, the process allowed them to learn what things they didn't have to do or be concerned about. As a result, the second prototype was a better product that took about half as long to build. By the time they started work on the sixth one, they fully understood the problem.

Terry Little, the project manager for the U.S. Air Force, explains that the use of prototyping by Lockheed Martin was one of the key factors in its ability to win the contract. As he explains:

> "Prototyping is a wonderful way of learning, yet we don't do enough of it because we would like to believe that if we simply get enough smart people together, we can run through the numbers, put them in the model, do the simulation, and it will all come out just like it is supposed to. But guess what? In the real world, it rarely happens the way we predict with our models. The reason people want it to be that way is because prototyping is not cheap—it is not cheap in terms of the money or the time required to do it. It is messy, and sometimes you are embarrassed with the results, but eventually you reach your goal. In the long run, it saves you money."

Management by Hands-On Engagement

In the transferring harbor cranes project, the two project leaders were closely involved with the workforce throughout the entire 24/7 operation. They worked on it in shifts, including weekends and holidays, staying together with the workers and even eating with them. As one of them underscored:

> "This was our norm for all the special projects we carried out, and our people expected it. We believed that this way we could learn quickly about changes and react in a timely manner, and not less importantly, we could naturally infect the entire workforce with our passion and energy. We promised large bonuses to the workers, but we believe that the role model approach is a more effective motivator."

Focus on Results

Sometimes even small gestures can take on far greater meaning than expected. Brian Rutledge, the JASSM financial manager, recalls the significance of such a gesture to promoting his results-focused orientation:

> "After Terry said that we were going to be on contract in six months, he directed someone to make a viewgraph stating this goal: *Be on contract by July 1.* That was it. He wanted it pinned up in everybody's cubicle. At first, I thought: 'Oh man, this is goofy. I know what we're doing. I don't need to have a reminder on the wall.' When I talked to other people working in the program office, I just rolled my eyes. 'What's this guy thinking?' I said. 'It's like we're in kindergarten.' But after a few months, I had to admit that there was something to it. I saw it there every day when I walked up to my desk. I eventually found myself stopping to think: 'What am I doing to get to that point, and what can I cut out of my work that's preventing me from getting there? How am I getting distracted from the goal?'"

So they kept a chart to measure their progress—not a chart that used the *project plan* to monitor specific tasks, but a chart that plotted the *results accomplished*. The final outcome was a mission accomplished in less than five months.

The importance of the focus on results is poignantly captured by Karl Weick, a distinguished university professor at the University of Michigan: "The argument, in a nutshell, is the one set forth by a Persian proverb: 'Thinking well is wise; planning well, wiser; doing well, wisest and best of all.'"

Practice Nine: Lead, So You Can Manage

In a world perceived as being in "geometric order," projects require only plan-driven management. The cases in this book, however, clearly demonstrate that in the real world of "living order," there is a need for both leadership and management.

Plan-driven management assumes a relatively predictable world and thus relies primarily on planning, control, and risk-management tools. A dynamic environment, where unexpected events are inevitable and the project is plagued with numerous problems, demands both leadership and management. Most of these problems are *technical*, that is, they can be solved with knowledge and procedures already at hand. Although solving these problems might require great flexibility and high responsiveness, they can still be resolved while *maintaining the status quo*. They just require good *managerial* skills. Other problems, however, are *adaptive*, that is, they are not so well-defined, do not have clear solutions, and often require new learning and changes in patterns of behavior. To address these adaptive problems, the project manager must be willing and able to make significant changes and to *challenge the status quo*. These problems, therefore, require *leadership*.

Another aspect that distinguishes between these two roles is that managers engage in routine activities, whereas leaders focus on and generate nonroutine interventions. Using this distinction, it is clear that the epilogue includes three practices requiring primarily routine activities and three that demand nonroutine interventions, as follows:

Practices requiring *routine* activities:

- Plan, monitor, and anticipate.
- Use face-to-face communication as the primary communication mode.
- Be action-oriented and focus on results.

Practices requiring *nonroutine* interventions:

- Challenge the *status quo*.
- Do your utmost to recruit the right people.
- Shape the right culture.

The remaining two practices, "embrace the living order concept" and "adjust project practices to the specific context," can be considered infrastructure practices that affect all other practices.

So which role is more dominant: leadership or management? Does one need to strive to be a manager who is also a leader or vice versa? On the one hand, without being involved in the ongoing management of the project, the project manager simply does not know when to intervene and what is the best way in which to do so. Moreover, to maintain stability, the project manager must selectively choose the cases for which challenging the *status quo* is vital. Thus, the project manager actually ends up spending much more time on routine management activities than on leadership activities. So maybe management is the dominant role?

On the other hand, as the cases presented here demonstrate, without challenging the status quo and solving the adaptive problem at hand, the project might simply come to a grinding halt. Only once the problem is overcome, using a nonroutine leadership intervention, can routine management actually proceed. That is, without leadership, there is no management! You must lead so that you can manage.

However, there is more to the debate of leadership versus management. Project managers are judged primarily not for what *they* do, but rather for what *their people* do. So far, we have discussed leadership and management as if performed by two different people. However, when these two roles reside within the same person, it is important to understand that leadership attitude and behavior inspire team members, even when the project manager performs just routine management activities. This is where the leadership role has the upper hand.

Dougal Maclise described Ray Morgan's effectiveness as the project manager of the Pathfinder project in this way: "Whether one meets the optimist developer, the experienced builder, the inquisitive engineer, or the energetic cowboy, one always immediately feels that each one of his personalities is an authentic and sincere person. His genuine spirit is contagious. You simply cannot *not* follow Ray."

As stated eloquently by an anonymous source, "Life is not measured by the number of breaths we take, but by the moments that take our breath away." Although most of the time project managers perform managerial activities, the few incidences in which they act as leaders are what define them in the eyes of their team members as leaders who they willingly follow.

Thus, distinguishing between management and leadership is helpful when you first begin shaping your attitude and developing your skills, but these roles are intertwined and indistinguishable once you become a successful project manager. What you actually become is a project leader.

INDEX

A

ABCs of project management, 176, 229

action orientation, 232-236

adaptability, 32-33

adaptive problems, solving, 8

Advanced Medium Range Air-to-Air Missile (AMRAAM), 125-147

adversity, reactions in, 49

AeroVironment Design Development Center, 76-78, 83, 95

Aldridge, C. Pete, 50

alliances, sharing within, 84-85

AMRAAM (Advanced Medium Range Air-to-Air Missile), 125-147

Amrami, Ishai, 54-55, 59, 67-69

analytical approach, fallacy of, 21-22

Anderson, Chuck, 132-135, 143-146, 224

anticipate (ABCs of project management), 176, 227-229

approval of plan, in evacuation case study, 149-151

architects, relationship with contractors and clients, 55-65

autonomy, trust and, 25-26

B

"Bad Management Theories Are Destroying Good Management Practices" (Ghoshal), 5

Baer-Riedhart, Jenny, 71-75, 78, 88-91, 100, 219

battalion personnel, in evacuation case study, 156-163

Bauer, Jeffrey, 83, 90, 94

Benjamin (dairy plant building case study), 194, 200, 211

Benjamin (evacuation case study), 160

Bergson, Henri, 214

Berlin, Isaiah, 220

best people (ABCs of project management), 176

Boeing, 39, 45

C

CAIG (Cost Analysis Improvement Group), 31-32

case studies

dairy plant building, 193-211
    planning and preparation phase, ending, 193-198
    schedule-driven project management, 198-203
    splitting and harmonizing the work, 203-211
descriptions of, 10-14
downsizing, 125-147
    challenges inherent in, 125-129
    partnership between government and contractors, 130-141
    trust between government and contractors, 141-147
evacuation, 149-169
    approval of plan, 149-151
    battalion personnel, 156-163

implementation phase, 164-169
  psychological preparation of
    defense forces, 151-159
  harbor crane transfer, 103-124
  constant vigilance phase,
    118-124
  entrepreneurial phase, 103-114
  risk reduction phase, 114-117
missile development, 19-50
  changing perceptions of
    business, 19-22
  mutual commitment to goals,
    22-37
  relationship among govern-
    ment, contractors, suppliers,
    38-47
  teamwork, 47-50
museum building, 51-70
  mutual commitment to goals,
    55-65
  splitting project into two parts,
    51-55
  versatility of team, 65-70
solar-powered airplane flying,
    71-101
  collaboration with local com-
    munity, 87-94, 100-101
  know your customers' needs,
    71-75
  relationships with people,
    importance of, 94-99
  systems and communication,
    importance of, 76-87
spacecraft building, 171-192
  culture of location, 175-183
  "good enough" requirements,
    171-175
  teamwork, 183-192
challenges inherent in downsizing,
  125-129
challenging the status quo, 218-222
chaos, order versus, 214-215
Chaskelevitch, Israel, 59-64, 67-68
Chiu, Mary, 179-182, 190-191
Churchill, Winston, 4
clients, relationship with contractors
  and architects, 55-65

collaboration with local community,
  87-94, 100-101. See also cooperation
commitment to goals, 22-37, 55-65
communication in ABCs of project
  management, 176
  among various locations, 175-183,
    203-211
  face-to-face communication,
    230-232
  within systems, importance of, 76-87
complex projects case studies
  dairy plant building, 193-211
    planning and preparation
      phase, ending, 193-198
    schedule-driven project man-
      agement, 198-203
    splitting and harmonizing the
      work, 203-211
  descriptions of, 13-14
  spacecraft building, 171-192
    culture of location, 175-183
    "good enough" requirements,
      171-175
    teamwork, 183-192
constant vigilance phase (harbor
  crane transfer case study), 118-124
context
  adjusting to, 216-218
  project management and leadership
    in, 8-9
contractors, relationship with
  clients and architects, 55-65
  government, 38-47, 129-147
  inspectors, 207-209
  suppliers, 38-47
control of project, role of, 227-229
cooperation, 87-94, 100-101. See also
  collaboration with local community
  between inspectors and contractors,
    207-209
  with various teams, 183-192
cost
  cutting, 45-46
  as requirement, 30-32
Cost Analysis Improvement Group
  (CAIG), 31-32

cost-driven project management,
   198-199
Creative Evolution (Bergson), 214
culture of location, 175-183, 224-227
customers, knowing needs of, 71-75

D

dairy plant building case study,
   193-211
   description of, 13-14
   planning and preparation phase,
      ending, 193-198
   schedule-driven project manage-
      ment, 198-203
   splitting and harmonizing the work,
      203-211
Daniel (evacuation case study),
   153-154
data memos, 83
David (evacuation case study),
   159-161, 167
David Packard Excellence in Acquisition Award, 50
Del Frate, John, 79, 82
Deming, W. Edwards, 98
de-scoping, 171-175, 189-192
disengagement. *See* evacuation
   case study
downsizing case study, 125-147
   challenges inherent in, 125-129
   description of, 12
   partnership between government
      and contractors, 130-141
   trust between government and
      contractors, 141-147
Dror (dairy plant building case
   study), 201, 210
Drucker, Peter, 5, 9
Dryden Flight Research Center,
   71-75, 88

E

Einstein, Albert, 5
entrepreneurial phase (harbor crane
   transfer case study), 103-114
Environmental Research Aircraft and
   Sensor Technology (ERAST), 71-75
European navigation, Trukese navigation versus, 232-233
evacuation case study, 149-169
   approval of plan, 149-151
   battalion personnel, 156-163
   description of, 13
   implementation phase, 164-169
   psychological preparation of defense
      forces, 151-159
experience, reflection on, 213

F

face-to-face communication, 230-232
The Fifth Discipline Fieldbook, 4
flat organizational structures, effect
   on project success, 124
flying solar-power airplanes. *See*
   solar-powered airplane flying case
   study
Forbes, Malcolm, 216
fox and hedgehog analogy, 220-222
Frandsen, Allan, 175-179, 185, 189,
   224-226, 229
Fuller, Buckminster, 4

G

geometric order, living order versus,
   214-215
Ghoshal, Sumantra, 5
Gillman, Tom, 135, 144-146
goals
   focus on, 35-36, 235-236
   mutual commitment to, 22-37,
      55-65

"good enough" requirements,
171-175
  when to ignore, 189-192
government, relationship with
  contractors, 38-47, 129-147
  suppliers, 38-47

H

hands-on management, 119, 235
Handy, Charles, 4
harbor crane transfer case study,
103-124
  constant vigilance phase, 118-124
  description of, 12
  entrepreneurial phase, 103-114
  risk reduction phase, 114-117
Harel, Dan, 153
harmonizing work after splitting,
203-211
Harpaz, Arik, 161-163, 169
hedgehog and fox analogy, 220-222
Heraclitus, 214
Holocaust History Museum, 51-70

I

Ilan (evacuation case study), 159
implementation phase (evacuation
case study), 164-169
implementation reviews, 187-189
independence in project management, 198-203
input on project requirements, 28-30
inspectors, cooperation with contractors, 207-209

J

Joint Air-to-Surface Standoff Missile
(JASSM), 19-50
Joint Direct Attack Munition (JDAM)
missile, 19, 22

K

Klein, Amos, 104-117, 120-124
Klein, Ofer, 104-114, 117-124
Kornfeld, Shimon, 52-61, 64-70, 223

L

Lawson, Larry, 40, 47, 216, 219,
227, 234
leadership in project management,
8-9, 236-238
leadership practices
  adjusting to context, 216-218
  challenging the status quo, 218-222
  face-to-face communication,
  230-232
  leadership versus management,
  236-238
  living order versus geometric order,
  214-215
  planning, monitoring, anticipating,
  227-229
  purposeful action, 232-236
  recruiting right people, 222-224
  shaping team culture, 224-227
learning
  from best managers, 7
  from stories, 1-4
Leitzel, Jackie, 27, 38, 50
Lewin, Kurt, 5
Little, Terry, 3, 19-50, 222, 227-229,
234-235
living order, geometric order versus,
214-215
local community, collaboration with,
87-94, 100-101
location, affecting culture by, 175-183
Lockheed Martin Integrated Systems,
38-44, 47-50

M

Maclise, Dougal, 93-94, 99, 238
Mallik, Dennis, 127, 136-137,
144, 231

management. *See* project
management

Margolies, Don, 172-174, 179-182, 190, 218-219, 224-225

Massielo, Wendy, 138

McCaman, Brock, 139, 142

McCready, Paul, 95-97

McDonnell Douglas Aerospace, 38-39

Mifram, 103-114

Mike (dairy plant building case study), 203-211

missile development case study, 19-50

    changing perceptions of business, 19-22
    description of, 11
    mutual commitment to goals, 22-37
    relationship among government, contractors, suppliers, 38-47
    teamwork, 47-50
monitoring, role of, 227-229

Morgan, Ray, 4, 76, 80, 84, 89, 94-99, 100, 222, 226, 238

Morris, P.W.G., 5

Murphy, Gerald, 184-187

museum building case study, 51-70

    description of, 11
    mutual commitment to goals, 55-65
    splitting project into two parts, 51-55
    versatility of team, 65-70
mutual accountability, 26-27

mutual commitment to goals, 22-37, 55-65

N

NASA, 71-87

navigation, European versus Trukese methods, 232-233

Nekomoto, Dave, 89-92, 100, 226

new product development case studies

    descriptions of, 11
    missile development, 19-50
        changing perceptions of business, 19-22
        mutual commitment to goals, 22-37
        relationship among government, contractors, suppliers, 38-47
        teamwork, 47-50
    museum building, 51-70
        mutual commitment to goals, 55-65
        splitting project into two parts, 51-55
        versatility of team, 65-70

O

Ofer (dairy plant building case study), 195-199

oral presentations, written proposals versus, 34-35

order, chaos versus, 214-215

organizational change case studies

    descriptions of, 12-13
    downsizing, 125-147
        challenges inherent in, 125-129
        partnership between government and contractors, 130-141
        trust between government and contractors, 141-147
    evacuation, 149-169
        approval of plan, 149-151
        battalion personnel, 156-163
        implementation phase, 164-169
    psychological preparation of defense forces, 151-159
organizational structures, effect on project success, 124

P-Q

Pacific Missile Range Facility (PMRF), 88

partnership between government and contractor, 130-141. *See also* teamwork

Pathfinder, 71, 85-87

people, importance of relationships with, 94-101

personnel, selecting, 156-163, 178-179, 222-224

PERT (Program Evaluation and Review Technique) charts, 84

plan approval, in evacuation case study, 149-151

plan-driven management, 236

planning
    by action, 234
    ending planning phase, 193-198
    role of, 227-229

Plans and Situated Actions: The Problem of Human-machine Communication (Suchman), 232

PMRF (Pacific Missile Range Facility), 88

practices. *See* leadership practices

preparation
    ending preparation phase, 193-198
    psychological preparation of defense forces, 151-159

procedures, developing, 80-83

product development. *See* new product development case studies

Program Evaluation and Review Technique (PERT) charts, 84

project examples. *See* case studies

project leadership. *See* leadership in project management, leadership practices

project management
    ABCs of, 176, 229
    leadership in, 8-9, 236-238

project management practice. *See also* leadership practices
    detachment from research, 4-6
    learning from best managers, 7

project management research
    detachment from practice, 4-6
    learning from best managers, 7

project management theories, outdated nature of, 4-6

project ownership, sense of, 26-27

project requirements
    cost as, 30-32
    "good enough" requirements, 171-175
    input on, 28-30

prototyping, 47, 234

psychological preparation of defense forces, 151-159

purposeful action, 232-236

R

recruiting personnel, 156-163, 178-179, 222-224

redundancy, risk and, 174-175

reflection on experience, 213

relationships
    with contractors, suppliers, government, 38-47
    with government and contractors, 129-141
    with people, importance of, 94-101

relocation. *See* evacuation case study

repeated and risky tasks case studies
    descriptions of, 11-12
    harbor crane transfer, 103-124
        constant vigilance phase, 118-124
        entrepreneurial phase, 103-114
        risk reduction phase, 114-117
    solar-powered airplane flying, 71-101
        collaboration with local community, 87-94, 100-101
        know your customers' needs, 71-75

relationships with people,
importance of, 94-99
systems and communication,
importance of, 76-87

requirements. *See* project requirements

research. *See* project management
research

results, focus on, 35-36, 235-236

risk, redundancy and, 174-175

risk reduction phase (harbor crane
transfer case study), 114-117

Rutledge, Brian, 22, 26, 31, 35, 38,
45, 223, 235

Rutledge, Lynda, 23, 33-34

S

Safdie, Moshe, 51-54, 65

SAMP (Single Acquisition Management Plan), 24

schedule-driven project management,
198-203

Schein, Edgar, 225

selecting personnel, 156-163,
178-179, 222-224

settlement relocation. *See* evacuation
case study

Shalev, Avner, 52, 65

sharing within alliances, 84-85

Sharon, Ariel, 149-151

Simon, Herbert, 231

Single Acquisition Management Plan
(SAMP), 24

Skunk Works, 43

Snow, Frank, 182, 192, 232

solar-powered airplane flying case
study, 71-101
     collaboration with local community,
     87-94, 100-101
     description of, 11-12
     know your customers' needs, 71-75

relationships with people, importance of, 94-99

systems and communication, importance of, 76-87

spacecraft building case study,
171-192
     culture of location, 175-183
     description of, 13
     "good enough" requirements,
     171-175
     teamwork, 183-192

splitting projects into parts, 51-55,
203-211

status quo, challenging, 218-222

Stokley, Judy, 125-134, 141-144, 219

Stone, Edward, 171-177, 189

stories, learning from, 1-4. *See also*
case studies

Suchman, Lucy, 232

Sudan, George, 126-128, 141

suppliers, relationship with government and contractors, 38-47

sustain (ABCs of project management), 176

systems, importance of, 76-87

T

Taylor, Fredrick, 9, 222

team members (ABCs of project management), 176. *See also* personnel

teamwork
     cooperation within, 183-192
     between government and contrac-
     tor, 47-50, 130-141
     shaping team culture, 224-227
     versatility of team, 65-70

technical problems, solving, 8

theories of project management,
outdated nature of, 4-6

Thurber, John, 180-181

transferring harbor cranes. *See* harbor crane transfer case study

Tri-Service Standoff Attack Missile (TSSAM), 20

Trukese navigation, European navigation versus, 232-233

trust

    autonomy and, 25-26
    between government and contractor, 141-147

TSSAM (Tri-Service Standoff Attack Missile), 20

U

UAV (Unmanned Aerial Vehicle) technology, 72-73, 76-87

"The Underlying Theory of Project Management Is Obsolete" (Koskela and Howell), 5

unlearning, 3

Unmanned Aerial Vehicle (UAV) technology, 72-73, 76-87

V

Vaill, Peter, 214

versatility of team, 65-70

von Mehlem, Judi, 184-185

W-X

Weick, Karl, 236

Westphal, Jon, 141

Whitehead, Bob, 74

Worsham, Jerry, 138

written proposals, oral presentations versus, 34-35

Y

Yad Vashem, 51-70

Yaron (evacuation case study), 156-163, 164, 167-169, 219, 223

Yitzhak (harbor crane transfer case study), 106-107, 112

Z

Zaleznik, Abraham, 214

Zvika (dairy plant building case study), 194-211, 217, 220, 225, 230